Reading Race

Reading

Race

White American Poets

and the Racial Discourse

in the Twentieth Century

Aldon Lynn Nielsen

The University of Georgia Press

Athens and London

© 1988 by the University of Georgia Press
Athens, Georgia 30602
All rights reserved
Set in Times Roman with Helvetica
The paper in this book meets the guidelines for
permanence and durability of the Committee on
Production Guidelines for Book Longevity of the
Council on Library Resources.

Printed in the United States of America

92 91 90 89 88   5 4 3 2 1

Library of Congress Cataloging in Publication Data
Nielsen, Aldon Lynn.
    Reading race: White American poets and the racial
discourse in the twentieth century / Aldon Lynn Nielsen.
        p.   cm.—(South Atlantic Modern Language
    Association award study)
    Bibliography: p.
    Includes index.
    ISBN 0-8203-1061-1 (alk. paper)
    1. American poetry—20th century—History and
criticism.   2. American poetry—White authors—History
and criticism.   3. Race in literature.   4. Race relations
in literature.   5. Racism in literature.   6. Afro-
Americans in literature.   I. Title.   II. Series.
PS310.R34N54   1988
811'.5'09355—dc19   88-3942
                                                    CIP

British Library Cataloging in Publication Data available

South Atlantic
Modern Language Association
Award Study

For My Family
Aldon,
Vivian,
Carol,
Dennis, and
Brian

Contents

Acknowledgments

This work was undertaken with none of the usual institutional supports which scholars so often acknowledge at the beginning of their finished texts, a fact I record simply to underscore the extent of my debt to those who gave encouragement to a scholar who had not yet been institutionalized. Had I not been required to carry out this research in moments stolen from my several wage-paying employments, this book would have been considerably longer. Had it not been for the people I am about to name, this book might not exist at all.

To begin, I must thank Anika Martin, whose example and patience helped me find a way to write, and whose generosity of spirit continues as a model for me.

I also wish to thank Abi Pereira and Sheila Humphrey for their faith and ministrations through the dire hours.

An earlier version of the manuscript was read by Robert Ganz, Judith Plotz, Christopher Sten, Robert Combs, Richard Flynn, Craig Werner, and David McAleavey, whose suggestions were of great help to me. The use I made of their suggestions is, of course, my own responsibility. Peter Schmidt read the section on William Carlos Williams and directed me to materials which allowed me to focus my thoughts about that poet with greater clarity. To Lilian Weber, and to Ron Weber, whose camera and eye found so many of my errors, I owe words which only they could possibly understand.

John Sekora and Jerry Ward also read this book at an earlier stage, made important suggestions, and were the first to encourage me to seek publication. It is largely due to their urgings that I now find myself in a position to thank the South Atlantic Modern Language Association for honoring *Reading Race*. Leota Lawrence and my colleagues at Howard University made it possible for me to travel to Atlanta to accept the award.

Karen Orchard, Nancy Holmes, Joanne Ainsworth, and the staff of the University of Georgia Press handled me and my work with good humor and kindness, no matter how many addresses I gave them.

Lou Lewandowski and my new colleagues at San Jose State University have given me an address with an institution attached to it, and I thank them for the future works this will make possible.

For serving as a multitude of muses I thank the students of the George Washington University, Howard University, and San Jose State University.

No author really ends where he began: a text is a copula, a mark of passage and predication. I wish here to acknowledge the care and affection of Anna Everett. Her kitchen table was the scene for my revising, and her gentle strength led me to any number of conclusions I could not have anticipated when I began this project. Where will it all end?

Excerpts from the following poems are reprinted in this book by permission of the publishers:

"A Negro Woman" by William Carlos Williams, *Pictures from Brueghel.* Copyright 1955 by William Carlos Williams. Reprinted by permission of New Directions Publishing Corporation.

"The Wildflower" and "The Descent of Winter" by William Carlos Williams, *Collected Poems, Volume I: 1909–1939.* Copyright 1938 by New Directions Publishing Corporation.

"one day a nigger" by E. E. Cummings. Copyright 1950 by E. E. Cummings. Reprinted from *Complete Poems, 1913–1962* by E. E. Cummings by permission of Harcourt Brace Jovanovich, Inc.

"Incident" by Countee Cullen, *On These I Stand.* Copyright 1925 by Harper and Brothers Company; copyright renewed 1953 by Ida M. Cullen. Reprinted by permission of GRM Associates, Inc., agents for the estate of Ida M. Cullen.

Reading Race

Chapter 1

Introduction

Accordingly, after they had been bumping one evening to the Captain's content, May-Day confidentially told Rose-Water that he considered him a "nigger," which, among some blacks, is held a great term of reproach.

Melville, *White Jacket*

Here, writing in 1850, Melville recognizes a disjuncture in American symbolic behavior that has been either ignored or denied through much of our history. In this scene, two black seamen have been engaged in a gladiatorial performance for the benefit of their white Captain, a performance which interestingly prefigures the "Battle Royal" episode in Ralph Ellison's *Invisible Man*. This performance, or "head-bumping," gotten up by the Captain, "consists," Melville informs us, "in two negroes (whites will not answer) butting at each other like rams" (*White Jacket* 263). Having completed their entertaining of the whites, the two black men repair to the privacy of their own racial realm to speak an actual insult followed quickly by a real battle. Melville seems the only one on the ship who fully appreciates the irony in the fact that the Captain orders these two to battle but punishes them for fighting. It is an irony which arises from dissimilar readings of outwardly identical acts. And the scene underscores the fact that the words spoken by the men on the ship signify differently as well, that signification being again dependent upon the racial context.

While there may still be found those who would insist that the use of the epithet "nigger" in times past by black and white alike denoted innocent affection, the author of *White Jacket* sees, before the Civil War, that it is taken no less as a term of opprobrium by those to whom it is directed. It was, and is, the signifier of a radical separation between linguistic communities. White and black Americans employ similar vocabularies, but they employ these vocabularies in disjunct signifying systems. Our language has come to act as that metaphorical veil of which W. E. B. DuBois speaks so often, separating two national groups and occluding our vision of one another. This veil is maintained between the two terms of a racial dialectic, one of which is privileged. Such privilege is evident even in the naming of the two terms. To the one side of the veil is the white thesis, which is given primacy, which is considered originary, and which names itself. To the other side of the veil, cloaked in darkness, stands the black antithesis, which is always seen as secondary, and which receives its name from the white term. That name is "nigger," and it serves as an organizing principle for the formation of discourse which I shall examine in this book.

The metaphor of veiling proved useful to DuBois, and to later writers such as Robert Burns Stepto in his study *From Behind the Veil,* because of that curious visual property of veils which allows them to operate much like two-way mirrors. The entity within the veil, in this case the second term of our dialectic, is near enough to the fabric that a choice is available between studying the mesh itself or directing the gaze outward, which act affords a clear view of what lies beyond while seeming to cause the veil itself to vanish. On the other side, those viewing from without, the representatives of the primary term of our dialectic, cannot clearly see who or what is within; they can see only the veil, which from a distance appears solid. The situation is overdetermined, and is overironized as a result of the fact that this linguistic veil has been initially fabricated by the white community, and now prevents that community from obtaining an unobstructed view of the object they would describe.

This book is an examination of white discourse, but I cannot proceed without noting, at least briefly, what occurs behind that discursive veil. Rose-Water fights May-Day, in the actual battle royal, because May-Day has spoken the white term from within the black discourse. Rose-Water's first response is to put into play a white term of his own, to invoke a white ancestor. But the insult lies in the fact that May-Day has said that the white man's name for Rose-Water is the correct one, that Rose-Water has no power over his own definition; he is just what the white man has said he is. This reinvocation of white language from within the black linguistic community is something Rose-Water must fight against. Yet, there is a power of ironization available to the linguistically disenfranchised. In an effort to regain control over their own speech and their own self-definition, the powerless minority move to reappropriate the terminology. From their position of secondariness, they attempt to wrest language away from their oppressors and to reverse the terms of the dialectic; to assume primacy at least within the realm of discourse they are themselves emitting. There is, then, a countermove to Rose-Water's refusal to accept the name applied to him by white language, and that is to appropriate that name as one's own creation, to fill it with a significance unavailable to whites, a significance which overturns the signifying gestures of the privileged term. Neither a strict decentering nor a mere reversal, such an appropriation and alteration of the signifying term has the effect of moving the power of nomination into the hands of the others. "In place of a simple reversal, it is necessary to effect a dialectical inversion that does not leave contrasting opposites unmarked but dissolves their original identities. Inversion, in other words, must simultaneously be a perversion that is subversive" (Mark C. Taylor 10). This motion of reversal becomes a ritual which has the effect of giving cohesiveness to the oppressed community. Richard Harvey Brown, in his article "Dialectical Irony," says of such ritual irony that "it is enacted or controlled by the very persons who are ironized. . . . Just as only Jews are permitted to tell 'kike' stories and only Blacks 'allowed' to say 'nigger,' so it would seem that ritual irony is offered as a kind of safety valve to those who are already committed to the values of the group" (558). One signifier, the word "nigger," can produce profoundly opposed effects within the community. When put into play as it is by May-Day in the passage cited from *White Jacket* it reaffirms white power and sunders interpersonal cohesion. When put into play in its ironic sense it denies the power of white language and permits the community to arrive at its own definitions of itself.

Our interest, however, is in the mode of operation of the dialectical term signified by the word "nigger" within the linguistic community which has constructed it, among white speakers of American English, who have no need of any such ironized term to describe themselves. "Nigger," though now less frequently spoken in polite conversation than in Melville's day, continues to exist as a linguistic nexus of white thought. And while we have come to understand that such a thing as institutional racism exists, that racist effects can emanate from structures inhabited by individuals striving to behave in a nonracist fashion, it is necessary that we recognize as well that racism exists as a discursive structure within our culture. Racist terms, summarized by the epithet "nigger," survive as frozen metaphors within American speech; thus whites who have never had any contact with blacks in their lives may still exhibit an essentially racist mode of thought, one which privileges them while demoting an invisible other to a secondary status. Though the individual terms of this discourse persist, and seemingly determine the course of much thought regarding race, it is this demotion which is the compelling force of racial language rather than the terms themselves. "The imperialist is not fixed on specific images or stereotypes of the Other but rather on the affective benefits proffered by the manichean allegory, which generates the various stereotypes" (JanMohamed 87).

All linguistic communities evolve systems of power relationships enforced by and reflected in language. In the white American linguistic community, this has involved the perpetuation of a relationship in which the white majority exercises power over the black minority. A part of this power relationship entailed the destruction of the languages that Africans brought with them to these shores and their subsequent replacement by English. But language has been employed further by whites to maintain a screen, or veil, between themselves and those whom they enslaved. There must be something said about the other which somehow differentiates him from yourself if you are to enslave him, or, after emancipation, if his condition is to be kept different from your own. A cultural hegemony has been developed through such acts of language. As Frank Lentricchia defines it, "hegemony . . . is fundamentally a process of education carried on through various institutions of civil society in order to make normative, inevitable, even 'natural' the ruling ideas of ruling interests" (76). Along with political, economic, and social power, the dominant white class has maintained its hegemony by maintaining its powers to describe and to enforce its descriptions. Its "ruling ideas" are formulated in discourse, and that discourse is distributed throughout the civil and cultural institutions. Edward Said, noting the same phenomenon as it operated within the discourse of orientalism, observes that "representations are embedded first in the language and then in the culture, institutions, and political ambiance of the representer" (*Orientalism* 272). Language is, in effect, the institutionalizing force, that which constructs representations and conveys them from one structure to another. And because language inhabits all its speakers, its representations come to seem universal laws; they acquire that naturalness of which Lentricchia speaks. That arrival at naturalness is indicative of the maturity of the representation. Like a frozen or dead metaphor, it no longer requires explanation among native speakers. It is, to refer once more to Lentricchia, "the mark of the stable, 'mature' society whose ideological apparatus is so deeply set in place, so well buried, so unexamined a basis of our judgment and feeling that it is taken for truth with a capital letter" (76). Just as ethnic jokes depend upon mutual assumptions for their humor (if they have to be explained they are not funny), white cultural hegemony rests upon a discursive formation which exists for the purpose of convincing all society that this is a "natural" state of affairs.

In order for this formation to succeed, the nonwhite must be constantly distinguished from the white, must be posited always as the most radically *other*. White culture is self-constituting; it views itself as the thesis which arises with its own self-made history, as opposed to an ahistorical antithesis. That antithesis, though seen as real, must be delineated out of nothingness by the privileged term. In his recent collection of essays, *The World, the Text, and the Critic,* Said describes this function as follows: "The dialectic of self-fortification and self-confirmation by which culture achieves its hegemony over society and the state is based on a constantly practiced differentiation of itself from what it believes to be not itself" (*World* 12). The language of white thought has had to create the boundaries of its existence and to determine what will not be allowed inside. The white subject has spoken to itself, and in so speaking has created its own racial consciousness. To follow Jacques Lacan's formulation in *The Four Fundamental Concepts of Psycho-Analysis,* "the consciousness is the sum of the effects of speech on a subject, at the level at which the subject constitutes himself out of the effects of the signifier" (126). White history long ago passed through a sort of racial-mirror stage, and the language of white culture continues to inscribe the effects of that passage. The signifier of whiteness continues to rewrite itself as a discourse into our institutions, including our literature, and we, as racial subject, continue to read it, to recognize it, to privilege it, and to enjoy its power. Thus, as Jean-Paul Sartre described a similar phenomenon in the language of colonialism, we pass linguistic tokens among ourselves in conversation, not to pass along information or to mean, but as a signifier of our serial relationship of race and power, as signs that we belong. "When two colonists, in conversation, appear to be exchanging ideas, they actually merely reactualize them one after the other in so far as they represent a particular aspect of serial reason" (Sartre n301).

This power that I speak of and through, the self-enforcing power of definition I am referring to as white discourse, is expressed largely, as my quotations from Said might indicate, in negative terms. The ability to constitute a structure of whiteness assumes, more often than not, the form of the constitution of antiwhiteness, the creation of some bad, other thing out of the mass of humanity. This entails the creation of a system of interlocking, self-supporting grids, which must be available at all points within society. Such a descriptive system, Hans Robert Jauss has said, "constitutes the paradigmatic level; it is interaction, 'image-fields,' . . . i.e. the associations called forth by certain words which have adequate connotative potential. They evoke in the reader a self-contained sphere of ideas which are often recognized when just one *single* element of such a system is presented" (264). Jauss's summary points to two particularly critical aspects of this discursive system. First, its speaking evokes a self-contained sphere of ideation. Because this discourse is self-constituting, because its purpose is to create the radically other, it is an entirely fictive discourse. The signifier of the racial discourse has no referent in the material world. It arises within whiteness as an attempt to sustain wholly artificial limitations, thus it gestures vaguely toward the real world without ever touching upon it, though the material effects of its manipulation are undeniable. It cannot provide a Wittgensteinian picture of the world because its intent is never to know an object but always to create and recreate the subject. In the formulation of Sartre: "These phrases were never the translation of a real, concrete thought; they were not even *the object* of thought. Furthermore, they have not by themselves any meaning, at least in so far as they claim to express knowledge about the colonized. They arose with the establishment of the colonial system and have never been anything more than this system itself producing itself as a determination of the language of the colonists in the milieu of alterity" (n301). That is to say quite simply that we are unlikely to find many actual black people who correspond at all closely to that image system known popularly as the stereotype. In this sense Felix Guattari is quite right to assert as "an example of a structure functioning as a subject . . . the fact that the black community in the United States represents an identification imposed by the white order" (117). While there certainly is a black community composed of living individuals, it is a different community that exists in white discourse as a set of self-confirming propositions. That second "community" is a structure of meanings, composed entirely out of language, which, like the elements of the phonetic system, have significance only in their relationship to one another. Through the power of white hegemony, the signifiers of that system have been placed into circulation within society such that they are distributed fairly evenly across the population. It is thus not necessary that the full discourse appear each time that its operations are to be manifested. It is required, as Jauss has pointed out, only that one element of the system be presented. No more do mature speakers of American English require a gloss when an element of this racial structure appears before them than do they require an explanation of the frozen metaphor in a phrase such as "I got loaded last night." Only one small portion of the imaging system, only a suggestion of blackness need appear for the entire structure to be articulated. It operates much as the "charged detail" of Pound, or the "objective correlative" of Eliot. And located at the vortex of this racial structure is the one signifier which, even when unspoken, serves as the organizing principle of the entire discourse, the white man's name for the nonwhite, the signifier "nigger."

While a complete history of the rise of this discourse is beyond the scope of this book, it is important to note in passing, precisely because hegemony has asserted the universal naturalness of its description, that the description of the nonwhite as it is currently constituted was not always the "natural" one in the West. Herodotus, following his journeys on the Nile, reported favorably on the civilization of the Ethiopians (Snowden 105). Diodorus reported that the

civilized Ethiopians "were the first to honor the gods whose favor [they en-
joyed]" (qtd. in Snowden 109). Homer says in the *Iliad* that "Zeus went to
the blameless Aithiopians at the ocean / . . . to feast, and the rest of the gods
went with him" (Homer 70). While the experience of battle between Christian
and Moor may have had a good deal to do with the development of an ideological bias against the nonwhite, it is evident that the institution of slavery
did more than anything else to constitute a system of belief in the inferiority of
black persons.* This can be seen as early as 1518 when Bartolomé de Las
Casas proposed to the Spanish Crown that Indian labor in the mines of the
New World be replaced with Negro slaves, based upon his belief that the
Negroes had a better tolerance for the rigors of such a life than did the native
Americans. He was later to confess that the enslavement of Africans was no
more just than that of Indians, but the pattern of positing differences in the
Africans which presumably suited them for the horrors that were to be in-
flicted upon them had been set (David Brion Davis 169–170). A fictive discourse evolved which closed the minds of the slave masters to the sufferings
that they were perpetrating. Language, as much as habit, accounts for the
ignoble ability the American slaveholders had achieved at the time Crèvecoeur described them: "Their ears by habit are become deaf, their hearts are
hardened; they neither see, hear, nor feel for the woes of their poor slaves,
from whose painful labors all their wealth proceeds. Here the horrors of slavery, the hardship of incessant toils, are unseen; and no one thinks with com-
passion of those showers of sweat and of tears which from the bodies of
Africans daily drop, and moisten the ground they till" (155). The fiction
which supported this deafness held the African to be, if not entirely inhuman,
at the very least less human than the other races of man. Hence Thomas
Jefferson, echoing Las Casas, advanced his suspicion that blacks are "inferior
to whites in the endowments both of body and mind" (138), then moved his
suspicion up to the status of natural law with his asseveration of the black's
"own judgment in favor of the whites, declared by their preference of them,
as uniformly as is the preference of the Oranootan for the black woman over
those of his own species" (133). No matter the extent of Jefferson's knowledge or lack of same on the subject of simian species, it is clear from this
passage that he participated in the creation of that white mythology which

---

*The extent of general ignorance regarding the connections between slavery and racism may
be judged from an astonishing remark by Tzvetan Todorov, an otherwise astute reader: "It was
the abolition of slavery which led to the rise of racism in the United States: we attribute to 'race'
what we no longer have the right to attribute to social difference" (372).

relegates the black to the position of a decidedly *sub*species, a subspecies that yearns for intercourse with whiteness and that exercises attraction only among the beasts. (One must wonder, given this infamous remark of Jefferson's, what to make of the preponderant lust of the white man for the black woman as testified to by the number of mulattoes sired in the South.)

As a subspecies, one of the marks of the black's otherness was his or her inability to participate fully in the aesthetic, as it has been defined by white culture. Within white discourse, the black is held to be an ahistorical creature with no tradition of art, and more particularly, though nearly overburdened with an intuitive, unreflecting sensuality, with no literature. Writing within that discourse, Jefferson was able to remark of Phillis Wheatley, the first Afro-American woman to publish a book of verse in English, and, following Anne Bradstreet, only the second woman from the thirteen colonies to have a book of poems published in England, that she was not worthy of the name "poet." Indeed, according to Jefferson, "the compositions published under her name are below the dignity of criticism" (135). From the first centuries of our history, then, beginning with our earliest and most canonical social critics, the nonwhite is seen as a nonparticipant in the creation of American literature. To be the other, to be outside whiteness, outside white discourse, was to be without a literature and to remain unheard. The fictive signified of the racial signifier, the image structure clustered about that most antithetical of all antithetical terms, "nigger," is marked by the absence of poetry.

George M. Frederickson, in *The Black Image in the White Mind*, has described the contours of white discourse about blackness as it existed in the period preceding that with which I am primarily concerned in this book. He conceives of this discursive development as the evolution, given impetus by the institution of slavery, away from individual prejudice against the unfamiliar, toward an ideological racism embedded in a culture. I shall quote from his work extensively here because he has outlined succinctly a series of statements out of which the discursive veil of white racism in the twentieth century has been fabricated. Frederickson offers the following as statements which, from the early part of the nineteenth century, dominated the white discourse about race among abolitionists and proponents of slavery alike:

> 1. Blacks are physically, intellectually, and temperamentally *different* from whites. 2. Blacks are also *inferior* to whites in at least some of the fundamental qualities wherein the races differ, especially in intelligence and in the temperamental basis of enterprise or initiative. 3. Such differences and differentials are either permanent or subject to change only by a very slow process of development or evolution. 4. Because of these permanent or deep-seated differences, mis-

cegenation, especially in the form of intermarriage, is to be discouraged (to put it as mildly as possible), because the crossing of such diverse types leads either to a short-lived and unprolific breed or to a type that even if permanent is inferior to the whites in those innate qualities giving Caucasian civilization its progressive and creative characteristics. 5. Racial prejudice or antipathy is a natural and inevitable white response to blacks when the latter are free from legalized subordination and aspiring to equal status. Its power is such that it will not in the foreseeable future permit blacks to attain full equality, unless one believes, like some abolitionists, in the impending triumph of a millenarian Christianity capable of obliterating all sense of human differences. 6. It follows from the above propositions that a biracial equalitarian (or "integrated") society is either completely impossible, now and forever, or can only be achieved in some remote and almost inconceivable future. For all practical purposes the destiny of blacks in America is either continued subordination—slavery or some form of caste discrimination—or their elimination as an element of the population. (321)

These propositions underlie American speech on the subject of race and form the medium in which racial stereotypes perpetuate themselves. One of the reasons that opponents of civil rights legislation and enforcement fall back upon the assertion that we cannot legislate morality is that they inhabit a language which continues to speak these propositions to them, rendering these ideas both natural and inevitable. Our language and our literature, since at least the time of Las Casas, have told us that the black is lesser. When, in 1900, Charles Carroll proposed in *The Negro a Beast* that blacks literally are simian, he was simply participating in the literary tradition of Thomas Jefferson (Frederickson 277).

With few exceptions, the racial images we will be tracing in the writings of white poets of the twentieth century have existed as frozen metaphors in American writing since at least Jefferson's time, and they exhibit many of the same contradictions that may be remarked in Jefferson's *Notes on the State of Virginia*. Blacks are depicted as being both brutes and innocent, childlike creatures dependent upon the white man for their guidance. They are seen as having innate rhythmic sense and an instinct for singing yet incapable of producing fine art. They are lacking in both intellect and an instinct for liberty, and yet their machinations in the pursuit of freedom require constant vigilance on the part of their oppressors. A writer such as Theodore Parker could express a militant egalitarianism on the one hand, while simultaneously writing such fictions as, "the African has the largest organs of generation in the world, the most exotic heat; he is the most polygamous of men" (qtd. in Frederickson 120). These knots of contradiction are nowhere more evident than in the image structures concocting the white man's black woman, who seems composed of equal parts beloved mammy and mindless sexual dynamo. Gertrude Stein's *Melanctha,* to which I shall return in this chapter, contains an instance of what Paule Marshall, in her address "Characteristics of Black Women in the American Novel," correctly identifies as the prototypical "nigger wench," a character who coexists easily in the white mind with such admiringly sketched, durable mammies as Faulkner's Dilsey (Marshall 76–77). This capacity to sustain contradiction is not totally attributable to the eccentricities of individual illogic; there are two aspects of the racial discourse which render such contradiction nearly inevitable. The first of these is the nature of the discursive project itself, which sets out from a visibly human object and concludes by obscuring that object behind the fiction that it is somehow other and lesser than human.

> [T]he slave acquires his animality, through the master, only *after* his humanity has been recognized. Thus American plantation owners in the seventeenth century refused to raise black children in the Christian faith, so as to keep the right to treat them as sub-human, which was an implicit recognition that they were *already* men: they evidently differed from their masters . . . in lacking a religious faith, and the care their masters took to keep it from them was a recognition of their capacity to acquire it. (Sartre 110–11)

While the fictive signifiers occlude the object which is their occasion, the speakers of these signifiers must constantly maintain the fictive discourse if they are to prevent the reality of the other from erupting through the veil and into their lives, as occurs when Ellison's invisible man places a visible fist in the face of a white man who has not acknowledged his existence. Edward Said comments in *The World, the Text, and the Critic* that "if we believe that Kipling's jingoistic white man was simply an aberration, then we cannot see the extent to which the white man was merely one expression of a science— like that of penal discipline—whose goal was to understand and to confine non-whites in their status as non-whites, in order to make the notion of whiteness clearer, purer, and stronger" (224). To constitute the purity of white self-consciousness, it is imperative that the white subject arrive at an understanding of the black object not *as itself* but in its status as fictive signifier of the nonwhite. As Said's reference to Kipling makes evident, the constitution of the white subject is to a great extent a literary project. The white man is a character in the narrative of Western history. The white American cannot exist as such without calling into being the nonwhite other. The second aspect of this discourse which yields seemingly contradictory image structures is a phenomenon discussed by Ursula K. Le Guin in an essay entitled "American SF and the Other." In that essay she remarks that "if you hold a thing to be totally different from yourself, your fear of it may come out as hatred, or as awe—reverence" (Le Guin 369). Fear expressing itself as awe or reverence produces that odd variant of racial discourse which Frederickson has termed "romantic racism," a variant which proposes the nonwhite as an exotic creature. This particular segment of discourse acquires renewed strength during the period of modernism in America, and as we shall see in a later chapter it produces structures which describe the black, often in admiring tones, as an unconstrained libido acting out the sexual and social fantasies of the white subconscious. It has obvious affinities to such precursor discourses as that which produces Rousseau's noble savage, and it leads to such fictions as Carl Van Vechten's *Nigger Heaven* and other works Frederickson describes as "emphasizing that the blacks [are] basically exotic primitives, out of place in white society because of their natural spontaneity, emotionalism, and sensuality" (327). Many of those who have written romantic racism into the monologue that is white literature seem to have believed that they were, in ascribing their own desires and fetishes to the nonwhite other, paying a compliment, but, as LeGuin again points out:

> If you deny any affinity with another person or kind of person, if you declare it to be wholly different from yourself—as men have done to women, and class has done to class, and nation has done to nation—you may hate it, or deify it; but in either case you have denied its spiritual equality, and its human reality. You have made it into a thing, to which the only relationship is a power relationship. And thus you have fatally impoverished your own reality. You have, in fact, alienated yourself (369).

My object in what follows is to examine the process of objectification of the racial other in the white discourse as it manifests itself in the writings of poets, and to see what that discourse has made it possible to say or not say. Poets, who we would like to think are enrichers of our reality, have in this regard often participated in its impoverishment. They have, for the most part, joined with the rest of white culture in creating the fiction of the black thing. They have joined in what Felix Guattari defines as "the dominant race ideology in the United States, with its puritanism and its myths of destroying the 'bad object'—that is, whatever is different, whatever tries to—or manages to—elude the American Way of Life" (205). The power relationships which exist in white language appear as a matter of course in white poetry. The white poet claims the power to describe the "bad object," to set it outside his own discursive empire, to maintain the poetic as a white project. It is not possible to create a mainstream without reconciling the enormous body around it to a lesser position, and the creation of the white canon has occurred to the exclusion of other possible literatures. That complex of frozen metaphors we are about to delineate has spoken itself over and over into our poetry; it defines what it is possible for a white poet to say and still remain a white poet.

As a first step along this course, I would like to offer a reading of one poem by a "mainstream" contemporary American poet for the purpose of demonstrating that the discourse of whiteness is still very much in operation, that the power relationships which that discourse describes are much as they always have been, and that the primary image structures, or frozen metaphors, of the past are still primary, and I wish to demonstrate that the poem cannot even be read adequately outside of that white discourse. Stanley Fish observes that "when we communicate, it is because we are parties to a set of discourse agreements which are in effect decisions as to what can be stipulated as fact. It is these decisions, and the agreement to abide by them, rather than the availability of substance, that make it possible for us to refer . . ." (242). We must activate such a set of discourse agreements before we can read even the title of a poem such as Henry Taylor's "De Gustibus Ain't What Dey Used to Be" (41), for this poem is essentially a white communication. Before we can "get" the pun in the poem's title, we must recognize a discourse agreement among white readers about black speech. Before the poet can communicate his joke to us, we must stipulate as fact certain assumptions about black dialect without subjecting them to any real-world tests. This has the immediate effect of determining who the readers of this poem can be. The nonwhite reader conversant with white discourse, as are most black readers in this country, cannot read this poem as being addressed to him or her without being swallowed up by that set of discourse agreements. The title serves as a sign to nonwhites that they are not invited to be readers of this poem; they cannot read it without subjecting it to the ritual ironies earlier described. This is particularly curious because the whole thrust of the poem is to liken poetry to the nonwhite.

The piece carries an epigraph, attributed to Marshall Fishwick, which reads: "Poetry, like the old darky mowing the lawn, can't be hurried." The epigraph puts the poem's controlling trope into action, glosses the title's joke for any who have read over it too quickly, and enforces another discourse agreement: that the nonwhite is lazy. Taylor's poem operates by seizing upon a number of the frozen metaphors of white discourse and employing them as symbols for the admirable project of poetry. In this fashion the poem again exhibits the inherently contradictory nature of white imaging systems. Poetry, a "good object," is good because it is in some ways like the nonwhite, or "bad object." How can this be? In part, it is because poetic inspiration is being viewed as in some sense having an outlaw, or desperado nature. It is dangerous; it chooses its own time and place to strike; it disrupts the normative life; it takes over. But while these qualities are considered attractive in the life of the arts, they are considered a nuisance when they manifest themselves in the character of the hired help.

Metaphor has its way with us, after all, by bringing together entities which are sometimes assumed to be dissimilar. Symbolic action in "De Gustibus Ain't What Dey Used to Be" enacts a power relationship by transferring energy from the nonwhite object to the white subject, from the vehicle to the tenor. Poetry receives positive energies by reason of its sharing certain qualities with that to which it is dissimilar. The same qualities operating as nonwhiteness are regarded as negative. Taylor's first stanza enacts the old stereotypes of negroid loyalty, slowness, and docility. The black has an "earthy charm" which is described as being "of its own," hence nonwhite. The poet positions himself in a relationship of power over both poetry and the nonwhite in the first two lines. Just as the nonwhite requires the special understanding of the white handler, poetry requires the special care and understanding of those who have come to an intimate knowledge. As southerners claimed for so long to "know their negroes," the poet acquires access to the same sort of relationship with poetry. If you "know" how to treat the recalcitrant object, you may be able to prod it into performance. The remainder of Taylor's poem is a catalogue of racial image structures:

It shuffles and makes excuses
and tells you the mower is dull,
but you know better than that:
never trust it with machinery.
   It makes room for itself in your life.

It breaks everything it touches,
and steals what isn't nailed down;
its speech is a savage mumble,
and it lies just to keep in practice.
   There are things it will force you to see.

It promises to come back next week,
but you know it probably won't;
it is liable to get its throat cut

by another one just like it.
It has settled in your life for good.

It shambles over the lawn
taking its own sweet time.
It can never be overworked;
it has a natural rhythm.
It will stay. It will finally own you.

Questions as to the extent of Taylor's personal belief in the correspondence of these image structures with any real black persons are irrelevant to this demonstration. The poem offers no critique of its own signifying structures and contains no overt ironizing gestures within its stanzas. What is of interest is the fashion in which the poem requires and strengthens the discourse agreements of white literature. As Martin Heidegger notes in *Being and Time,* "any interpretation which is to contribute understanding must already have understood what is to be interpreted" (194). To understand Taylor's poem, one must have already understood the racial imagery it uses. In this sense, white discourse is given a preexisting privilege which the poem does nothing to subvert. For this poem to communicate at all, its stipulations must be read as if true; the existence must be assumed of a referential category of nonwhite life which can be described as shuffling, deceitful, clumsy, thieving, savage, inarticulate, violent (particularly against its own kind), as always concocting excuses for itself, as constantly in need of white supervision, and, here is the romantic tinge, as exhibiting along with all these qualities an innate sense of rhythm. The metaphor has an effect other than that we might normally anticipate. Rather than bringing two entities together on the basis of a hitherto unperceived similitude, this metaphor seizes upon the realm of the nonwhite only to eject it in the end from its significations. It describes a sort of hermeneutic circle. The poem proposes once more the fiction of the nonwhite, links certain of its image structures to the process of poetic creativity, and draws a boundary around that newly described process which the nonwhite cannot enter. We must read racism if we are to read this poem. We must be fluent in racism's idioms and repeat them over to ourselves. We must constitute ourselves as white and oppose ourselves to a blackness which we have also constituted. Even if we reject the truth value of the images which comprise the vehicle of Taylor's trope, we must perform these operations if we are to read that trope. We then find ourselves confronted with a poem that tells us poetry is valuable because it is like those descriptions of black life which we know to be untrue. Finally, within the boundaries of Taylor's metaphor, if we ourselves would be poets we must hold ourselves in a superior position with respect to the nonwhite we have created so that we can "understand" and "handle" it.

While it is a more than usually egregious example, Taylor's poem and its publication in the post–Civil Rights Act era indicate the extent to which this system of white discourse still functions in our literature. Given the persistence of this discursive formation within our language, it might seem that the nineteenth-century assumptions about its inevitability, or at least its unalterable nature, are correct. Such a discourse is, however, susceptible of dissolution. Where there have been breakthroughs in the self-confirming chain of racial signifiers, they have come about as the result of a massive deconstruction of the discourse from within. The white subject has had to have been part of a reversal of the terms of the dialectic it has itself set in motion, to have removed itself from the position of primacy, and to have reconstituted itself as something other. It has had, in effect, to rewrite itself as a consciousness by rewriting the language that it writes *in*.

While the domain of this book is the twentieth century, it is necessary to reach outside that time boundary to locate the last major instance of an attempt to break through white discourse in the fashion I have suggested. "History," writes Felix Guattari, "is not the history of repetition, anti-historic history, the history of kings and queens; it is finding the signifying breakthrough, recognizing the point when the scales were tilted. But that signifying breakthrough is as hard to identify as the underlying meaning of a dream; what precisely was broken" (179). It is in the mid-nineteenth century that the clearest disruption within white discourse occurs, and it occurs in Herman Melville's "Benito Cereno." Melville's views on slavery and race, as Carolyn Karcher demonstrates in *Shadow over the Promised Land,* are not invariably consistent, but they are often linked to his concerns with the operations of signification. Melville frequently appears to share in some of the beliefs about racial relations outlined by Frederickson. But just as often he can be found puzzling out the way in which race appears in our representations to ourselves. In his poem "Formerly a Slave," for instance, he seems to be writing the same poem Whitman writes in "Ethiopia Saluting the Colors." Both poets look upon the face of a black woman, formerly a slave, try to read in it the history and destiny of her race, and find the reading somewhat obscure. What gives Melville's offering its unusual interest is that the face he is interrogating, whose meaning he finds "sibylline," is a painting, by E. Vedder, which Melville describes as an "idealized portrait" (*Battle Pieces* 154). It is the representation of a former slave, rather than the former slave herself, to which Melville puts his questions. Much of the power of his short novel "Benito Cereno" derives from the fact that representation and its effects serve as a plot device. Melville will make use of his protagonist's blindness within white discourse to generate dramatic irony. That one character represents the nonwhite to himself in such a way that he is unable to read properly danger signs which confront him, and he very nearly loses his life as a result.

Like Edgar Allan Poe's "The System of Doctor Tarr and Professor Feather," "Benito Cereno" presents a sort of inverted captivity narrative in which those normally in confinement have taken over the direction of their place of confinement. Both works make use of dramatic irony, allowing the reader to make out what has occurred in the place of imprisonment before it occurs to the protagonist. But where Poe uses his familiar first-person narrative form, Melville adopts the third person, centering the narrative in the thoughts of Captain Amasa Delano, from whose point of view most of the tale proceeds. Readers are then permitted to look through, or overlook as the situation requires, the prejudices of Captain Delano. Arguing against a number of earlier, inadequate readings of the work, Carolyn Karcher has stated that she does "not believe that 'Benito Cereno' is primarily a dramatization of slave revolt, let alone a psychological study of the slave rebel, but rather an examination of the white racist mind and how it reacts in the face of a slave insurrection" (128). More important, though, "Benito Cereno" ("BC") is a dramatization of the white racist mind *not reacting* in the face of a slave insurrection; for the dramatic irony of the novel derives from Delano's inability to recognize that which is palpably before him. He is so much inhabited by the discourse agreements of white mythology, his consciousness is so much the production of that discourse, that he can see no more than the signifiers of the nonwhite, which he holds in his mind, and he cannot see the actuality of the slave revolt he has happened upon.

Even in the earliest stages of the novel, Melville posts signs to alert the reader to the fact that Delano's perceptions are imperfect. His character, to begin with, supposedly inclines him away from "the imputation of malign evil in man" ("BC" 107). Further, he is quick to form impressions based on insufficient sensory evidence. For example, when first drawing near the crippled ship with its load of slaves, he takes the dim, dark figures appearing at portholes and on the decks for a shipload of monks. Later, and much more significantly, Melville describes his character as "a man of such native simplicity as to be incapable of satire or irony" (127). Such cautions with regard to Delano's reliability come from our narrator's descriptions, but the indicators of the more crippling flaw in Delano's powers of perception come from his own thoughts. He may be presented as unwilling to impute evil to men, but he will impute evil to the hapless Benito Cereno before he will concede to himself that black slaves are capable of formulating designs at all.

Melville takes sufficient pains to see to it that most readers will catch on to what has transpired aboard Cereno's vessel well before the climactic scene in which Delano finally realizes what is up. He uses symbolism to this end when narrating Delano's first view on shipboard. The vessel, fallen into an extreme state of disrepair, features a "castellated forecastle [which] seemed some ancient turret, long ago taken by assault, and then left to decay" ("BC" 110). Someone who is not susceptible to irony might easily miss the import of such a romantic symbol, but Delano even misses the deliberate signs made frantically to him by the now captive whites on the ship. He notes that one of the Spanish sailors keeps his eyes fixed upon him "with a sort of covert intentness" (128) and later observes the same sailor looking toward the place where he and Cereno are whispering with a "lurking significance, . . . as if silent signs, of some Free-Mason sort," were being interchanged (128). Later still, he sees a sailor "peering from behind a great stay, like an Indian from behind a hemlock, . . . a marlingspike in his hand, . . . who made what seemed an imperfect gesture towards the balcony, but immediately, as if alarmed by some advancing step along the deck within, vanished . . ." (141). Delano meditates upon the possible significance of all this. He asks himself, "what means this? Something the man had sought to communicate unbeknown to anyone . . ." (141). The import of all these signs escapes Delano, but it is easily apprehended by the reader. It is as if the sailors were gesturing frantically past Delano to the consciousness of each reader as an alarm, having failed with the somewhat thick Captain. In one last instance, an aged sailor hands Delano a complicated knot, one that Delano describes as "Gordian," and pleads covertly with the Captain to "undo it, cut it, quick" (142–43). But such subtlety is lost upon Delano, despite the fact that the blacks on the deck who witness this scene are visibly perturbed by it and evidence suspicion about what has transpired between the two whites. Given these signals, the only way that a reader can be surprised by the ending of this tale is by making the same errors of analysis made by Delano.

Like the signifier "nigger," all scenes in "Benito Cereno" are polysemous, though Captain Delano consistently reads them for their literal sense. Upon boarding the ship he sights a group of older blacks posted "sphinx like" ("BC" 111) above the turmoil on the decks. These men are acting as lookouts and supervisors, but Delano sees in them only doddering old laborers. Likewise, the quarterdeck is occupied by six blacks who spend *all* of their waking hours polishing hatchets. Again, Delano's suspicions do not rise, because his prejudices are so powerful. He notes that "with the peculiar love in negroes of uniting industry with pastime, two and two they sideways clashed their hatchets together, like cymbals, with a barbarous din" (112). Even when Delano gets as far as surmising that the old men at times act "the part of monitorial constables to their countrymen, the blacks" (116), or that the hatchet polishers seem to brandish the weapons as much as use them for percussive instruments, he quickly dismisses the thoughts, because they would impute abilities to the Africans which he cannot concede. For he believes whites to be the shrewder race, and blacks to be "too stupid" (142) even to be acting in complicity with piratical white leaders.

The complex of assumptions which so deludes Delano is most succinctly set out in the scene in which he looks on while Cereno is shaved by the man who seems to be his body servant, Babo. This scene brings out Delano's belief that "there is something in the negro which, in a peculiar way, fits him for avocations about one's person. Most negroes are natural valets" ("BC" 151). The negro's natural avocation for such tasks appears to stem from his good humor and "the docility arising from the unaspiring contentment of a limited mind" (152). Add to that the blind attachment of servile loyalty and we have the paternalistic image of the childlike black which has proved so persistent in white consciousness. That this image structure was pervasive in Melville's time is shown in his description of Delano's reaction to the scene of master and servant assuming their proper places: ". . . like most men of good, blithe heart, Captain Delano took to negroes, not philanthropically, but genially, just as other men to New Foundland dogs" (152). More heavily laden with dramatic irony than any other in the book, this scene draws added force from the fact that it is an ironic repetition of a daily ritual of subservience. Prior to the uprising, the servant ran a razor across the throat of his master at a certain specified time each day. Subsequent to the uprising, the power relationship has been reversed. The shaving ritual is continued, but it is now an instance of ritual irony. The scene is now *consciously* enacted, for two purposes. First, it is repeated as a sign of normality, meant to be read by Delano as signifying that life is following its usual course on the ship. This produces a literal reading of a fictive sign. But it is unlikely that Delano would have remarked the absence of the daily shave had the subject not been brought to his attention, which leads one to conclude that the ritual's second purpose is its most important. The ritual is an enactment of the new power relationship. The former slave holds the emblem of his newly won authority, the sharpened razor, to the most vulnerable point on the former master's person. Looking on at this ritual enactment, the analogy to a scene of execution momentarily crosses Delano's mind; he briefly sees Babo as "a headsman, and in the white a man at the block" (153). Even that brief flash in Delano's imaginings will be overironized in its turn later in the course of the narrative when Babo is beheaded by the white power structure. But again, Delano's participation in white assumptions causes him immediately to dismiss the analogy as an "antic conceit."

Delano does entertain suspicions about the occurrences he witnesses, but his prejudices turn these suspicions further and further from the truth. He would sooner discern in Cereno a deceitful pirate than attribute intelligence or cunning to the blacks. In fact, it is that very unwillingness to concede mental capacities to the nonwhite that causes him to abandon his suspicions of Cereno. At one point, he questions the veracity of Cereno's highly questionable explanation of the events that have transpired. It occurs to him that "if Don Benito's story was, throughout, an invention, then every soul on board, down to the youngest negress, was his carefully drilled recruit in the plot: an incredible inference" ("BC" 134), an inference Delano ends by laughing at because of the capacity for intrigue it would assume among the Africans.

Melville's ironic narrative follows this pattern to the very end. Signs are offered which allow the reader to conclude that Delano is dangerously unperceptive, signs such as the several scenes in which black men, ostensibly slaves, behave in an abusive fashion toward the whites on the ship, the ostensive masters. By his use of this technique, Melville effectively explodes the discourse agreements of racism within the consciousness of the reader through demonstrations to the reader that those agreements afford an inadequate means by which to read the text of the real world. "Benito Cereno" is an instance of what Bakhtin has termed parodic stylization, a novel which effectively destroys the language of racial representation in a "type of internally dialogized interillumination of languages. The intentions of the representing discourse are at odds with the intentions of the represented discourse; they fight against them, they depict a real world of objects not by using the represented language as a productive point of view, but rather by using it as an exposé to destroy the represented language" (Bakhtin 363–64). The "slumbering negress," described by Delano, "like a doe in the shade of a woodland rock" ("BC" 138), is not, the reader finds, an example of "naked nature" as the Captain would have it, but a participant in a grand conspiracy. This explosion of the racial dialectic in "Benito Cereno" becomes most acute in the characterization of the leader of the slaves' uprising. Babo is not the hulking, savage brute lashing out without thought that filled the nightmares of the South, quite the opposite. When Delano first encounters Babo in the company of Cereno, he beholds "a black of small stature, in whose rude face, as occasionally, like a shepherd's dog, he mutely turned it up into the Spaniard's, sorrow and affection were equally blended" (112). But as in the shaving scene, it is the black who is master of the situation, and his power over his fellows and former masters is one of ratiocination, not one of physical prowess. As Karcher points out, "Melville's portrayal of Babo as an almost disembodied brain . . . reverses the conventional racist stereotype of the Negro as all brawn and no brain" (Karcher 130). None of this is apparent to Delano, however; so ill-equipped is he to see past his own racist propositions that even when Cereno has leapt for his life into Delano's departing boat, and a knife-wielding black has leapt after him, Delano perceives in the black "a servant . . . in the act of leaping, as with desperate fidelity to befriend his master to the last" ("BC" 169).

The dialectical reversal that began in slave revolt is carried through to Melville's depiction of the final execution of Babo. This figure who so confounded racial stereotypes, "whose brain, not body, had schemed and led the revolt" ("BC" 192), is beheaded, his body is burned, and his skull is fixed to a pole in the plaza. This ritual execution and dismemberment is meant by the white authority as a sign of its power and as warning to those who might be tempted to follow Babo's example. But it has the effect within the narrative of elevating the brain of the nonwhite in warning to the white term itself. Babo's head, which Melville refers to as a "hive of subtlety," so much in contrast to Delano's imperviousness to subtlety, is said at the close to have "met, unabashed, the gaze of the whites . . . and looked towards the monastery, on Mount Agonia without; where, three months after being dismissed by the court, Benito Cereno, borne on the bier, did, indeed, follow his leader" ("BC" 193). Babo's eyes gaze out from the text of "Benito Cereno" in stark announcement, not only of the terror which the slavers must have anticipated, but of a terror which must be faced by white culture generally, the dread that culture must face of having the "bad other" it has called into being suddenly break through the abstraction of white description. Melville has forced just such a rent in the veil of racial discourse. And through that rent, the reader may glimpse, in the unblinking gaze of Babo's torment, what James Baldwin has offered as his diagnosis for the future of white discourse: "The real terror that engulfs the white world now is a visceral terror. . . . It's the terror of being described by those they've been describing for so long" (Baldwin 24).

Babo's skull posted in warning over the corpus of American literature was, for all its symbolic power, largely ignored by those white poets who came after. As effective a disruption of the white monologue as it is, "Benito Cereno" has proven to be an isolated incident in the adventure of white letters. More nearly paradigmatic for the writing of white poets has been Gertrude Stein's *Melanctha: Each One as She May*, first published in 1909. *Melanctha*, while presenting a broader range of black characters than contemporary novels such as Thomas Dixon's *The Leopard's Spots* and *The Clansman*, repeats with little variation the same images of the nonwhite which those propagandistic fictions brought over from the nineteenth century into our own, and in this respect it represents the kind of impoverishment of the imagination that Ursula Le Guin speaks of. What sets Stein's novel apart from the works of Dixon is that it stands as an early instance of modernism and that its black characters are treated sometimes sympathetically rather than condemned as subjects fit for genocide. But Stein's sympathy is the sympathy of romantic racism, and it is this that marks it as the signpost of modernism's discourse on the nonwhite.

Melanctha's centrality as a text was quickly recognized by the emerging modernist writers, black and white alike. By the time the black American poet Claude McKay visited Paris, he reports, the black artists considered Stein's home a sort of cultural port of call. This was in part because of her having acquired the reputation of someone who "does not mind Negroes" but primarily because of the influence of *Melanctha*. McKay was advised by acquaintances within the émigré community that Stein had "written the best story about Negroes, and if you [meant] to be a modern Negro writer, you should meet her" (McKay 248). And yet Stein's interest in blacks was an oddly distanced one, one which remained informed by the view of nonwhites as being ahistorical and without an art of their own. The disparity between the common perception of Stein's attraction to Africans and Afro-Americans and the much less clear views displayed in her writings appears as well in the public reception of *Melanctha*. There have been many, Richard Wright among them, who chose to look upon *Melanctha* as the most realistic portrayal of black life and language to have come from a white author to that date.* McKay, on the other side, "could not see wherein intrinsically it was what it was cracked up to be" (248). To the contrary, he found it to be a reproduction of "the common phrases relating to Negroes." "Melanctha," he concludes, "seemed more like a brief American paraphrase of Esther Waters

---

*For an excellent discussion of the strange relationship between Wright and Stein see Eugene E. Miller.

than a story of Negro life" (248). Another Afro-American poet, Sterling Brown, has said of the language of *Melanctha* that "the characters talk in a mannered dialogue; they all sound like each other, and like the white people in the other two stories" of *Three Lives* (111).

Stein's own attitudes toward the nonwhite are everywhere problematic. *Tender Buttons* may be composed of nonreferential, cubist, prose poems, but it is difficult to read a line from it such as "needless are niggers," from "Dinner" (494), as being wholly unmotivated. At a time when several of the artists she championed were championing, and copying African art, she continued to relegate such art to a secondary, even tertiary position, refusing to believe that what attracted the likes of Picasso to it could have proceeded from the black African aesthetic. Writing in *The Autobiography of Alice B. Toklas,* she remarks of herself: "She had a definite impulse then and always toward elemental abstraction. She was not at any time interested in African sculpture. She always says that she liked it well enough but that it has nothing to do with europeans, that it lacks naivete, that it is very ancient, very narrow, very sophisticated but lacks the *elegance of the egyptian sculpture from which it is derived*" (Stein 60, emphasis added). Again, speaking specifically of Picasso and the development of his various periods, Stein notes that during one of them his creative activity was dominated "by negro ritual expressed in negro sculpture (which has an arab basis the basis also of spanish ritual) . . ." (199). While perceptive enough to have observed that Picasso's affinity for African art may have come partly out of the influence of the African continent, via the Moors, upon Spanish culture generally, she is never willing to concede that the black Africans may have influenced Arabic culture as much as they were influenced by it, because she is unwilling to concede the breadth of the nonwhite aesthetic. That aesthetic has the quality of being ancient, but it is, for Stein, narrow.

Despite her mixed feelings about Africa, there is evidence to suggest that Stein held Africans to be at least, somehow, more authentic than the American Negroes who figure in *Melanctha*. Claude McKay, in his autobiography, *A Long Way from Home,* recounts an episode involving his friend Carmina and a young white man who had been a protégé of Stein's. Carmina had always felt welcome at Stein's salon, until she and the young man became romantically attached, at which time Stein visibly cooled toward both of them. Finally, Stein scolded Carmina's young man: "telling him that if he were seriously interested in Negroes he should have gone to Africa to hunt for an authentic one. Carmina said she did not know what more authentic than herself Miss Stein desired. For besides having some of the best white blood mingled with black in her veins, which were blue, she came from the best Negroid middle-class stock, and Gertrude Stein was also only middle-class" (McKay 335). Carmina did not realize that she had stumbled upon exactly the reason for Stein's dislike of her. The same question of authenticity appears to have troubled Stein's relationship with Paul Robeson, one of the "quantities of negroes" sent to her by Carl Van Vechten. Speaking as Alice B. Toklas, Stein says of Robeson that "as soon as any other person came into the room he became a negro. Gertrude Stein did not like hearing him sing spirituals. They do not belong to you any more than anything else, so why claim them, she said. He did not answer" (224). Stein's narrative, like so much of white writing, strips black Americans of their history, their art, and their song, and then hears no answer from them. Further, it has seemed to encourage many of its educated readers to follow in Stein's path, using her novel as a means for the continued denial of Afro-American artistic history, as evidenced in Richard Howard's recent asseveration that one of *Melanctha's* claims upon our attention as an innovative fiction is that in it Stein "invented . . . the first American novel of black life" (9), a remark that not only "forgets" the history of the Afro-American novel but also erases a tradition in white letters going back beyond Stowe's *Uncle Tom's Cabin.*

In fact, Stein leaves the nonwhite precious little room to answer in the cascades of her white language, for she confines them to a psychic ghetto from which no answer can emanate. I refer particularly here to Stein's frequently quoted assertion, still in *The Autobiography of Alice B. Toklas,* that the nonwhite is "suffering from nothingness." Echoing her earlier comment about African sculpture, she contends that "the african is not primitive, he has a very ancient but a very narrow culture and there it remains. Consequently, nothing does or can happen" (224). This last comment reflects the dominant intellectual suppositions of Stein's culture, and could as well have been written by Hegel, who dismisses Africa from his *Philosophy of History* with the remark that Africa "is no historical part of the world: it has no movement or development to exhibit" (99). It also asserts once more the fatalism about the situation of the nonwhite which George Frederickson outlined in *The Black Image in the White Mind,* and at least in part attributes the "naturalness" of that fatalism to blackness itself. The ancient narrowness of African culture is presented as not only constricting the potential of the nonwhite but as being a far greater restraint upon that potential than anything resulting from the murderous measures still being taken by whites against blacks at the time Stein was writing. Much less often quoted than Stein's more widely known phrase about nothingness is the horrific bit of intellectual perversity that leads into it.

Stein offers her conclusion "that negroes were not suffering from persecution, they were suffering from nothingness" (224).

However difficult it may be to conceive of anyone who holds such a structure of belief ever managing a realistic description of the lives of black Americans, it may be that the argument over the issue of realism has been misdirected all along. For one thing, Stein's experience of blacks prior to her expatriation was severely limited. Her medical training and clinic experience in Baltimore was brief. Far more important, there is evidence that Stein was never terribly interested in achieving realistic portrayals of individual characters in her novel. On at least one occasion she said of *Melanctha* that the realism of the composition of her thoughts in making that novel outweighed the realism of each character; that she was more interested in the "essence" than in making the people real (Eugene E. Miller 109). Carl Van Vechten once prepared a questionnaire on the subject of how the Afro-American should be portrayed in art, which included the inquiry: "Is not the continued portrayal of the sordid, foolish, and criminal among Negroes convincing the world that this and this alone is really and essentially Negroid, and preventing white artists from knowing any other types and preventing black artists from daring to paint them?" (Van Vechten 64). Had this question been put to Stein following publication of *Melanctha* she might well, no matter her possession of what we have seen to be strong personal notions regarding what is essentially Negroid, have responded that it was neither her place nor her purpose to instruct the world in such matters. We might, in turn, feel authorized by her own, actual commentary to disregard the question of what she may or may not have intended with regard to the degree of realism in the portrayal of her black characters and to concentrate more closely on the question of what characterizations of blacks she did in reality compose. Such an operation will discover that the same image structures of white discourse earlier discussed in this chapter manifest themselves again, without the deconstructive ironizings of Melville, albeit with interesting complications, in *Melanctha*.

Examining these same issues in his article, "Black Brutes and Mulatto Saints: The Racial Hierarchy in Stein's *Melanctha*," Milton A. Cohen has proposed the following generalizations about Stein's manipulations of racial imagery:

First, Stein clearly links skin tone to personality traits. Second, her associations follow many of the established stereotypes that whites held of blacks: the "black" end of the scale represents coarseness, stupidity, and a "half-savage" childishness. Images of the fearful, eye-rolling, exaggerating Negro also appear at this end. The "white" end of the scale brings intelligence, complexity, and courage. In between, the "light brown" shade denotes seriousness, hard work, decency, kindness, and religiosity, while the "pale yellow" is complex, mysterious, uncertain, sweet but somewhat vague. (120)

This system of differentiation along the spectrum from black to white begins on the very first page of Stein's novel when Melanctha, a lightskinned Afro-American, is described as patient, submissive, soothing, and untiring, as opposed to her "real black" friend, Rose Johnson, who is described as sullen, childish, cowardly, unmoral, shiftless, promiscuous, stupid, goodlooking, well built, and as having acted, during the birth of her child, "like a simple beast" (Stein 340–49). The bestial aspect of Rose Johnson's character is emphasized in Stein's presentation of that birthing. Having made herself an abomination during the birth, black Rose proves a negligent mother in the following days. Indeed it is Rose's negligence that causes the baby's death when Melanctha, who has been caring for both mother and child, has to leave for a few days. In her treatment of this episode, Stein has made use of one of the most pernicious images in the entire structure of white discourse, for she repeats once more Thomas Jefferson's portrait of the nonwhite incapable of feeling the same degree of familial devotion felt by whites, an image which must have proved useful to traders in slaves. Following the death of Rose's infant, Stein says, "Rose Johnson had liked her baby well enough and perhaps she just forgot it for a while, anyway the child was dead and Rose and Sam (the child's father) were very sorry, but then these things came so often in the negro world in Bridgepoint that they neither of them thought about it very long" (449).

A similar discrimination of personality traits based on skin tone is operative among the male characters in *Melanctha* as well. Thus, Melanctha's father is a "big black virile negro" (343), who comes around to the house Melanctha occupies with her mother only once in a while and is described as common, decent enough, "brutal and rough to his one daughter," powerful, loose built, hard handed and angry (343–44). (Melanctha's mother, a pale yellow, is pictured as pleasant, sweet appearing, mysterious, uncertain, and wandering.) This father, James Herbert, is readily contrasted with Melanctha's doctor boyfriend, Jefferson Campbell, "a strong, well built, good looking, cheery, intelligent and good mulatto" (371). Campbell is given the role of "race man" in this book and is constantly expounding moral observations of the type put forward by Booker T. Washington. This seems to proceed from Stein's having awarded him middle-class status among the panoply of figures she has created. Jefferson Campbell, in addition to bearing the name of a white American president, and bearing the blood of white Americans, had a father who was a servant to white families, and thus had the opportunity to imbibe deeply the white middle-class value system. As an Afro-American doctor, he has committed himself to that value system, and he would like to see other non-whites cease embarrassing him and start following the same code. And so it is Campbell who is heard to worry continually over the way "the colored people just keep running around and perhaps drinking and doing everything bad they can ever think of . . . just because they want to get excited" (368).

Certain qualities and skills are, however, apparently generic, without regard to skin tone, as may be seen in the scene in which Melanctha's black father battles a "light brown negro." "Suddenly between them there came a moment filled full with strong black curses, and then sharp razors flashed in the black hands, that held them flung backward in the negro fashion" (Stein 346). This is, of course, another reinscription into American literature of the motif of nonwhite violence to its own kind that we have seen in the later poem by Henry Taylor.

In addition to the assignment of discrete stereotypical attributes to individual characters, Stein has attempted to give her entire novel an atmosphere of negroness (I hesitate to use the construction "negritude" because of its additional political connotations) through the use of just such generic traits, suffusing her narrative with a white sense of nonwhiteness. Production of this atmosphere is accomplished by continual return to the image structures of animallike simplicity and joy loosed from the constraints of Western socialization. That image structure is usually brought into being in the novel through the presentation of the feature of black laughter. Like Sherwood Anderson in his novel *Dark Laughter,* Stein has filled the interstices of her narrative with "the wide, abandoned laughter that makes the warm broad glow of negro sunshine" (340). That link between laughter and sunshine is significant, for Stein will not only depict blackness as being at some diminished level of civilization closer to the natural than is the white bourgoisie; she will present it as being a part of nature, a suggestion which was to be replicated in the film *Borderline,* which the poet H.D. helped to create. She will speak of "the warm air of the sultry, southern, negro sunshine" (399). Blackness comes to be, like the robin, a harbinger of such good weather, a natural sign of abundance and lush growth: "the buds and the long earthworms, and the negroes, and all the kinds of children were coming out every minute farther into the new spring, watery, southern sunshine" (425). Once they have emerged in this way, one may "listen with full feeling to the yowling of the free swinging negroes, as they [run], with their powerful loose jointed bodies and their childish savage yelling" (352). So much in tune with nature are these non-whites that, during the summertime, they are not even subject to the normal course of human illnesses. Dr. Jefferson Campbell, our narrator informs us, has the leisure to pursue his romances because "it is summer now, and Jeff Campbell had more time to wander, for colored people never get sick so much in summer" (393). But as always there is an inherent contradiction here, and one might well adduce Derrida's comment on a similar position of Hegel's to illuminate later turns in *Melanctha:* "A strange interpretation: one has just been told that the Negro merges with nature, and in a moment one is going to learn that nature dominates the Negro" (Derrida 207).

There exist within this narrative odd, complicating factors, instances in which the image structure of the nonwhite folds over on itself in unexpected ways. Despite her general adherence to racial stereotype, some of Stein's black characters exhibit anomalies. Rose Johnson, for example, though displaying the "blackest" traits of childishness, slowness, selfishness, and lack of familial devotion, is a nonparticipant in that universal nonwhite laughter; Stein says of Rose that she "was never joyous with the earth-born, boundless joy of negroes. Hers was just ordinary, any sort of woman laughter" (Stein 340). In contrast, Jane Harden, who is whiter still than Melanctha herself, whose whiteness makes "her see clear" (354), is a loose, rough, reckless drinker. Milton Cohen has offered an explanation of these anomalies by articulating Stein's racial hierarchy with the hierarchy of her conception of "bottom natures" running from the "nervous and easily aroused to the phlegmatic" (Cohen 119). So even though she associates increasing complexity and intelligence with an increased quantity of white blood, Stein does not necessarily "associate 'superior' skin tone (white) with moral restraint" (Cohen 121). An individual's bottom nature, if we follow Cohen following Stein, may play along with or against the expectations of the racial imagery within which it is confined. But there is yet an additional complicating factor to which Cohen fails to allude. Rose Johnson, who stands somewhat apart from the natural abandonment of black laughter, "had been brought up quite like their own child by white folks" (Stein 339). The two women who serve as Melanctha's guides into the world of sexuality and earthy experience have both received infusions of whiteness, one by blood and one by contiguity. The white heredity of the one complicates her and lends her intelligence. She, like Jefferson Campbell, has been to college, but in her case the middle-class socialization process is overcome by both her bottom nature and her nonwhite nature. The direct experience of white society had by Rose, Melanctha's second guide, acts as a restraint upon her psyche, though not upon her libido, and inhibits her full participation in the natural exoticism of blackness. Still, though Rose knows "very well, she (is) not just any common kind of black girl, for she had been raised by white folks" (430), her "white training had only made for habits, not for nature" (340). And so for both women the encounter with whiteness is subjugated to their nonwhite nature, to the "promiscuous unmorality of the black people" (340). And it is this natural unmorality, this refusal of white bourgeois mores, which is the major motif of Stein's narrative, a motif which again is characteristic of white thought as embodied in Hegel: ". . . it is manifest that want of self-control distinguishes the character of the Negroes. This condition is capable of no development or culture, and as we see them at this day, such have they always been" (98).

When we hear the moralizings of Jefferson Campbell, we are hearing what Milton Cohen has called "the voice of the white bourgeoisie coming through a black manikin" (121). When we hear the libidinous blues of *Melanctha* in response, we are hearing the stirrings of white desire passed through a fictive veil of blackness, a passage which has been integral in the most despicable of racist cant. "It is only the black African that Gobineau and other writers seek to depict as a pure human machine stripped of reasoning faculties and moved only by a blind sensorial *desire*" (Miller, *Blank* 18). In this sense, Gertrude Stein called the tune that would resonate through the chambers of high modernism. Rather than the ironized signpost left by Melville, Babo's mute stare, white discourse in the twentieth century has been presided over by the sign left at the close of *Melanctha*. Melanctha sings her blues and then simply dies away, fading from the white view behind a narrative veil, unable to answer for herself.

Chapter 2

Poets

of the

Transition

Once riding in old Baltimore,
    Heart filled, head filled with glee,
I saw a Baltimorean
    Keep looking straight at me.

Now I was eight and very small,
    And he was no whit bigger,
And so I smiled, but he poked out
    His tongue and called me "Nigger."

I saw the whole of Baltimore
    From May until December:
Of all the things that happened there
    That's all that I remember.

Countee Cullen, "Incident"

A reading of white American literature of-
tentimes resembles this "incident" recounted by the black American poet
Countee Cullen. One sets out upon the project, "head filled with glee," only
to be assaulted by insult, insult which is no whit lesser because committed
sometimes unwittingly. Having failed to learn the lessons offered by
Melville's "Benito Cereno," American poets repeated the example of
Gertrude Stein's *Melanctha* quite readily. For the white poets who mark the
transition from nineteenth-century modes of composition to those of high
modernism, poets such as Carl Sandburg and Robert Frost, the vocabulary of
white racism was one they spoke with fluency and with few signs of self-
consciousness. Only one major poet of the transition, Edwin Arlington Robinson, has left a poem of any importance which looks upon the nonwhite without the blindness of white mythology. And lesser poets, such as Vachel
Lindsay, even when attempting to deal honestly and sympathetically with the
Afro-American as subject, were so much captives of white discourse that they
not only failed to speak their way to a new discourse, they were absolutely
incapable of recognizing that their efforts admitted of any objections from
nonwhite readers, or from white readers opposed to racism.

Perhaps the most widely known of such incidents is Vachel Lindsay's long
poem "The Congo," which he first recited publicly at the Lincoln Day banquet in Springfield, Illinois, on February 12, 1914. While apparently not an
overwhelming success with his immediate audience, Lindsay went on to re-

peat the poem on March 1 at a banquet sponsored by Harriet Monroe's magazine *Poetry*, attended by Yeats and Sandburg, where it met with a much
warmer reception and went on to become one of the most popular performance pieces in his repertoire; so much so that as late as 1931 he was driven
to ask his agent to include a clause in all his future contracts for recitations to
the effect that he would no longer do "The Congo" (Ruggles 411). One of his
earliest biographers, fellow poet Edgar Lee Masters, claims that "the poem
called 'The Congo' is Beethoven jazz with the greatest success. The Negroes
are to have their place in the City of the Perfect" (Masters 324). Even having
been awarded a reserved seat in Utopia, there were many nonwhite readers
who responded unfavorably to the poem, including W. E. B. DuBois, whose
Crisis magazine had already published an interesting short story by Lindsay,
called "The Golden Faced People," which dealt with racial oppression and
stereotypes.

Vachel Lindsay had the experience common to many white Americans of
his era of hearing several sides of America's racial controversy expounded at
home from his earliest years. His father put forward the view that Lincoln was
a reprobate and that Harriet Beecher Stowe's book appealed only to infidels,
while his mother, though possessed of "many Southern ideas was all for
Lincoln." Looking back upon this experience in "An Autobiographical Foreword" to his *Collected Poems*, Lindsay observes that "Mason and Dixon's
line runs straight through our house in Springfield still, and straight through
my heart" (23). Though it is true that Lindsay's early life brought him into
contact with a greater variety of black people than did Gertrude Stein's, it is
especially significant for this inquiry that when asked by "elegant ladies" how
he had acquired his knowledge of the Negro, he begins his response with a
purely literary source. He remembers clearly that his father used to read to the
children from *Uncle Remus*, and so, even before Lindsay began to have significant contacts with blacks, he was internalizing a primarily linguistic structure of thought about them. All his future experiences would be filtered
through a metaphorical veil, and the nonwhite could speak to him only
through the concocted idioms of Joel Chandler Harris.

The manner of Lindsay's acquisition of the racial language structures is
particularly interesting because in this instance we are faced with a poet who
sincerely wished Afro-Americans well and took steps, where he could, to be
of assistance to them. It was Lindsay, after all, who brought wider public
attention to the works of Langston Hughes after that younger poet, then a
waiter at Washington's Wardman Park Hotel, served him a manuscript along
with his dinner. And following race riots in Springfield in 1909, during the

course of which two men were lynched, Lindsay composed his short story, "The Golden Faced People," which is another attempt to deconstruct the white mythology of race, this time by casting its action in a distant future when white Americans are subjected to the domination of Asian occupiers similar to the subjugation of African slaves to white American owners. But even responding sincerely to his shock at these riots, even when arguing for the obliteration of racial boundaries, Lindsay seems unable to escape from a self-confirming white viewpoint. He says in his "Autobiographical Foreword" that "we have so many negroes in Springfield we had race riots for a week" (23). To begin with, the proportion of black citizens of Springfield at the time was closer to 6 percent (Massa 162), not the 20 percent that Lindsay claims (Lindsay 23). Yet far more revealing than that overestimation is what is going on with the syntax of Lindsay's comment. For the statement sets up a cause-and-effect relationship between the rising numbers of nonwhites and the attacks upon them by whites, moving the responsibility from the lyncher to the lynchee. Lindsay is so much the product of the set of discourse agreements operating in *Uncle Remus* that he quite simply cannot hear the objections of those who exist outside that set of agreements. Writing in 1916 to Joel E. Spingarn, a white associate of W. E. B. DuBois, Lindsay complains: "My 'Congo' and 'Booker T. Washington Trilogy' have both been denounced by the colored people for reasons that I can not fathom. As far as I can see, they have not taken the trouble to read them through. The third section of 'The Congo' is certainly as hopeful as any human being dare to be with regard to any race . . . and 'King Solomon and the Queen of Sheba' is a prophecy of a colored Utopia. Yet the *Crisis* took the trouble to skin me not long ago." Spingarn replies to this patiently and elegantly, in part *because* Lindsay was valued as a liberal voice, pointing out that the objection arises from the poet's adoption of the metaphorical contraptions positing the exoticism of the nonwhite. He says to Lindsay, "you look about you and see a black world full of strange beauty different from that of the white world," and goes on in the same letter to chide Lindsay for his apparent belief that "black men and women are not like others who have been mocked and scorned and wounded, but beings a little different from other sufferers . . ." (qtd. in Massa 169–70). What Spingarn detected in Lindsay's "The Congo" is nothing more complicated than the poet's involvement in the ongoing project of white literature of separating itself from that which it regards as being not-itself. That project is everywhere evident in "The Congo," for Lindsay, in writing that poem, portrays "the concern of a savage, childlike race with religion, a concern that in the end will redeem the soul of the race. The

Mumbo-Jumbo refrain is a symbol of 'the ill fate and sinister power of Africa from the beginning,' yet this fatality, which enters the Negro's history at all points, is eased by his high spirits, his incomparable gift of expressing joy, and is finally overcome by his religious faith, shown most of all in his capacity for emotion and vision" (Ruggles 214; the words in quotation marks are Lindsay's own). Composition of "The Congo" begins from such readily identifiable discourse agreements, and never leaves them, and it is for that reason that the Negro utopia is a utopia of otherness, located surely in some place other than white America.

"The Congo" is an importantly resonant poem. Inspired by a sermon describing the life and death of Ray Eldred, a missionary who drowned while swimming in a branch of the Congo River, it beckons in one direction to Joseph Conrad's *Heart of Darkness*. At the same time it serves as a precursor poem, with its assumption of the fatality of Africa and its people, to Wallace Stevens's "Owl's Clover," with its equally savage invocations of fatal Ananke. "The Congo" is subtitled "A Study of the Negro Race," but it might be more aptly described as a brown study clouding the white imagination. Section I of the poem, "Their Basic Savagery," proceeds to link a vision of contemporary Afro-American life to an African source. This is a common enough artistic device, one which bears clear resemblance to Jean Toomer's use in *Cane* of the Southern Road that grows out of a goat path in Africa. But Lindsay follows that route from "Fat black bucks in a wine-barrel room" to a source in cannibalistic frenzy, a journey which must have caused many blacks to ask, along with Countee Cullen in his poem "Heritage," "what is Africa to me?" (Cullen 88). Lindsay's imagined Africa is so much like Conrad's because both men are writing from within the same white mythology about the same fatal darkness:

THEN I SAW THE CONGO, CREEPING THROUGH
    THE BLACK
CUTTING THROUGH THE FOREST WITH A
    GOLDEN TRACK.
Then along that riverbank
A thousand miles
Tatooed cannibals danced in files
Then I heard the boom of the blood-lust song
And a thigh-bone beating on a tin-pan gong.
                                    (Lindsay 178–79)

As Conrad's narrator leaves us with "the horror," this section of "The Congo" leaves the reader with the word "blood" repeating itself over. Also to be noted is the concatenation of that blood lust with the black aesthetic. Lindsay makes of the richness of African music a one-note threat as witch doctors and warriors with whistles, fifes, and rattles all proclaim their desire for blood. That one note is elaborated into "A roaring, epic, rag-time tune / From the mouth of the Congo," but it remains a message of fatality. Where the sophistication of Wallace Stevens will image a fatal Ananke, here we get the far less interesting but every bit as fatal Mumbo-Jumbo, "god of the Congo," who, if you, the white reader, are not careful, "will hoo-doo you."

The second section of the poem, which studies "Their Irrepressible High Spirits" (Lindsay 180–82), again opens with a scene of black revelry, this time employing the stereotype of the crapshooting Negro. Lindsay here describes a type of black Xanadu, an ebony palace, which he at least concedes is a product of the imagination. It is "A negro fairyland . . . / A minstrel river / Where dreams come true," but that dream is one that occurs within the white mind. As in the preceding section, a link is established between the American revelry and an African source. The party is attended by a baboon butler, recalling Thomas Jefferson's orangutan, and dances to a "parrot band," which conceit, while calling up jungle images, seems to be making a statement about the originality of black music. Mumbo-Jumbo intrudes upon this scene, as it did upon the last, just as fatality is seen to enter black experience at all points, giving the cakewalk an air few would have thought of. (At this stage, for the first time, Lindsay's marginal directions to the reader indicate that "a touch of negro dialect" is to be adopted.)

It is not until we reach section 3, "The Hope of Their Religion" (Lindsay 182–84), that we encounter "A good old negro." The rhythms are unchanged in this section, but now they signify the blood of redemption rather than the blood of cannibalism, a crime which early Christians were sometimes accused of having committed. Mumbo-Jumbo, Fatal Ananke, is routed in this passage by "their" religion, which is the religion of white people, and the Negroes are seen repenting their crimes of "stupor and savagery and sin and wrong." Marginal directions instruct the reader to follow the parabola from darkness to whitened deliverance as the refrain reappears; we are told to *begin with terror and power, and end with joy,* as we arrive upon the golden track of Christian redemption. Just as the earthly utopia Lindsay envisoned for the nonwhite in section 2 was a pure product of white American imaginings, the spiritual paradise sketched in section 3 is a white man's idea of a black heaven, an advance copy of *Cabin in the Sky,* an eternal camp meeting up yonder. The twelve apostles are depicted driving away all the Mumbo-Jumbo, as everything Lindsay had posited as "native" to the nonwhite is driven off in the moment of redemption. Even the jungle is stripped from the blacks in their apotheosis:

> Then along that river, a thousand miles
> The vine snared trees fell down in files
> Pioneer angels cleared the way
> For a Congo paradise, for babes at play,
> For sacred capitals, for temples clean.

It is evidently not enough that the nonwhite be freed from the snares of sin, the snares of naturally occurring vines must also be thrown off. The "skull-faced witch-men," who, one supposes, must have constituted some sort of priesthood within the "native" religions, are swept away along with their rattles and drums and blood lust. Clearly, in Lindsay's view, only the recalcitrant would resist this generalized cleansing, which even redeems the forest and its creatures. At the poem's close, only one continues to chant "Mumbo-Jumbo" out of the darkness of radical otherness; only the vulture continues to cry the Congo tune: "Mumbo-Jumbo will hoo-doo you," prefiguring a like taunt delivered by a buzzard in Robert Penn Warren's "Pondy Woods." Given that conclusion, Lindsay's dismay at the reluctance of "the colored people" to embrace his "prophecy of a colored Utopia," takes on a yet more disturbing cast.

Carl Sandburg, one of the initial auditors of "The Congo," would have found little to dismay him in any of this during his early years, because he too was operating within the poetic tradition of white speech. This is evidenced by such poems as his "Mammy Hums," which adds little to the well-established image structures of black femininity. The poem speaks of the "nigger mammy humming" of songs and goes on to make the same sort of connection between the black and nature that we saw in Stein's *Melanctha.* The mammy's "murmurs run with bees' wings / in a late summer sun" (Sandburg, *Complete Poems* 128). Sandburg was a child of the early Scandinavian and Irish immigrations to the American Midwest and belonged to a social class that sometimes resented deeply the later massive influx of Mediterranean peoples and southern blacks. Much of that resentment seems to have still been lodged in Sandburg's consciousness while he was performing his journalistic tasks following the brutal race riots that took place in Chicago almost contemporaneously with his emergence as a public poet. Those riots began with the murder by a white mob of a black who had inadvertently violated the segregated waters off the city's beaches, and ended only after roving bands of men had stoned and killed dozens of Chicagoans. The extent to which Sandburg, in his early years, subscribed to the structure of the racial beliefs we have been examining may be gauged from two letters he addressed to his brother-in-law, Edward Steichen, shortly after the violence had subsided. In the first of these letters the poet tells the photographer that he has "spent ten days in the black belt and [is] starting a series of articles . . . on why Abasynnians, Bushmen and Zulus are here" (Sandburg, *Letters* 166). He of course did nothing of the sort and would have been hard pressed to locate a bushman in Chicago in any event. What was really bothering Sandburg was the, to him, unjustifiable increase in black population in his city. Like Lindsay after the Springfield riots, Sandburg seemed to think the blacks brought all this on themselves by failing to stay where they belonged. The second letter discussing the series of articles Sandburg set out to write is dated six months later and exhibits stark racism. In it, Sandburg reports: "The last figures I heard as to the race riot death toll was 35 negro dead and 20 white men. . . . The stories of many niggers being killed and hidden are bosh. It's a damn hard job to get rid of one corpse in a big city" (*Letters* 175).

Other poems from this period, including "Nigger," and "Singing Nigger," again show Sandburg resorting to the same dead metaphors for his treatment of the nonwhite subject. "Nigger" is a monologue which sounds as if spoken by the dead metaphor itself: "I am the nigger, / Singer of songs, / Dancer . . ." (*Complete Poems* 23). Through the speaker's veins courses the "Red love of the blood of women, / White love of the tumbling pickaninnes . . . / Lazy love of the banjo thrum." To this lazy, musical sensuality, Sandburg adds the by now expected "breaking crash of laughter / . . . / Loud laughter with hands like hams," which could have been lifted entire from the pages of *Melanctha*. The African of this poem must not only toil in Babylon, he must also laugh and perform for his captors. Sandburg finds the laughter to be innate to the black man "smiling the slumber dream of old jungles, / Crazy as the sun and dew dripping, heaving life of the jungle," and he proposes that the black's elemental kinship with the earth has rendered him "softer than fluff of cotton . . . / Harder than dark earth." These images recur two years later in "Singing Nigger," as Sandburg finds his way into the exoticism of the jazz age. Here, the subject is addressed as "bony head, Jazbo, O dock walloper," and is advised that it was heard shooting (what else?) craps and singing "My baby's going to have a new dress" (*Complete Poems* 108). Physical labor, earthy play, gambling, and jazz music remain the only areas of activity open to the black subject in this poet's verses.

Each of these poems takes a turn at the end which indicates that Sandburg may have begun to examine more closely the racial idioms he spoke so natively; each closes with a sudden introduction of irony. "Nigger" ends with the defiant image of the New Negro as defined from the hopes of a people after World War One by such black intellectuals as W. E. B. DuBois and Alain Locke. It is an image not calculated to please the other members of Sandburg's social caste. It is as if the stereotype suddenly stood up on its own and gestured threateningly toward its maker:

> Brooding and muttering with memories of shackles:
>> I am the nigger
>> Look at me.
>> I am the nigger.

It is a muttering that would find its answer later in the Afro-American poet Margaret Walker's heavily Sandburgian "For My People," and in Sterling Brown's "Strong Men," a poem directly influenced by Sandburg. The newly arrived blacks, crammed into tenements on Chicago's South Side, forced Sandburg at the last to an uncomfortable self-examination. In "Singing Nigger," he admits at the end that he knows what experience the songs of Afro-America grow out of and why God listens to them. The poet touring the Black Belt observes a group of men forming a brief fraternity around their single can of beer and departs, wondering to himself where *he* has come from.

It is moments like these that account for the rare occasions in Sandburg's poetry when the nonwhite breaks through the veil of the poet's internalized systems of speech. The times that Afro-America is heard most clearly in his poems are the times when Sandburg stops speaking of or for them and simply listens to the voice of the nonwhite. One such instance is the posthumously published "Sojourner Truth Speaking" (Sandburg, *Breathing* 61), in which Sandburg seems simply to have created verse arrangements out of the recorded statements of that eloquent struggler for her people's freedom. Another similar effort is the poem, "Sayings of Henry Stephens" (Sandburg, *Complete Poems* 691–94), a poem datelined, coincidentally enough, Springfield, Illinois, 1917. In this piece, Sandburg practices the secretarial skills he had acquired and takes down the monologue of a black, workingclass speaker:

> You're a white man
> an' I'm a negro.

Your nationality don't make no difference.
  If I kill you
  Everybody says:
"Henry Stephens, a negro, killed a white man."
  .   .   .   .   '.   .
If I buy a house right next to the Peabody mine
That won't do no good.
Only white men digs coal there.
I got to walk a mile, two miles, further
Where the black man can dig coal.

Without subjecting his persona to the contortions of the white man's black dialect, Sandburg takes the nearly unprecedented step of allowing the non-white to speak his own experience into the ruminations of white poetry. While he was never able wholly to free himself of the discursive blinders he wore when writing, Sandburg was, at least on these two occasions, capable of stilling the river of white speech long enough for his readers to hear the voice of suppressed otherness calling to them across the abyss. Nevertheless, there is a troublesome aspect to such poetic transcriptions, a sense in which the poet, through citation, exercises the greatest power over the other. In the view of Michel de Certeau, "the written discourse which cites the speech of the other is not, cannot be, the discourse of the other. On the contrary, this discourse, in writing the Fable that authorizes it, alters it" (78).

Robert Frost's father seems to have adhered to political sentiments resembling those of Vachel Lindsay's father, but in Frost's case there were few mitigating counterarguments in the household, and he grew to maturity with a fully matured set of prejudices. One of his biographers, Lawrance Thompson, reports in *Robert Frost: The Early Years* that

> Frost's own Copperhead sympathies expressed themselves during the first fall at Harvard, as he participated in a band-led victory procession through Cambridge streets, following a football game. The only person he recognized in the procession was the Negro from his Greek class, and they talked together as they marched. When they were joined by three other Negro students, Frost decided that he had marched long enough. He made excuses and dropped out of the parade. His attitude toward Negroes, and their sympathizers, conveyed to him in boyhood by his Copperhead father, stayed with him throughout his life. (236)

Frost's behavior during the course of that procession formed a pattern which would repeat itself in his later life; the poet would form an alliance with an Afro-American when it suited his purpose, only to turn his back on that relationship when he either no longer required it or found that it embarrassed him. That he had completely internalized a bitter prejudice against the aspirations of the nonwhite and against whites who sympathized with those aspirations is manifest in a letter he later wrote to Richard Thornton in which Frost discusses the aims of the Committee of Vermont Traditions and Ideals: "I don't know what their ideals may be, but possibly one of them is to stay black Republican, set the nigger free and elect Taft retroactively as of 1912" (qtd. in Thompson, *Triumph* 384). This letter characterizes Frost's mode of response to nonwhite ambitions throughout his public life, and the term "nigger," which he so easily employs here, was to remain his favored term of abuse, the term by which he would signify an area of darkness he felt to be foreign to and beneath him.

On one of those few occasions that Frost chose to strike up an acquaintance with a black writer, the episode became a near reenactment of his march away from blackness during that Cambridge parade. William Stanley Braithwaite, poetry editor of Boston's *Evening Transcript* and one of the more popularly read poets of his day, was what has sometimes been called a "voluntary" Negro, that is, he could easily have passed for white had he had any inclination to reject his nonwhite heritage and ancestry. The popularity of his own verse and articles had made it possible for him to edit and publish an equally successful *Anthology of Magazine Verse* annually, and he was always in search of bright, new talents to feature in his essays and anthologies. Nathan Haskell Dole, who had only just become acquainted with Frost himself, arranged a meeting between the two poets, the result of which was Braithwaite's determining to do an article on Frost with the assistance of notes prepared and sent to him by Frost. With this assistance, Braithwaite eventually produced two articles which appeared in the *Transcript,* and which did much to further Frost's growing reputation (Thompson, *Triumph* 15). Indeed, when Edmund J. Wheeler undertook to refute the charges brought by Ezra Pound, a man who would have his own encounters with Braithwaite, that America had been delinquent in its recognition of Frost, it was Braithwaite's articles he cited as evidence to the contrary.

But Frost, having enjoyed Braithwaite's attentions, was soon to turn violently against him and to turn to the structures of racist discourse for his armament, a turning which Lawrance Thompson believes was brought on by Braithwaite's preference for Edwin Arlington Robinson. In a Christmas letter to Louis Untermeyer, Frost promises his colleague: "Sometime at a worse season I will tell you what I think of niggers," and later in the same letter he draws a definition which displays the deep-seated nature of his prejudice:

And again: to be niggerly is not necessarily to be niggardly. It is niggerly for instance to single out Fannie Stearns Davis for dispraise, but it can't be called niggardly to name nobody else in the world but to praise them. In the case of Fanny you can't help suspecting something in the woodpile, a nigger scorned or slighted or not properly played up to.

   Mind you I haven't read Fannie and I haven't read Braithwaite's g.d. book [that year's *Anthology*]—I got one of the children to read it for me and tell me about it. (Qtd. in Thompson, *Triumph* 64)

In still another letter to Untermeyer, commiserating with him over an unfavorable comment Braithwaite had made about Untermeyer in the *Transcript*, Frost refers to the Afro-American poet simply as "the Transcript Nigger" (qtd. in Thompson, *Triumph* 163) and with that one epithet expels the representative of blackness from the realm of white letters.

   There are very few references to blacks in Frost's verse, and when they occur they are usually confined within the same bounds of otherness as they are in his personal papers. One poem, "The Discovery of the Madeiras: *A Rhyme of Hakluyt*," features a Dantesque narrative nested within the primary narrative, a story of two enslaved lovers undergoing the middle passage. The tale is told by a ship's captain who shares the perceptions of blacks held by Captain Delano in "Benito Cereno," that the black woman is "a savage jungle cat," for example (Frost 345). In this interior narrative the male lover takes sick "when at length the fever struck / That spoils the nigger-trader's luck." The crew, to cut their losses, determine to throw the sick man overboard alive before the disease can spread to others. Then, the thought enters

> into someone's head
> Of the ocean bed for a marriage bed.
> Some Tom said to Dick or Harry:
> Apparently these two ought to marry.
> We get plenty funerals at sea.
> How for a change would a wedding be?—
> Or a combination of the two,
> How would a funeral wedding do?
> It's gone so far she's probably caught
> Whatever it is the nigger's got.
> (Frost 345–46)

The African lovers are bound naked facing one another and, in a horrific replication of the image of Paolo and Francesca, are tossed overboard to the waiting sharks. That Frost intends this story to be terrifying is clear from the reaction of the woman to whom it is repeated within the poem, and the nested narrative could serve, in a fashion somewhat like the early pages of "Benito Cereno," as a check upon the internal system of racial thought of its readers. But it is interesting that while this stream of signifiers flows from the racist mind of the sea captain with no textual signals of irony, on each occasion that Frost purports to represent the views of those opposed to racism in his verse, he makes them sound foolish. In "The Literate Farmer and the Planet Venus" he has a generic "liberal," speaking for an entire realm of political discourse, report that:

> As liberals we're willing to give place
> To any demonstrably better race,
> No matter what the color of its skin.
> (But what a human race the white has been!)
> (Frost 369)

This same liberal voice goes on to imply fairly forcefully that those who act to assist blacks in their struggles do so for their own glorification: "The slave will never thank his manumitter; / Which often makes the manumitter bitter!" (Frost 371) While the line shows a recognition that the slave has no obligation to thank the dominant powers for relinquishing their immediate power over him, this line, put forward as a liberal position, renders ludicrous the motivations of whites active in the freedom movements. Even when Frost attempts to pillory the proponents of evolutionary theory, in "Accidentally on Purpose," he represents that theory as speaking in a voice of ignorance and racism:

> They mean to tell us all was rolling blind
> Till accidentally it hit on mind
> In an albino monkey in a jungle . . .
> (Frost 425)

Frost here depicts the evolutionists as having pushed the color bar even further back than Jefferson did, so that it operates among the simian species as it operates among humans. My point is not that no one ever made such a claim but that Frost selects this most perverse position as his straw man in his argument with evolution, and in so doing lends the most eccentric fringe of Social Darwinism a status it never actually claimed in scientific discourse. He knocks over evolutionary "accident" but leaves white primacy standing, "accidentally on purpose," in suggesting the white origins of human thought.

A reader might turn to the author of *John Brown's Body* for a respite from these patterns of abuse, for Stephen Vincent Benét, though no longer considered in a class with Frost as a poet, was possessed of clearly more sympathetic politics on questions of race. In his foreword to Margaret Walker's *For My People,* a volume he had selected for the Yale Series of Younger Poets award in 1942, Benét demonstrated his sensitivity to the type of patronizing reading with which white readers might greet such a volume. He declared that Walker's is not "interesting and moving poetry because it was written by a Negro. It is too late in the day for that sort of meaningless patronage—and poetry must exist in its own right" (Benét, Foreword 8). Years before, at the close of his own epic poem of the American Civil War he had presented his vision of a United States healing the wounds of slavery, racial hatred, and warfare through the image of a black soldier, Spade, wounded in the Battle of the Crater, going to work in the fields with the white veteran Jake Diefer, who had lost an arm in the war (Benét, *John Brown's Body* 356–58). Further, Benét saw more plainly than many the dangers attendant upon attempting to appropriate the voice of the other. In one of the most often cited passages of *John Brown's Body* (*JBB*), Benét pulls back from the temptation to try in his own voice to utter the saga of black America:

> Oh, blackskinned epic, epic with the black spears,
> I cannot sing you, having too white a heart,
> And yet, someday, a poet will rise to sing you,
> And sing you with such truth and mellowness.
>
> (337)

That part of Afro-American history which Benét does essay he undertakes with an impressive understanding. In terse lines he is able to indicate the ironies of the postemancipation exploitation suffered by black workers, as in the scene where the economies of liberation are delineated for a former slave:

> That shovell'l cost five dollars.
> Remember that—it comes out of your first week's pay.
> You're a free nigger now
>
> (*JBB* 220).

More important, throughout the verses of his account Benét foregrounds his own awareness of the extent to which white literature and speech have supported the structures of oppression. In an apostrophe to the character Aunt Bess, the poet observes: "They have made you a shrine and a humorous fable, / But they kept you a slave while they were able" (153). Perhaps most significant in this regard is Benét's inclusion within his poem of an example of the fashion in which literary imagery comes to serve as a screen which to a large measure determines what the white consciousness will be able to encompass. As was the case with Vachel Lindsay, many white poets of the twentieth century tend to view Afro-America through the metaphorical veils of Joel Chandler Harris, Harriet Beecher Stowe, and others whose imaginary Negroes seized the imaginations of American readers. Almost as a warning of this process, Benét produces a character in his poem, Ellyat, whose imagined American Southland comes entirely from literary sources:

> The South, that languorous land where Uncle Toms
> Groaned Biblically underneath the lash,
> And grinning Topsies mopped and mowed behind
> Each honeysuckle vine.
>   They called them niggers
> And cut their ears off when they ran away,
> But then they loved their mammies—there was that—
> Although they sometimes sold them down the river—
> And when the niggers were not getting licked
> Or quoting Scripture, they sang funny songs,
> By the Swanee river, on the old plantation.
>
>   (21)

However, for all his insight into the effects of racial mythology upon the national psyche, in many of his portrayals of black characters Benét quotes racial scripture, falling back again and again on clichéd imagery. His attempts at reproducing black dialect seem to be signifiers of deficiency. Benét's use of dialect, rather than capturing the fullness of African-American speech, demonstrates the inconsistencies of Benét's own writing. The character Spade, for instance, is perfectly capable of pronouncing the final "th" sound of words like "with" (*JBB* 165), and yet he constantly speaks of "de Norf" (the cleaving to rules of capitalization is interesting). The physical descriptions provided of black characters by Benét stand as a catalogue of stereotypes. A former king in Africa, Tarbarrell is said to be "the image of black stone / Whose eyes were savage gods" (12). But while some blacks are gods, albeit after strange gods, most are characterized by tropes derived from a considerably lower link in the chain of being. A fugitive slave glimpsed by Ellyat in Boston is described as "the black man with the eyes of a tortured horse . . ." (21). Slaves told by John Brown's raiders that they have been freed are said, by the narrator, to have "heard the news / With the dazed, scared eyes of cattle before a storm" (30). Lastly, like Sherwood Anderson, Gertrude Stein, and so many others, Benét's imaginary blacks are marked, or masked as the case may be, by their resilient laughter:

> . . . all through the scare, and before and after,
> Their voices are rich with the ancient laughter,
> The negro laughter, the blue-black rose,
> The laughter that doesn't end with the lips
> But shakes the belly and curls the toes
> And prickles the end of the fingertips.
>
> (151–52)

Only Edwin Arlington Robinson among this group of writers has left us a poem of major proportions taking a nonwhite subject matter and attempting to treat it in its own terms rather than as the phantom production of self-constituting whiteness, and that poem is his "Toussaint L'Ouverture." Importantly, Robinson's poem arises from the same sort of dramatic situation which drives "Benito Cereno," a slave rebellion and its aftermath. Unlike Melville's novel, however, "Toussaint L'Ouverture" is not narrated by a white, nor is it centered in a white consciousness. It is instead a dramatic monologue spoken to the reader by Toussaint L'Ouverture himself, the major figure in the revolution of San Domingo which began in 1791 and resulted, following the defeat of Bonaparte's 1803 invasion, in the creation of the modern state known as Haiti. The immediate occasion of Robinson's writing this poem was his reading of Percy Waxman's biography of L'Ouverture, *The Black Napoleon* (Wallace L. Anderson 123), a biography which the author of the most widely acknowledged history of the San Domingo revolution has described as "superficial" (James 388). But as has happened so often in the past, major poetry has in this case proceeded from an inferior prose source.

The monologue is datelined from the Château de Joux, 1803, which is the location and date of Toussaint's imprisonment by Bonaparte, an imprisonment which led to the black man's death on April 7, 1803. As a subject matter, this has obvious attractions for a poet of the likes of Robinson. In the background is the high drama of the revolution itself, which C. L. R. James describes as follows: "The transformation of slaves, trembling in hundreds before a single white man, into a people able to organize themselves and defeat the most powerful European nations of their day, is one of the great epics of revolutionary struggle and achievement" (ix). James is meticulous in pointing to the fact that Toussaint L'Ouverture "did not make the revolution," a point which Robinson follows carefully. But neither does James deny any of Toussaint's personal greatness, for he submits "that between 1789 and 1815, with the single exception of Bonaparte himself, no single figure appeared on the historical stage more greatly gifted than this negro, a slave till he was 45" (x).

The facts of Toussaint L'Ouverture's imprisonment are much as they appear in Robinson's work. Toussaint was incarcerated in the Fort-de-Joux in the Jura Mountains by Bonaparte, and it was the Frenchman's intention that he should die there of "natural" causes. To this end, Toussaint was denied all companionship, placed on a starvation diet, and given an insufficient supply of wood to heat his quarters. Medical attention was eventually withdrawn because, his jailer reported, "the construction of Negroes being totally different to that of Europeans, . . . [it] would be useless to him" (qtd. in James 363). Such abuse quickly reduced the prisoner's ability to endure. "The hitherto unsleeping intellect collapsed periodically into long hours of coma. Before the Spring he was dying. One April morning he was found dead in his chair" (James 365).

This then is the dramatic situation into which Robinson introduces his readers. The veil of darkness, the darkness of the prison and the darkness of white discourse, is pierced through by the voice of this revolutionary who, not being able to see his auditor, addresses us familiarly:

> Am I alone—or is it you, my friend?
> I call you friend, but let it not be known
> That such a word was uttered in this place.
> You are the first that has forgotten duty.
>
> (Robinson 227)

Direct address is in this case made problematic by the fact that the speaker cannot tell to whom he is speaking. He begins by addressing to the reader the starkest of questions from the racial prison house of language, "Am I alone?" It is not, yet, a rhetorical question. The poem seems to anticipate an answer at this point, an answer from us; it wants to know whether we can so far forget the duties laid upon us by our discourse agreements as to abandon their stipulations and address this caged black leader as a friend. Toussaint's voice reaches out to the reader, assuring him that what has been said of the nonwhite is not true; he is not a brute incapable of finer feeling. "Yes," he declares out of the blindness of his crypt, "I can feel and hear." And he demands to know if we too can feel and hear.

The situation is ironized when we who have come to interrogate the poem, as Caffarelli came under Bonaparte's orders to interrogate Toussaint, end by being interrogated by the poem. We are warned, not as we were in Vachel Lindsay's "The Congo" with threats of hoo-doo, but with threats of what might proceed from our own violation of white agreements.

> You must be careful,
> Or they will kill you if they hear you asking
> Questions of me as if I were a man.
>   (Robinson 227)

The facts that this voice issues such a warning to us, and that we *can* ask questions of it as if it emanated from the mouth of a man, deconstruct the Jeffersonian agreement upon the bestiality of the nonwhite. The poem forces us away from the Steinian assumptions of the earthiness of the black and causes us to consider the nonwhite "as more than a transplanted shovelful / Of black earth, with a seed of danger in it— / A seed that's not there now, and never was" (227). The threat whiteness has constituted as existing is a fictive threat. The danger of blackness which we have encrypted in our language is a self-reflecting signifier of dread. "The only danger that was ever in" blackness "was food that . . . hate made to feed itself" (227).

As the first lines show, the poem concerns itself greatly with our words, and with our speaking of them. There are words that it is not safe to utter. The voice of the poem challenges us to speak them, while itself speaking them into us:

> Are you still there? Are you afraid to speak?
> You are the first thing fashioned as a man
> That has acknowledged me since I came here—
> To die, as I see now—with word or motion
> Of one man in the same world with another
> And you may be afraid of saying to me
> Some word that hurts your tongue.
>   (Robinson 228)

Afraid because to say that hurtful word would destroy the fiction we keep alive in our language, the story we have told ourselves in our literature of the world we inhabit, as men, by ourselves, a world the blackness cannot enter. Words, as I have attempted to show, create and maintain relationships of power as surely as do prisons and arms, and Toussaint tells us that "the few that have the word / Are mostly the wrong few in the wrong places, / On thrones or chairs of state too high for them" (230). And having established this, he goes on to put to us two questions that are rhetorical in the classic sense: "Is power a breaking down of flesh and spirit? / Is foresight a word lost with a lost language?" (231). As at the outset Toussaint begins by assuring us of his ability to hear; the poem emphasizes hearing throughout. "Hear me," Toussaint implores, "and I will tell you a strange thing" (229). And again still later, "Hear me, and I will tell you what I saw" (231).

There are several passages in which Robinson uses Toussaint's statements specifically to throw over the image structures of race we have identified so far. To the stereotypical representations of black laughter, Toussaint simply points out the obvious, that his white jailers have taken away from him "a way to laugh." To the repeated assertion that the black is something other than and less than human he offers his auditor his thanks for seeing in him:

> . . . a remnant of mankind,
> And not a piece of God's peculiar clay
> Shaped as a reptile, or as a black snake.
> A black man, to be sure; and that's important.
>
> (229)

Most attention is directed, as at the close of "Benito Cereno," to the assertions of white discourse about the nonwhite intellect. As Babo's head was elevated on a pole in punishment for having contained a mind capable of conspiring for its own liberty, so for Toussaint "France was a place where they were starving me / To death, because a black man had a brain" (234). Not just a brain, but a brain far more subtle than that possessed by the hapless Captain Delano; Toussaint boasts a mind fully capable of recognizing the ironies of his position in the prison house of language, and of calling these ironies to the reader's attention.

> Is it not strange, my friend, for me to see
> So clearly, and in the dark, more than he sees
> Who put me here?
>
> (233)

It is a poetic instance that is overironized. The person who put Toussaint here, in the poem, is Robinson as much as it is Bonaparte, and all of these words about words of blackness are streaming from the imagination of a white artist. The white artist has, as de Certeau asserts in *Heterologies,* altered the speech of the other, repossessed it, and has hence rewritten his authorizing fable. But our project is exactly to uncover the ways that the white mind represents blackness to itself, and it is therefore important to pursue this counterexample to the black heaven of Vachel Lindsay. In the black hole of white thought in which Toussaint finds himself, from which there is no escape, he must continue to ask himself why he can see what others cannot see:

> . . . Is it not strange, my friend—
> If you are there—that one dishonored slave,
> One animal owned and valued at a price,
> One black commodity, should have seen so early
> All that I saw?
>
> (230)

As if directly responding to Frost's "Accidentally on Purpose" in a sort of prolepsis, the speaker insists upon his createdness and the validity of his perceptions: "my prophetic eyes, where God has fixed them / In this black face, could see in front of them" (230). What Toussaint's eyes see, "out of this cold and darkness," is the condition of our being, the state we have placed ourselves in by our acts of language, "a place where black and white are dark together" (232).

Robinson is at his most eloquent in this poem when he contrives to have Toussaint L'Ouverture speak directly of the self-constituting nature of white imaginings, and of their effect upon the ability of the white mind to apprehend anything outside of the boundaries it has set to describe itself. Building upon the passages that show the vacuity of white discourse agreements regarding black intelligence, Toussaint offers the reader a demonstration, a reading of the operations of the reader's own thought:

> Can a black man be wise? He would say not.
> Having his wisdom, he would have to say it
> To keep his hate alive; and without that
> He would soon hate the sound of his own name.
>
> (232)

This quotation effectively makes Bonapartes of us all, and we can see in it again the accompanying emphasis upon the soundings of words and upon the power over the name. Such emphasis is cause for the reader to reflect with a certain anxiety upon his own place, and possible complicity, within white speeches and silences, for Toussaint promises, as Robinson writes to fulfill the promise, that "this will all be told; / And it will not sound well when men remember" (232). From the altitudes of his imprisonment, Toussaint proffers a challenge, calling attention to the fact that white privilege rests upon a construction which eliminates all that lies outside itself:

> Say who shall answer for a world where men
> Are mostly blind, and they who are the blindest

Climb to cold heights that others cannot reach
And there, with all there is for them to see,
See nothing but themselves.

(228)

It is the man locked away in solitary confinement who points out the tragic
solitude of his jailer. It is the nonwhite encrypted within our discourse that
indicates to us our self-imprisonment. The senselessness of this state of affairs
is a puzzlement to Toussaint, partly, he says, *because* he is black, because he
understands that he is not the creature of white dreams but a man locked away
out of sight. But he has only the reader to convey his puzzlement to, and the
reader may not have ready answers for Toussaint's pointed questions. The
bondage Toussaint finds himself in, that he struggled to free his people from,
is something that "will go on as long / As men capitulate who feel and see, /
And men who know say nothing" (231).

"Toussaint L'Ouverture" closes upon a symbol every bit as disturbing as
that which closes "Benito Cereno." Melville's final trope, the eloquent head
of Babo, looks out from the text upon a reader who is assumed present to
himself. Stein's *Melanctha* closes upon an equally present reader but with-
draws the black subject from the reader's view, pulling it voicelessly behind a
textual veil. What causes the disturbance at the conclusion of Edwin Arlington Robinson's poem is that he problematizes the status of the reader himself.
Having demonstrated that Bonaparte's Toussaint is a fiction, a white dream of
nonwhite dangers, Robinson leaves the status of the person addressed by his
poem in question. Toussaint suddenly raises the possibility that the person he
speaks to is as much a fiction for him as he has been for Bonaparte. His story
may have been encrypted and silenced as he has been. There may be no one
listening. "Now I see," he says to the lively darkness, "You were a dream,
my friend" (233). At poem's end the reader is neither here nor there. As
Toussaint's monologue approaches through the silence whiteness has imposed
upon black discourse toward the silence of death, the silence of whoever
might be listening from the other side of the veil finally engulfs the text.
Toussaint's last cry is an affirmation of his own being, directed against the
discursive veil:

You are gone.
Where are you? Is this the night again?
I cannot see you now. But you are there—
You are still there. And I know who is here.

(234)

Chapter 3

Modernism

But what a pity
that
the poet
the priest
and the revolution
never seem
to arrive
for the black woman,
herself.

Only for her black lips
or her black leg
does one or the other
arrive
only for her
devouring mouth
always depicted
in the act
of eating
something colorful

only for her breasts
like coconuts
and her red dress.

Alice Walker,
Horses Make a Landscape
Look More Beautiful

High modernism's hopes to arrive at the thing itself, freed from the encrustations of the language of romance, did not always succeed even in arriving at new ways of writing about the thing, especially if the "object" under consideration was a living race. As a case study of such failure, a history of modernism's representations of blackness serves to demonstrate that, for all their contributions to revolutionizing form, white modernist poets have only infrequently managed to approach the representation of black life without reerecting the terministic screens of racist imagery.

Seldom in our literary history has blackness so occupied the imaginations of white artists as during the rise of modernism. Indeed, that jazz age that found a sort of spokesman in F. Scott Fitzgerald derives its name from America's primary indigenous art form, one created by Afro-Americans. It was an age in which, as noted in an earlier chapter, visual artists turned to what was widely viewed as an African primitivism to gain impetus for their own creations. Additionally, the ascent of modernism had its inevitable effects within the black community in America, and the period of that artistic movement's consolidation coincides with the period of intense creative ferment among Afro-American artists that has come to be known as the Harlem Renaissance. Many of the elements of exoticism and primitivism which are to be found in white writing about blacks during this era may also be found in works by black authors, sometimes heavily ironized and sometimes not. To some extent this phenomenon represents the internalizing by the oppressed of the language and image structures of the oppressors; to some extent it represents the realities of writing for a market directed to a white readership, as Paul Dunbar had learned to his consternation when the success of his dialect verse overwhelmed his work in standard literary English. There were instances, like the episode from Melville's *White Jacket* featuring May-Day and Rose-Water, when black speakers simply meant something quite different from what white authors intended by the same words. And there was, always, a lively critique of that exoticism from within the discourse of the black intelligentsia, emanating most audibly from the writers associated with *Crisis* magazine under DuBois's editorship. In any event, more works by and about blacks appeared than at any time since Reconstruction, but this renewed attention to Afro-American life and expression did not serve to expel from our discourse the old myths of the bad other. It served instead to foster among white writers a curious combination of romantic racism with the most egregious elements of antiblack sentiment from the nineteenth century. Writing of this era, George M. Frederickson observes that "the cultural revolt against 'Puritanism' and 'repression' in the 1920's could lead some whites to believe that they were being complimentary to blacks when they described them as naturally naive and primitive creatures who characteristically gave free rein to all their passions" (328). And such compliments were produced as Carl Van Vechten's *Nigger Heaven,* DuBose Heyward's *Porgy,* and Edward Sheldon's theatrical sensation, *The Nigger.* Whites attended black-cast musicals like *Shuffle Along* on Broadway, and streamed to Harlem. But the black life which they saw depicted in *Shuffle Along,* or on the stage of Harlem's whites-only Cotton Club, was organized always along the lines of white expectations. Whites tended to see only that which they had all along told themselves to see. It was the white sociologist Melville J. Herskovits, not a white poet, who, writing of his trips to Harlem for the special "New Negro" issue of *Survey Graphic* edited by Alain Locke in 1925, identified those expectations: "Should I not find there, if anywhere, the distinctions of the Negro, of which I had heard so much? Should I not be able to discover there his ability, of which we are so often told, to produce unique cultural traits, which might be added to the prevailing white culture, and, as well, to note his equally well-advertised inability to grasp the complex civilization of which he constitutes a part?" (676). Herskovits visits Harlem and purports to find instead a typical American community. While he may be overcompensating in his declaration that Harlem, or any other part of Manhattan, is typically American, he at least has not trained himself to see only exotic primitives engaged in unthinking lives.

But Herskovits's questioning of the racial image structure in America was anomalous; the intellectual trend of the times was supportive of traditional white discourse. More typical were scholars such as New York University's Henry Pratt Fairchild, who said in one of his several books on the subject that there "can be no doubt that if America is to remain a stable nation it must continue a white man's country for an indefinite period of time" (qtd. in Gossett 387), a remark which only puts more explicitly what later remarks by T. S. Eliot and Allen Tate will also assert. And, despite the proliferation of anthropological and sociological information available to white intellectuals, they were always already so gripped by the preexisting discursive formation that they were disinclined to devise more adequate new explanations of America based upon such information. As one example, when the army's newly instituted programs of intelligence testing began to be replicated widely, results began to turn up which indicated that northern blacks did better than southern blacks, and better even than the whites of particular southern states, phenomena which would seem to suggest the necessity of a nongenetic accounting for the measured intelligence levels of various racial groups. As Thomas F. Gossett points out in *Race: The History of an Idea in America,* however, respected white thinkers chose to explain these data as the result of a supposedly greater amount of white blood among northern blacks. "Dr. Robert M. Yerkes, who had been in charge of the Army tests . . . endorsed the thesis that the tests proved that the Negroes were inferior in intelligence" (376) in a foreword which he wrote for *A Study of American Intelligence,* a volume authored by Dr. Carl C. Brigham of Princeton which argued for the superiority of the Nordic race over all others. This inability to arrive at adequate understandings of evidence due to the constraining influence of established racial imaging systems even afflicted those like Ezra Pound and his mentor in things African, Leo Frobenius, who were more willing than many of their fellow intellectuals to give a hearing to evidence at all. It is indicative in this regard that in Nancy Cunard's *Negro: An Anthology,* published as late as 1934, a number of the white poets we shall be discussing here contributed pieces which are clear instances of romantic racism.

The evidence offered by the writings of white poets during the era of high modernism demonstrates that they, like most other white intellectuals of the time, though writing more and more often of the nonwhite, were frequently guilty of a type of aesthetic slumming. Many seemed to feel as did Carl Van Vechten that "the squalor of Negro life, the vice of Negro life, offer a wealth of novel, exotic, picturesque material to the artist" (64). While appropriating to themselves what they thought to be the spirit of the jazz age, their writings again served to relegate the ostensible origin of that spirit to the periphery of culture. Black art was a "primitive" artifact placed in the museum of white discourse, detached from actual black communities.

Most immediately available as a precedent for this sort of writing is Gertrude Stein's *Melanctha,* and E. E. Cummings, who spoke favorably of Stein's early works while he was still a university student, is one of her apparent successors in this tradition. Nonwhites appear frequently in his works, and they nearly always appear veiled in the same romanticized and colorful terms as were deployed by Stein. Cummings repeats Stein's notion of the nothingness which is the condition of blackness, and in one poem uses that posited nothingness to question the validity of emancipation:

Clamored Clever Rusefelt
to Theodore Odysseus Graren't
We couldn't free the negro
because he ant
                    (*Poems* 321)

Also, Cummings offers a replay of the imagery employed by Stein and Vachel Lindsay in their descriptions of the primary modes of black life, descriptions in which the black, conceived of as giving over much of his or her life to jitterbugging, crapshooting, and lovemaking, is somehow held to be more the product of animated libido than is the "civilized" white. Cummings appears to believe, as does Stein, that there is something in this unreflecting approach to life he considers blacks to embody which has been lost by Caucasians in the confusions of modernity: a direct relationship to one's environment that circumvents the overly rational scientism of the bland, urban society. His poem, "Theys sO alive," proposes that:

        some folks aint born
    somes born dead an

```
somes born alive (but
                niggers
         is
        all
       born
    so
Alive)
                ump-A-tum
                tee-dee
            um-tum
             tidd
                 -id . . .
            (Poems 622)
```

The only original element here is Cummings's typography. The black-face speech he writes belongs to a worn tradition of white mimickry, an orthographic marking of difference which John Edgar Wideman has described as "a way of pointing to the difference between blacks and whites; the form and function of black speech as it was represented was to indicate black inferiority. . . . *Difference* in the dialect tradition clearly signified *deficiency*. Afro-American speech had been devalued, robbed of those mature aesthetic and functional dimensions it had developed in the New World" (60). Further, Cummings's notion that blacks are by birth more animated than other peoples is in keeping with the elemental figurations of *Melanctha* and other such exercises. It continues the inscription of Afro-America's radical otherness into the literature. The Afro-American, like Africa itself, "has been made to bear a double burden, of monstrousness *and* nobility, all imposed by a deeper condition of difference and instability" (Christopher L. Miller, *Blank* 5). While he depicts the nonwhite as existing in a more symbiotic relationship to nature, Cummings's work continues to enforce white privilege; he portrays blacks as being aspirants to a state of whiteness, as is the protagonist of this little fairy tale:

```
one day a nigger
caught in his hand
a little star no bigger
than not to understand

"i'll never let you go
until you've made me white"
so she did and now
stars shine at night
            (Poems 622)
```

Oddly enough, in this oddest of explanations of star-fire, requiring as it does the elimination of darkness, the star-catcher's wish is the only instance I have located in Cummings's poetry in which he uses standard English to represent black speech. In his other works blacks usually pronounce their lines within the limits of minstrel tradition. This poem evidences forthrightly the fact that Cummings still speaks white mythology's proposition that negritude is a diminished state from which all blacks should desire elevation.

All this converges in the second act of Cummings's play, *Him,* which is comprised of nine loosely associated farces mounted by the play's main character. In the fifth scene of this act, Cummings appropriates the standard blues ballad, "Frankie and Johnie," staging it as a "coon" show complete with jazz band and an acting out of the ballad's narrative, as embellished by Cummings. As they enact this tale of black love and loss, Cummings's characters enact their white audience's discourse agreements about black exoticism and male-female relationships. The six "coalblack" figures who constitute the chorus are costumed in "vermillion suits with white shirts and socks, emerald green neckties, lemoncoloured gloves and silk hats" (*Him* 53), and they are said to sing "darkly" (51). The characters speak in a more than usually distorted minstrel-style dialect, particularly the "Negress," Cummings's reiteration of the black female exotic we have seen in Stein. This Negress, dressed in a red kimona, "willows" down the stairs and says to the play's representative of puritanical white morality who arises from his place among the audience to confront her, "Gway yoh poor whytrash" (56). Frankie, the Negress, refuses the moralizing influence of whiteness, refusing to be defined by this white "Personage's" assignment of ladyhood to her: "Doan call me 'young lady' yoh bowlegged fish: ah ain no 'young lady,' thang Gawd!" (56). Apparently our Negress is fully capable of speaking whitely when she chooses.

All of this seems to have been received without objection by contemporary white critics. The reviewer for *Hound and Horn* treasured the use of dialect and reported favorably upon Cummings's version of "Frankie and Johnie" (Dendinger 94). Margaret E. Lawless, writing for the *Norfolk Pilot,* reported that "the only really illuminating feature of the whole play is the inclusion in this act of a less expurgated version of the Frankie and Johnie ballad than has hitherto come to this reviewer's attention" (qtd. in Dendinger 107). This raises the interesting question of how the received version of this folk ballad comes to be considered expurgated by a white critic who admits that she has never heard a "less expurgated" version. What has plainly occurred is that Cummings's version has supplied the reviewer with an element which her participation in white discourse agreements has led her to want to find in black folk expression. Though there is nothing at all unusual in one culture's adapting the artistic products of another, Cummings's version is exemplary of the political-social effects of such translations. Cummings has taken the normal sexual tensions of this ballad of male-female relationship and exaggerated them to the point that they constitute the whole story, rendering it quite literally phallocentric. When the scene closes with the Negress brandishing a bloodied object the size and shape of a banana, an object which, it is announced, is the "BEST PART OF THE MAN / WHO DONE [HER] WRONG" (56), Cummings's play is doing nothing more than supplying the stolen signifier of black maleness, enacting on the stage what white discourse has done symbolically to the black man, and reemphasizing the purported rampant sexuality of black life. And it is evidently these significations which the critic Lawless felt lacking, expurgated, or castrated from the more familiar, "blacker," versions.

One later scene in the second act of *Him* carries the use of blackface dialect, so treasured by the reviewer for *Hound and Horn*, to the ridiculous sublime. It must be admitted that all the figures of this scene, in which meetings are arranged between centurions and Mussolini, speak in modern American stage dialects and that the dialect spoken by the several "fairies" in the scene may be every bit as stereotypical and objectionable as is minstrel dialect. In scene 8, two Roman centurions are found shooting craps. Not surprisingly, this crapshoot quickly enough attracts a representative of blackness, in the person of an Ethiopian slave who enters the circle "lazily" (65). Cummings's Ethiopian slave is notable as another iteration of the lazy, gambling representation of black maleness which enters into the white American mind throughout its history. This Ethiopian is interchangeable with the cinematic figure of "Sleep-N-Eat," or with the character of minstrelsy, "Mr. Bones," even with the ever-popular Amos and Andy. The Ethiopian, upon joining the game, announces to the centurions: "Yoh faded. Now len me dem dice, fellah, ah feels de speerit on me" (66). And when encountering the "fairies," he pronounces his opinion that "if daze anything worse dan Christians, it certainly am peddyrasts" (66). This syntax, like the banana cum phallus of scene 5, finds its source in white imaginings; it is not a representation of speech but the signifier of otherness manifesting itself in art.

Such manifestations were not confined to the artistic creations of white poets, they occasionally erupted within the dream reports of those poets. Hart Crane, who shared many of Cummings's preoccupations with black sexuality, was for a time troubled by recurring dreams emblematic of racial sexual stereotypes. In one of these dreams, Crane reported to friends, he was menaced by a black man displaying enormous and threatening genitalia (Unterecker 567). This penetralia of Crane's dreaming may be recognized as the same sexual representation bodied forth before by Theodore Parker, Thomas Jefferson, and innumerable others. Like those predecessors in white letters, and like Cummings, Crane perceived the nonwhite to occupy a position of inherent *aesthetic* inferiority to whites, even if certain aspects of their image were susceptible to romanticizing. And apparently like Vachel Lindsay, Crane learned much of his prejudice at home. In his correspondence with his family, the standard repertoire of white racism is put into play, often with no visible signs of self-consciousness. There is, for an instance, the letter to Crane from his mother dated January 30, 1917, in which she tells her son of the previous night's annual Cake Walk at a hotel, "given in the dining room after dinner by the real 'coons.' . . . How I wish that you could have seen those darkies parade and dance back and forth down through that long room" (*Letters* 34). Crane, while sharing his mother's curiosity about black song and dance, seems to have felt that blacks themselves, as he perceived them, were aesthetically displeasing. This can be seen in the letters that arise from his trips to Cuba and to Cayman Island. Of one boat trip he writes to his mother: "It was not until the island was cleared that I realized how many there were on that schooner. Thirty-five! and all of them niggers who proved to have no idea of ordinary decent cleanliness. . . . There was no shade from the intense blaze of the sun unless one could brave the stinks and fumes of a dozen odd sick and wailing nigger females below decks" (*Letters* 500). Part of his distaste for these Cubans also results from his sharing with so many other whites a strong feeling against what has been habitually termed "mongrelization" when blacks of mixed blood are discussed in white discourse. Crane described the Cubans to his father as a "trashy bastard people—without any sense of direction or purpose" (*Letters* 493). That this description is racially determined is transparent when the statement is contrasted to his descriptions of the skins of the Indians he had observed in Mexico as exhibiting "various depths of rich coffee brown, always so clear and silken smooth, [that] are anything but Negroid" (qtd. in Unterecker 688).

The poems themselves are considerably more problematic than these naked and less formal pronouncements, as Hart Crane wavers between an empathetic approach to the black man's seemingly untenable position in American society and a more denigrating tone. The empathetic moments are most in evidence in an early poem, "Black Tambourine," which grew out of a period spent in his father's employ as a furnace worker, displacing a black employee:

The black man, forlorn in the cellar,
Wanders in some mid-kingdom, dark, that lies
Between his tambourine, stuck on the wall,
And, in Africa, a carcass quick with flies.

(Poems 4)

The premise of the first three lines is an unusually accurate image of the purgatory to which white discourse banishes blackness to be coming from a white poet in the era of high modernism. The "underground" image is apt and was adopted independently by a number of black authors, including Richard Wright in "The Man Who Lived Underground," Ralph Ellison in *Invisible Man,* and Jean Toomer, with whom Crane briefly shared lodgings, in the final segment of *Cane.* The image of the tambourine attached to the wall of the workplace is again remarkably on target, suggesting on Crane's part at least partial understanding of the black worker's relationship to an ongoing culture. It suggests as well his awareness of the longing for a black homeland that is discernible throughout the history of Afro-American literature and in social movements such as Garveyism. And yet, there is a troubling sense in the last line of the quatrain that Crane shares Stein's position on the nothingness that is Africa, that he shares with Lindsay and Conrad an idea that Africa is a dark continent of hellish decay. The final fly-ridden image is just one more of the horrors.

We know from another letter that Crane was aware of some of the problems raised by this poem. Discussing the matter with Gorham Munson, Crane summarizes his poem as "a bundle of insinuations, suggestions bearing on the negro's place somewhere between man and beast. . . . A propagandist for either side of the negro question could find anything he wanted in it. My only declaration in it is that I find the negro (in the popular mind) sentimentally or brutally 'placed' in this midkingdom" (qtd. in Unterecker 190–91). Such is certainly the place awarded to blacks by Thomas Jefferson, Gertrude Stein, Pound, Eliot, and Williams. But so long as Crane saw in this a "negro question" about which sides could be drawn, rather than a problem created and perpetuated by whites, he could continue to equivocate. He may only declare the existence of a placement that has occurred in "the popular mind," but the form of that declaration tends to contribute to the continuation of that placement.

But in other poems Crane is much less equivocal, more in the voice we find him assuming in his letters home, and this results in lines that may seem

puzzling when we know of his friendship with an Afro-American artist like
Toomer. In part 2 of "For the Marriage of Faustus and Helen," following
upon a not terribly well realized attempt to use jazz rhythms in his lines, there
occurs an odd plea to the Olympians to "know . . . we are breathless / While
nigger cupids scour the stars" (*Poems* 30). This image with its astral "pickaninny" grows yet more curious if contemplated while holding in mind Cummings's similar moment invoking the little Negro who held a star and wished
for whiteness; what is this cosmology of astral blacks all about? But then this
sort of imagery comes facilely to Hart Crane. In the "River" passage of *The
Bridge*, he turns for a suggestion of eternity to the same bloodied source to
which Eliot would turn in "The Dry Salvages." Crane's lines read: "You are
your father's father, and the stream— / A liquid theme that floating niggers
swell" (*Poems* 69). Crane arrives at these moments in which he sounds so
much like a Cummings in the one instance and an Eliot in the other, not
because these poets all read one another's work, though surely they did, but
because they all shared a common vocabulary of racial images. When they
thought blackness, their thoughts were confined *within* the frozen metaphors
of the language that they thought *in*.

T. S. Eliot, who once described himself as having been in childhood "a
small boy with a nigger drawl" (qtd. in Spender 16), liked to speak of purifying the language of the tribe, and there was little question which tribe he was
concerned with. It is that tribe in which you feel well looked out for if you can
say, along with one of the canceled characters from "The Waste Land,"
they've "treated me white" (*Waste Land* 5). And for all his appropriations of
shards from other tribes to shore up his ruins, Eliot was generally unwilling to
admit that other tribes had contributed to the cultural richness of his own. This
was well known to his friend and advisor, Ezra Pound. When Pound was
preparing the manuscript for his study *Kulchur*, he wrote a letter to Faber and
Faber wondering how to keep Eliot "in his feedbox when I brings in deh
Chinas and blackmen in a bukk about Kulchur" (Pound, *Letters* 288). And in
a letter to Eliot himself Pound remarks "I know you jib at China and Frobenius cause they ain't pie church; and neither of us likes sabages, black
habits, etc." (Pound, *Letters* 336).

Eliot's juvenilia, when it touches upon blackness, evinces the same image
of sexual anima we have seen in Cummings. While still in America he composed lines for the *Harvard Advocate* concerning "King Bolo and his big
black queen / whose bun was as big as a soup tureen" (qtd. in Matthews 22).
But in later years the nonwhite was to become for Eliot a Conradian area of
spiritual darkness associated, as was sexuality on occasion, with death. In

"The Dry Salvages," perhaps drawing upon memories from his childhood in St. Louis, Eliot constructs an image uncannily similar to Crane's in *The Bridge,* an image in which Eliot likens Shivaite time, the preserver and destroyer, to ". . . the river with its cargo of dead Negros, cows and chicken coops" (*Poems* 133). These associations of death with the nonwhite are continued in Eliot's verse play, *The Cocktail Party,* which presents an imagined area of darkness, a far-off land called Kinkanja, in which unlogical jungle "natives" venerate monkeys and eat native Christians. They don't eat many Europeans because "when these people have done with a European / He is, as a rule, no longer fit to eat" (*Poems* 375). Thus literally as well as figuratively, Eliot's negative utopia demonstrates the accuracy of Christopher Miller's observation that "from earliest times, Black Africa was experienced as the literal end of European knowledge" (*Blank* 22). Kinkanja is little more than a breeding ground for plague where Europeans are dismembered (Eliot, *Poems* 380–81).

On the whole, Eliot tends to view the nonwhite as a disruptive element infringing upon the development of Western tradition. Characteristic, and perhaps more revealing than Eliot realized, is his comment during a Cambridge dinner that "because of the Negro influence on American music, no American could waltz properly" (Matthews 53). More seriously to be taken are the remarks he made in *After Strange Gods: A Primer of Modern Heresy,* a volume more frequently cited for its anti-Semitism. The most often quoted anti-Semitic remark is the one in which Eliot stresses the importance of "unity of religious background," in the course of which he asserts that "reasons of race and religion combine to make any large number of free-thinking Jews undesirable" (qtd. in Kirk 209–10). The inclusion of race as a factor has been too readily passed over in the past; it makes it clear that Eliot's remarks are not applicable only to Semitic peoples. His deprecation of what he terms "excessive toleration" is in fact directed against toleration of anything that lies outside European whiteness, as is indicated by statements immediately preceding the one about "free-thinking Jews." Eliot here makes known his appreciation of the stand taken by the Southern Agrarians, and then ties their position to his own definition of tradition: "You are hardly likely to develop tradition except where the bulk of the population is relatively so well off where it is that it has no incentive or pressure to move about. The population should be homogeneous; where two or more cultures exist in the same place they are likely to be fiercely self-conscious or both to become adulterate" (qtd. in Kirk 209). That Eliot is sounding again the same old warning against racial amalgamation is evidenced in a note he appends at this point, in which he reveals that a distinction exists in his mind between castes and social classes "which presuppose homogeneity of race and a fundamental equality" (qtd. in Kirk 209), which may be taken as his approving description of the situation he found in Virginia at the time he delivered these lectures in Charlottesville.

Wallace Stevens, our premier propagandist for the imagination, was not above the occasional "polack" joke (*Collected Poems* 210), or poetic side-swipes at squealing "dagoes" (*Opus* 36), and Randall Jarrell once said of Stevens that he "treats with especial sympathy Negroes, Mexican Indians, and anybody else he can consider wild" (*Poetry and the Age* 138). But whenever Stevens approaches the nonwhite as subject, his discursive practice renders the nonwhite as an objectified lesser thing in a fashion that runs counter to some of his stated intentions. In a letter of 1907 this poet, who sometimes signed himself "Sambo" (Stevens, *Souvenirs* 199), spoke of the social aspects of art in these terms: "We must leave it to the aesthetic critic to explain why . . . it is easier for nearly everyone to recognize the meaning of common reality after it has passed through another's brain—why thousands of kindly people should have contemplated negro slavery day by day for years without emotion, and then have gone mad over "Uncle Tom's Cabin." It is because common reality is being exhibited. It is being treated objectively" (*Souvenirs* 179). And in a later letter to his wife, writing from Johnson City in Tennessee to describe the movements of troop trains carrying black draftees he has observed, he attempts to view the black soldiers as they are viewed by the southern whites in the station, as "absurd animals." He ends, though, finding himself thrilled at the sight of the men. He tells Elsie, "I want to cry & yell & jump ten feet in the air; and so far as I have been able to observe, it makes no difference whether the men are black or white" (Stevens, *Letters* 223).

In other informal writings, however, we find testimony more characteristic of Stevens's poetic practice, a practice which serves to reinforce white racial mythology in the same way that so much white writing from Jefferson to Stowe's time had helped to make it possible for kindly people to contemplate slavery without emotion. A journal entry of 1905 defines a razorback hog as being "no account unless it can outrun a nigger" (Stevens, *Souvenirs* 152). In a letter written from Havana, Stevens displays the same sort of American ethnocentrism directed toward the Hispanic nonwhite as that seen in the letters of Hart Crane. Stevens reports his surprise at having found Cuba to be "infinitely more Spanish" than he had supposed, then goes on to complain: "I went up to a nigger policeman to get my bearings and found that the poor thing could not even understand me" (*Letters* 234). One supposes Stevens equally poor in his failure to understand the policeman. While he does not find an appreciation of the aesthetic to be foreign to blacks, he patently dislikes having to share aesthetic space with the lower-class black, and in a note written in the spring of 1906 he shows himself to be possessed of an appreciation of the mechanisms by which the dominant social order indoctrinates the lower orders in its own aesthetic: "Parks . . . are, generally, filled with the lower classes. Our park here, today, was thick with Italians and negroes. So, too often for the aesthete, museums, etc. are visited by the lower classes to the exclusion of the upper. Undoubtedly these things are important in modifying the natures of those who frequent them; & are, thus, a phase of that police system upon which order, very largely rests. (*Souvenirs* 166–67).

There are still other letters which are virtual glosses upon Stevens's use of the nonwhite in his verse. One of them, addressed to José Rodriguez Feo, draws a comparison between Feo's black cook and Pompilio, a mule: "Possibly the Negro & Pompilio are interchangeable. The truth is that I have been thinking about the position of the ignorant man in what, for convenience, may be called society. . . . Pompilio is the blank realist who sees only what there is to see without feeling, without imagination, but with large eyes that require spectacles" (Stevens, *Letters* 512). The "feeling" that Stevens speaks of here is not the same feeling that Stein and Cummings believe the nonwhite possesses in abundance but rather the "finer" feelings of the poet. Stevens did hold the same notions of the exotic, fun-loving black as did his contemporaries, as may be seen from his belief that "to lose faith in the existence of the first rate would put one in the situation of the colored man at a church picnic losing his bottle of whiskey" (*Letters* 844). People of color are, though, for Stevens, brutish as a mule and hence have little of importance to accomplish in Stevens's poetic republic. They can be seen mowing lawns, hanging wash, carrying things from here to there, and timelessly "playing football in the park" (Stevens, *Collected Poems* 270). When they appear in a group, as is the case with the football players, it is as a mass noun, "the negroes."

The generalized exoticism of the black subject that we have been tracing in American letters is a frequent quality of Stevens's work. In "The News and the Weather," he evokes "Solange, the magnolia to whom I spoke, / A nigger tree and with a nigger name" (Stevens, *Collected Poems* 265). In the fifth section of "The Auroras of Autumn," Stevens has a presumably white father fetching "negresses to dance / Among the children" (*Collected Poems* 415). *Owl's Clover* contains a trope of Chicago as "a Kaffir Kraal" (Stevens, *Opus* 63), perhaps the place where Sandburg was going to find his bushman. And

"An Exposition of the Contents of a Cab" degenerates into an Amos and Andy routine as "Victoria Clementina, negress, / [takes] seven white dogs / to ride in a cab" (*Opus* 20).

In this last passage we encounter the kind of juxtaposition of shades which also appears in Pound and Williams. "In the South" could have been titled "In a Station of the South":

> The black mother of eleven children
> Hangs her quilt under the nim-trees.
> There is a connection between the colors,
> The shapes of the patches,
> And the eleven children. . . .
>
> (*Opus* 9)

This is certainly inoffensive, but it fits into Stevens's pattern of employing nonwhites as local color, a pattern which goes so far as to incorporate the debris that black people might leave behind them. The title to the justifiably admired poem, "Like Decorations in a Nigger Cemetery," Stevens has advised, "refers to the litter that one usually finds in a nigger cemetery" (*Letters* 272). Why a graveyard for Afro-Americans should "usually" be more interestingly littered than one for whites, or why separate and unequal cemeteries should exist at all are questions which Stevens's explication does not address.

The ascription of colorful exoticism is emblematic of the apartness of the African races in Stevens's world view. It is part of a terminology which places blacks in a position of homelessness outside the cultural tradition that the poet sees himself as operating within, if not, as in Eliot's case, purifying. Having assigned blacks to that position, Stevens places himself in the role of instructor to them. In "Two at Norfolk" he advises, "Mow the grass in the cemetery, darkies, study the symbols and the requiescats" (*Collected Poems* 111), thus limning the cemetery as a sort of "slovenly wilderness" like that of the "Anecdote of the Jar," and the black man as the benighted caretaker of that wilderness. (Perhaps the darkie mowing the lawn in the epigraph to Henry Taylor's "De Gustibus Ain't What Dey Used to Be" moves so slowly because he is taking Stevens's advice and studying the symbols around him.) Elsewhere Stevens preaches "Blackest of pickanines, / There is a master of mud" (*Collected Poems* 148) and, in a "Prelude to Objects," admonishes that "the guerilla I should be booked / And bound. Its nigger mystics should change / Foolscap for wigs" (*Collected Poems* 195). How Stevens himself reacts to such preaching may be measured by the complaint he sent to Richard Eberhart in 1954: "I rode to the office this morning with one of the colored boys from the office who preached about one thing & another all the way in" (*Letters* 815).

But on the whole, Stevens's preachments are intended for other ears; he pushes black readers into the role of eavesdropper as he sings: ". . . I play my guitar. / The negro with laundry passes me by" (*Opus* 72). Blackness is at the periphery of Stevens's world and requires the attendance of imaginative missionaries. Just such missionary work occurs in the section of *Owl's Clover* titled "The Greenest Continent."

"The Greenest Continent" (Stevens, *Opus* 52–60) conjures up an Africa every bit as fantastic as Eliot's Kinkanja or Lindsay's Congo. Stevens's Africa in this major poem is also reminiscent of Sandburg's somnolent jungle and Crane's "corpse quick with flies," a region of radical wilderness, far more other than any imaginable Tennessee. It is an Africa over which no god rules singly. Stevens feels that "there never was the heaven of Africa, which had / No heaven, had death without a heaven." The Negro thus suffers not only the Steinian nothingness of this earthly life, but another in the hereafter. Stevens's Africa is a region where "fear might placate / And the serpent might become a god, quickeyed, / Rising from indolent coils," just as the monkeys became gods in Kinkanja. In order to create a trope for his contrast of order and chaos, Stevens calls into being an Africa "basking in antiquest sun," which I do not think reflects Stevens's intuiting of Leakey's discovery of the antiquity of African hominids, containing "for its children not a gill of sweet," dominated by death, which "sits upon the serpent throne."

Stevens has said of "The Greenest Continent" that "the specific subject is, I suppose, the white man in Africa. But it may be that no one will ever realize that" (*Letters* 307–308), and into this deathly wilderness of the spirit he introduces European "angels" with their jars, statues, reliquaries, and weapons:

Forth from their tabernacles once again
The angels come, armed, gloriously to slay
The black and ruin his sepulchral throne.

. . . .

Angels tiptoe upon the snowy cones
Of palmy peaks sighting machine guns? These
Seraphim of Europe?

These seraphim may, as Joseph Riddel suggests (129–30), represent missionary colonials, but the date of publication, 1936, indicates that Stevens also had the Italian expedition against Ethiopia in mind while composing "The

Greenest Continent." The Africa of the poem is symbolic, for Stevens, of a primitivism of the self, Pompilio the mule's sort of unfeeling blank realism, and the symbolic expedition of the angels with machine guns has been said by Stevens to "concern the difficulty of imposing the imagination on those that do not share it" (*Letters* 369). But the "filleted angels" that invade part 2 of the poem were palpably real to the "bushmen" they combatted "for a patch of gourds" (does Stevens know anything about geography?), and to the black "slaves" they loosed to "make black infantry." And Stevens's casting the invasion in these terms, trivializing as they do the stakes of the war and implying that the Italians were acting for the liberation of the Africans, is propaganda concocted by a politically naive individual. This business in American letters of portraying the African as someone who would be infinitely better off once rescued violently by whites is exactly the kind of discourse that made it possible for generations of readers to view slavery with equanimity.

Section 6 of the poem sets out the oppositions between art and formless chaos, between primitive libidinal force and rationality, and between Western civilization and Stevens's African disorder. The invaders have placed their jars and statues in the midst of the Africans' slovenly wilderness, but Stevens wonders:

. . . could the statue stand in Africa?
. . . .
could marble still
Be marble after the drenching reds, the dark
And drenching crimsons, or endure?

Perhaps, it is thought, the African wilderness, unlike the hills of Tennessee, may be too wildly primitive for the statue to persist. Perhaps the exotic colorings of the jungle shall end this time by overwhelming and transforming the marble rather than being themselves transformed. The conflict is resolved in the trope in section 8 of the deity "Fatal Ananke." This is the necessary divinity who rescues man from chaotic bush, who:

. . . sees the angel in the nigger's mind
And hears the nigger's prayers in motets, belched
From pipes that swarm clerestory walls.

Stevens's use of racist imagery to put across his philosophic points is a process ordered by his conception of African peoples as being beyond the scope of Western tradition, and salvageably human only insofar as they are susceptible of "finer" feelings, imagination as figured forth by the "necessary angel." The black in America is Stevens's homeless cosmopolitan, as he is to Eliot. Stevens could hold such notions and still consider himself rational because he was ignorant of Africa's contributions to culture, because he chose to ignore the means by which the Africans had been rendered homeless, and because he thought within structures of belief which supported such conceptions and shrouded them in scientificity. Witness the works of Dr. Carl Brigham and and Dr. Robert Yerkes. The extent to which Stevens was serious about all this can be ascertained from his explanations of his position to Ronald Latimer in October and November of 1935. First he establishes the Italians as having had "as much right to take Ethiopia from the coons as the coons had to take it from the boa-constrictors" (Stevens, *Letters* 289–90). And then later, employing a logic that is even more tortured than that of Cummings or Eliot, he goes on: "While it is true that I have spoken sympathetically of Mussolini, all my sympathies are the other way: with the coons and the boa-constrictors. . . . A man would have to be pretty thick-skinned not to be conscious of the pathos of Ethiopia or China. . . . But that Mussolini is right, practically, has certainly a great deal to be said for it" (*Letters* 295). In this aspect of his thought Stevens is much closer to Pound than he is ordinarily considered to be. Both poets could have used more of the kind of reflection Stevens engaged in some thirty years prior to the publication of "The Greenest Continent": "It must be a satisfaction to be without conscience. Even in that cell where one sits brooding on the philosophy of life, half decided on 'joyousness'—one observes one's black brother in a corner, and hears him whisper, 'The joyous man *may* not be right. If he dance, he *may* dance in other people's ashes' " (*Souvenirs* 164).

Ezra Pound once made a remark that demands to be placed alongside a reading of *The Cantos*. He claimed that "no reader of the *Golden Bough* is likely to relapse into bigotry" (*Letters* 134). Pound was one of the very few publishing white poets of his time who had bothered to acquire any scholarly knowledge at all about Africa and Africans. At the very least, we know from his own note on Leo Frobenius, published in Nancy Cunard's *Negro* anthology, that he had studied the seven volumes of *Erlebte Erdteile* (*Negro* 393), and from his correspondence with a Viennese bookshop we know that he had purchased in 1930 a copy of the separately published *Paideuma* (Stock 30). And Pound knew, from his readings in the classics, of the favorable opinions of Africa sometimes found in those sources. In canto 94, for example, he has Apollonius saying that "The Africans have more sense than the Greeks" (*Cantos* 640), Pound's rendition of reports made by Apollonius of Tyana after a trip on the Nile. Further, he spoke often, and on occasion eloquently, against abuses suffered by blacks both in times past and in the present. In canto 34 Pound disparages the bad treatment Americans afforded Claude Gabriel, a black who had come to the United States on a diplomatic mission for the Russian emperor (*Cantos* 166). *The Cantos* abound with denunciations of slavery and of slave traders. Pound reports approvingly of ancient Greeks in canto 98 that "No man in Greece will sell a slave out of his country" (*Cantos* 684). In canto 65 Pound repeats a conjecture made by John Adams:

> "I have often wondered that J's first draft has
> not
>   been published
> suppose the reason is the evident philippic
> against
>   negro slavery."
>   (*Cantos* 367)

And during his stay in the wards of the army detention center in Pisa after the Second World War, Pound came to see an analogy between his own situation and the middle passage. He saw "The wards like a slave ship" (*Cantos* 436), and his position as being akin to that of the slave: "in limbo no victories, there are no victories— / that is limbo; between decks of the slaver" (*Cantos* 470). And he recognized the intentions of the dominant power, in this case his own white nation, to indoctrinate him "amid the slaves learning slavery / and the dull driven back toward the jungle" (*Cantos* 431). Pound's denunciations were not confined to abuses of the past, moreover. In a letter to Langston Hughes he thanks the black poet for having sent him a copy of his work, "Scotsboro Limited," supports the struggle around the Scottsboro case, and thoroughly derides the governments of the southern states for their unjust racial policies (*Letters* 241). And Pound, always the activist, did not restrict himself to letter writing. He also made a financial contribution to the British Scottsboro Defense Committee through its honorary treasurer, Nancy Cunard.

Nonetheless, Ezra Pound was given to blistering racial insult both in his informal writings and in his verse, and his representations of blacks often invoke the same power relationships and image structures that have typified the other modernist poets so far examined. Pound's general feelings against racial amalgamation may be inferred from the fact that in a letter to Margaret Anderson in which he speaks of Amy Lowell, he inquires, "Is she yet weary of B——, and the mulattoism, mental and physical?" (*Letters* 130). I have not been able to ascertain whether "B——" is a reference to William Stanley

Braithwaite, but in any event, Pound patently feels "mulattoism" is a bad thing. Not long before, Pound had unloaded on Braithwaite, the hapless anthologist, in relation to the article about Frost by Edmund J. Wheeler mentioned in the last chapter, in which Wheeler had repeated Braithwaite's comment that Frost had accomplished more in England than any other poet of his generation. Pound fired off a letter to the editor of the *Boston Transcript* responding, "Now seriously, what about me. Your (?negro) reviewer might acquaint himself with that touching little scene in Elkin Mathews's shop some years since" (*Letters* 62), as if Braithwaite's race bore any conceivable relationship to his preference for Frost. (The scene Pound mentions was one in which Mathews asked Pound to subsidize publication of Frost.) In less polite terms, Pound wrote of this incident several months later to Harriet Monroe, saying, "I didn't know it was the coon I was answering. . . . Most certainly I did not write the letter to Braithwaite. He isn't the editor of *The Transcript!!!*" (*Letters* 67), a remark that is more than a little self-serving. While Pound might use the polite, lowercase "negro" when addressing an editor of a Boston paper, he seems to have much preferred the epithet "nigger." When he was desirous of impressing upon William Carlos Williams the extent to which he had exerted himself to "break the clutch of the old" he says that he "sweated like a nigger" (Pound, *Letters* 156). And this same poet who employed the dialects of Uncle Remus in his translations of the Classical Anthology would go to equally great lengths with the *Agamemnon*. "I twisted, turned, tried every ellipsis and elimination," he says of that effort, "I made the watchman talk nigger . . ." (Pound, *Kulchur* 92–93).

The tone adopted in these last remarks is the dominant tone in *The Cantos* whenever blackness appears, and it ends by diminishing the effect of his political opposition to slavery and racial abuse. Though Pound will include elements of his learning about African anthropology such as his reference to talking drums in canto 38 or his reference to the African derived tale, "The Legend of Gassire's Lute," which he uncovered in Frobenius (Stock 76–77), in canto 74 he seems to have shared Frobenius's reluctance to credit Africa with having generated its own culture and generally favors racial insult over anthropological inquiry. This begins as early as canto 8 with Pound's observation of Alessandro di Medici, son of Pope Clement and a Moorish slave: "*That Alessandro was negroid*" (*Cantos* 28), which Massimo Bacigalupo reads as a disparaging contrast to Henry James, who was "biondo" (Bacigalupo 42). In canto 12, speaking of Baldy Bacon, an American businessman Pound met in 1910, Pound tells of Bacon having slept "with two buck niggers chained to him, / Guardia Regia, chained to his waist / to keep 'em from slipping off in the night" (*Cantos* 53). Later Pound refers to a certain Mustafa, whom Carroll F. Terrell conjectures may have been a merchant Pound encountered in Gibraltar (Terrell 91), as "the nigger in the red fez" (*Cantos* 105). Reporting one of the annual games that had been held in times past in Mantua, Pound indicates in canto 27 that one year "the prize went to a nigger from Mantua" (*Cantos* 123). The pattern shows that Pound tended to refer to persons of color as "niggers" no matter where he found them, no matter what their nationality, and that, as his reference to Alessandro would indicate, his use of this term of darkness, as is true of the terminology by which he refers to Jews, is meant in a derogatory sense.

It is in the Pisan cantos, subject of much discussion because of their anti-Semitism at the time they won for Pound the Bollingen Prize, that blacks appear most often, for, imprisoned in the army detention center, Pound for the first time since he exiled himself had daily contact with a group of persons of African descent from his own homeland. He evidently enjoyed these contacts and even preferred certain aspects of his contacts with the blacks to those with whites, as in his contrast in canto 74 of "a black delicate hand" to "a white's hand like a ham" (*Cantos* 440). But Pound is often making use of the non-whites, and their speech, as local color for the landscape of his poem. He was self-consciously aware of what he was doing in this regard, and even speaks of it directly in canto 79:

> I like a certain number of shades in my landscape
> as per / "doan' tell no one I made you that table"
> or Whiteside:
> > "ah certainly dew lak dawgs,
> > "ah goan' tuh wash you"
> > > > (*Cantos* 484)

Which last gives some impression of the ridiculous lengths to which white poets will carry their representations of Afro-American speech as being some gross distortion. In the midst of Pound's orthographic minstrelsy we find the substitution of "dew" for "do," a substitution that makes no phonetic sense at all, coming as it does before "lak," rather than before "you," and in close proximity to such clearly enunciated words as "certainly;" it occurs only as an inscription of the otherness of black language. There are a number of these passages in which Pound reduces the Afro-American soldiers to abstract blobs of color. In canto 74 he watches "niggers scaling the obstacle fence / in the middle distance / and Mr. Edwards superb green and brown" (*Cantos* 434).

In canto 77 he returns to the same sight of "niggers comin' over the obstacle fence / as in the insets at Schifanoja" (*Cantos* 473). That tendency to see blacks as part of a composition is replicated when Pound notices that "those negroes by the clothes-line are extraordinarily like the / figures del Cossa" (*Cantos* 477).

The blacks in these lines, when they do step out of the colorful mass Pound has pressed them into, seldom step out of stereotype; they speak and behave much as do the blacks of Cummings or Stein. We see, for example, a "young nigger at rest in his wheel barrow / in the shade back of the jo-house" who addresses the imprisoned Pound, shouting out to him, "Got it *made,* kid, you got it made" (*Cantos* 506). Or we are presented with:

Mr. G. Scott whistling Lili Marlene
    with positively less musical talent
    than that of any other man of colour
      whom I have ever encountered
                (*Cantos* 484)

This remark would not be comprehensible unless one had agreed beforehand that men of color are expected to be possessed of great musical talent. Some of these invocations of stereotype tend to undercut Pound's denunciations of the slavers. When we read lines like " 'C'mon small fry' sd / the coon to the big black; of the slaver as seen between decks" (*Cantos* 436), the Amos and Andy type of comedic dialogue at the army detention center subverts the effectiveness of the analogy to the slave ships.

Pound also falls into the old custom in white discourse of distinguishing the "good" black from the "bad." "Whereas the sight of a good nigger is cheering," he declares in canto 79, "the bad 'uns won't look you straight" (*Cantos* 484). The good ones are like the "cheerful reflective nigger" of canto 78 (*Cantos* 479), or those who show signs of being cultured, like the "black boy / from the jo-cart" who yells out his greeting to Pound in German (*Cantos* 523). For Pound, after all, "What counts is the cultural level" (*Cantos* 518), and it is in this connection that his knowledge of Africa, such as it is, enters *The Cantos*. He sees "a jacent benignity" in the good blacks, like the one who converted a packing box into a work table for the caged poet, and in the visage of that benign black Pound finds reminders of the masks Leo Frobenius had gathered into the ethnological collections at his Institute for Cultural Morphology. Pound finds the face of the man who made his table a "baluba mask," which he compliments by mimicking: "doan you tell no one / I made you that table" (*Cantos* 434). And again in canto 81, speaking of cultural levels, Pound tells himself:

> Thank Benin for this table ex packing box
> "doan you tell no one I made it"
>   from a mask as fine as any in Frankfurt
> "It'll get you offn th' grown"
>   (*Cantos* 518–19)

But just as his mimicking of black speech is reductive, this nod to the culture of the civilization of Benin is reductive in ways that his comments about the traditions out of which European culture is held to rise seldom are. Pound's inclination to compare the faces of the men to the museum masks also indicates that he misread the intentions of the African artists. The masks Pound speaks of are not representational in the European sense, and indeed it is this very aspect of African art that exercised such attraction for Picasso. We nowhere find Pound making the same kind of error with regard to the masks made in the Tirol, which he seems to like (*Cantos* 448). He is never found being reminded of those masks when looking at a white European's face.

Pound's practice in his poetry tends, then, to push against the effect of his pronouncements against slavers, and his support for the notion that the American Civil War was not fundamentally about slavery, "the slaves were just red herring" (*Cantos* 732), as if the issue of slavery could be so neatly detached from the other causes of the war, tends to lessen the horrors of slavery. His misunderstandings of black culture and mimicking of black American speech serve not to increase attention to the history of African-derived culture but to continue the white myth of the emptiness of black life. And Pound's inclination to link Africa to Judaism entangles black culture in the maddening discourse of anti-Semitism. Pound lived to regret some of his pronouncements, if not repent them. There is a certain lingering wistfulness in the lines he wrote from Saint Elizabeth's about a particular black man, an Elder Lightfoot, identified by one source as one of Pound's fellow patients at the hospital, one heard to observe that the process of evolution appeared to be running in reverse (Terrell 2:588):

> Elder Lightfoot is not downhearted,
>   Elder Lightfoot is cert'nly
>   not
>   downhearted,
> He observes a design in the Process.
>   (*Cantos* 645)

There is, however, another Elder Lightfoot associated with Pound's Washington years whom the poet was almost certainly aware of; an Elder Lightfoot Michaux, who was known widely for, among other things, holding mass baptisms in Griffith Stadium using holy water shipped directly to the District of Columbia from the river Jordan. Pound's search for intelligent design in the universe brought him at length to an asylum from whence he could watch the black evangelist in the distance bring word of his own design to an audience far larger than any ever commanded by the poet.

Pound's role in America's racial discourse has not been greatly attended to in the extant criticism, even in much of the criticism that takes Pound's social thought as its focus. Telling on this point is the symposium sponsored by the *Partisan Review* in April and May of 1949 on the subject of the Bollingen Committee's award of its prize to Pound in honor of his *Pisan Cantos*. Given the proximity of this award in time to the Holocaust and to Pound's trial, it is not surprising that the discussion is concentrated upon Pound's anti-Semitism. What is surprising is that such a discussion of prejudice and poetry entirely omits Pound's racial thought, especially since Pound himself links the Jew to the nonwhite. As Robert Casillo has established in his essay "Pound and Fascist Ideology," the author of *The Cantos* tends generally in his verse to associate the Jews with a miasmic Africa. None of the contributors to the symposium, all of whom are white, makes note of this fact, a fact which has received later reinforcement with the emergence of letters such as the one Pound wrote to Nancy Cunard in the middle of the Italian campaign against Ethiopia, in which Pound seizes upon the historical links between Israel and Ethiopia to declare that "the Abyssinians are *black* Jews" (Cunard 129). This connection between Pound's anti-Semitism and his feelings about blacks was largely invisible to the writers in the symposium because, while they rejected Pound's virulent Semitic imagery, some of them participated in the same system of shared image structures of the nonwhite that Pound employs. Allen Tate, a member of the Bollingen Committee, said in his response that he considered anti-Semitism "to be both cowardly and dishonorable" (Tate, "*Partisan Review* Symposium" 91) but demonstrates in other of his own writings that he is substantially in agreement with Pound on the subject of Afro-Americans. Karl Shapiro, also on the Bollingen Committee, who voted against the award to Pound, makes no mention of Pound's anti-black remarks or use of black dialect, partly, I believe, because he himself was possessed of peculiar notions of what it means to "speak Negro" (see chapter 5). Only one of the contributors, Robert Gorham Davis, so much as broaches the subject of Afro-Americans and literary tradition, and his reference is no more than a passing jab at Tate and other southern writers, in the context of an examination of the large question of critical responses to modernist anti-Semitism: "most critics have accepted this in Eliot's terms. As homeless cosmopolitans and usurers, the Bleisteins and Sir Ferdinand Kleins represent the debasements of modern commercialism. As intellectuals, the Jews are the foremost carriers of disintegrative rationalism, earthly messianism. For the Southern Regionalists, Negroes are less interesting ideologically, but equally outside the tradition, and not to be made part of it by any liberal rhetoric" (Robert Gorham Davis 87). So far outside the traditions of white discourse is the nonwhite other that Pound's manhandling of African tradition and his insulting terminology and imagery about blackness meet with no audible objections from the other disputants in the *Partisan Review* colloquy. This may be taken as further evidence of the extent to which white hegemony operates within literary discussion to render its own assertions natural and inevitable.

Neither did Pound's manner of speaking of the nonwhite encounter objections from his friend William Carlos Williams, who had no qualms about objecting to much else in Pound's social thought. Williams shared with Pound the tendency to employ blacks as objects of local color, as he shared with Stein and so many other modernists an intense and highly romanticized interest in the purported sexuality of black people. While Williams had far greater contact with individual Afro-Americans than did many of his contemporaries, in part due to his years as a general practitioner in the working-class neighborhoods of New Jersey, and while he formed friendships easily with many black individuals, Nancy Cunard's musician lover Henry Crowder among them, blacks appear again and again in his work as the sort of colorfully animated exotic object Alice Walker complains of in the epigraph to this chapter, this despite occasional arguments against the practice made by people with whom Williams worked. Fred Miller, for one, who for a time collaborated on a novel with Williams, attempted unsuccessfully to convince Williams that "to regard the black as an object of aesthetic interest was still to regard him as an object, . . . and to do that was to deny him his humanity" (Mariani, *New World* 516).

The preparation for Williams's adult practice of regarding the nonwhite as an objectified area of sensual anima began in his early childhood. As Vachel Lindsay recalled being read to from *Uncle Remus* by his father, Williams, in his *Autobiography,* remembers his own father reading to him from the dialect verse of Paul Laurence Dunbar (15). These idyllic plantation choruses combined with the instruction received from his mother to form Williams's early impressions of Afro-Americans, impressions which are firmly in the tradition of white racism. In part 2 of *Kora in Hell,* section 17, a son muses over his mother's past and imagines "the darkies . . . dancing in Mayaguez" (Williams, *Imaginations* 62), a passage clearly making reference to Williams's own mother. In a book celebrating his mother's history, *Yes, Mrs. Williams,* the poet has declared that his "family is among those who came to America from Europe through the West Indies—so that in the United States—since they still owned slaves in Puerto Rico—I feel more southern than the southerners" (*Imaginations* 28). The anecdotes that Williams recollects having heard from his mother represent a type of oral tradition that has helped to perpetuate racist discourse from one generation to the next. In one of these anecdotes, Mrs. Williams joyfully recounts an afternoon when her childhood home had been filled with dancing and singing Negroes. Her father, angered by the commotion, took after them with his stick, scattering the group to various sections of the house, an action which fits in with the dichotomy Williams likes to draw between the puritanical, civilizing authority of the white, and the libidinal freedom of the nonwhite. In another anecdote of the same type, Williams's mother remembers watching her grandmother, who "used to slap the little colored servant and then go and wash her hands afterward" (*Imaginations* 75–76). Williams's fascination with black sexuality is also traceable to these early years. The prose piece that he contributed to Nancy Cunard's *Negro* anthology, "The Colored Girls of Passenack—Old and New," tells how Williams stole a peek at the house servant, Georgie Anderson, as she bathed (*Negro* 71). This was, in fact, Williams's first recollection of having seen a nude woman, and his voyeuristic interest in the black servant serves to illuminate that disturbing passage of his *Autobiography* where he remembers "as a young medical student falling in love with the corpse of a young negress, a 'high yaller,' lying stripped on the dissecting table before" him (55). Taken together, these passages are indicative of the fact that black womanhood held a special place within Williams's larger schemata of symbols of fertility and creativity and mortality, a place which is finally identified in lines from the poem "Adam:"

> But there was
> a special hell besides
> where black women lie waiting
> for a boy—
> > (*Earlier Poems* 372)

Additionally, as Joan Nay has recently pointed out, in his enthusiasm for what he sees as the black woman's closeness to a source of sensual and emotive powers, he elides any serious consideration of the social context within which any such powers, if real, would have to be exercised: " 'The Colored Girls of Passenack—Old and New' portrays black women as strong, self-reliant vigorous servants who survive smiling and who have 'tremendous furnaces of emotional power.' But the price they pay for enjoying life, for exercising their 'emotional power' (Williams' term for sexual power and enjoyment), is high: . . . Their submission to men, to their need for enjoyment, denotes a quality of passivity that contradicts their supposed strength and undercuts the narrator's admiring tone" (52).

There are other instances in Williams's history that point to a liberal political development on racial matters which contrast oddly with this last necrophilic image. One time he and his brother Ed "were watching an old colored man spading up the ground," and "noticed that the palms of his hands were as white as" their own (Williams, *Autobiography* 7). But such moments are far outnumbered by others in which his liberal spirit is ironized by his involvement in racist discourse. Exemplary of this latter trend is the letter he wrote to his son Bill in anticipation of the 1936 Olympic games in Berlin, the games many American liberals hoped would help put the lie to the Nazis' theories of Nordic superiority. In this letter, Williams looks forward to the "performances of our niggers. They may get so scared that they'll jump clean out of the stadium. I'd love to be there just to watch them for if anybody's going to bust a gut it'll be those boys" (Mariani 413).

Out of this background Williams fashioned an intellectual foundation for the racial objectifications of his verse, a foundation strikingly similar to that which lies behind Stein's *Melanctha*. The plainest statement of this rationale in prose occurs in the chapter titled "Advent of the Slaves," from *In the American Grain*. Here Williams follows Stein literally in her stripping away from the nonwhite their own history and the breadth of their culture. He reduces the experience of the middle passage and of centuries of slavery to a simple matter of immigration: "There is little use, after all—save in a title—of speaking of the advent of the slaves; these were just men of a certain mettle who came to America in ships, like the rest. The minor differences of condition were of no importance—the mere condition of their coming is of no importance—" (*American Grain* 208). This statement is also notable for the fashion in which it converts the experience of slavery into another aesthetic object, a title, to be manipulated by the poet. Williams also reasserts the Steinian notion of the nothingness out of which the black proceeds. He speaks of Christianity as "a thing to replace their own elephant-, snake- and gorilla-filled jungles—on which to fasten for stability, blowing it into the soul of their own darkness" (*American Grain* 208), a series of images common to the work of Crane, Eliot, Lindsay, and Stevens. Williams does posit a unique racial character of the nonwhite, but he sees it arising out of this ahistorical experience of nothingness: "All the rest is to keep from having to say anything more—like a nigger: it is their beauty. When they try to make their race an issue—it is nothing. In a chorus singing *Trovatore, they are nothing.* But saying *nothing,* dancing *nothing, 'Nobody,'* it is a quality—" (*American Grain* 209). This last is a reference to the famous performances of the song "Nobody" by the black entertainer Bert Williams, who often was required to black up with burnt cork so that his face would be dark enough to meet the expectations of his white audiences. Any consideration of white responsibility for the state of affairs described by "Advent of the Slaves" is absent from Williams's historical musings; it is as if this fertile nothingness ("nothin' makes much difference" [210], Williams says) is some sort of generic benefice. All of this must be seen finally as an ahistorical history concocted to serve as a foundation for the contemporary discursive formation and for Williams's poetry. When he speaks here of "a racial irreducible minimum," what he has in mind is no more than: "dancing, singing with the wild abandon of being close, closer, closest together; waggin'; wavin'; weavin'; shakin'; or alone, in a cabin, at night, in the stillness, in the moonlight—bein' nothin'— with gravity, with tenderness—they arrive and 'walk all over God's heaven—' " (*American Grain* 209).

The literary nature of this construction must not be overlooked. In the midst of this historical improvisation, Williams suddenly recalls having read "with thrilling pleasure and deep satisfaction E. K. Means's tale, *Diada Daughter of Discord,* an outstanding story of a wild nigger wench" (*American Grain* 210). This "wild nigger wench," whom Williams reincarnated in Georgie the maid and in his patient, Mabel Watts, is a pure product of the white imagination and is contiguous with the character of Melanctha. She is the beautiful thing who takes a beating at the heart of *Paterson,* that black Kora inhabiting the hell of New Jersey, a figure of white mythology.

William Carlos Williams, adamantly American in language and in his sense of place, remained also in the American grain with respect to his assimilation of the American language's racial image structure, and this assimilation manifests itself at key points within his verse. These manifestations may sometimes be read as parody, as in the second part of section 1 of *Kora in Hell: Improvisations,* where a "woman of marked discernment" makes trite remarks to the strange companions she finds herself among, and desire, it is said, "skates like a Hollander as well as runs pickaninny fashion" (*Imagina-*

tions 49–50). But later, in part 3 of the same section, all indications point to Williams himself as the one who observes while "a darky parts his wool" (50). Williams admits of the relativity of aesthetic standards across racial boundaries, and remarks in this same work, using again a disparaging epithet, that "kaffirs admire what they term beauty in their women but which is in official parlance a deformity. A kaffir poet to be a good poet would praise that which is to him praiseworthy and we would be scandalized" (42). And yet, having said this much, Williams makes no apparent effort to examine a non-white aesthetic but rather continues the white habit of viewing black beauty through the veil of Caucasian discourse agreements.

In the widely anthologized piece "A Negro Woman," the woman is seen:

carrying a bunch of marigolds
    wrapped
        in an old newspaper:
She carries them upright,
        bareheaded,
           the bulk
of her thighs
    causing her to waddle
        as she walks
looking into
    the store window which she passes
        on her way.
What is she
    but an ambassador
        from another world
a world of pretty marigolds
    of two shades
        which she announces
not knowing what she does
    other
        than walk the streets
holding the flowers upright
    as a torch
        so early in the morning.
        (Williams, *Selected Poems* 156)

As so often occurs in the poetry of Pound and Stevens, here we have more poetry in which black people simply carry things about while white writers experience them. "A Negro Woman" continues the notion of the black as an elemental figure that was earlier remarked in Stein. This woman is all physical motion, unreflecting, an "ambassador" from another world, unaware of her mission, a mission which requires the white poet's presence to be made manifest. The other world which she presages is one of pretty marigolds of two shades, and what is this if not another restatement of the theme Pound propounded with his preference for different "shades" in his landscape? The description of the bulk of the woman's thighs causing her to waddle is evidently an example of Williams's conception of "kaffir" beauty.

Much the same instincts inform poem 27 from *Spring and All:*

Black eyed Susan
rich orange
round the purple core

the white daisy
is not
enough

Crowds are white
as farmers
who live poorly

But you
are rich
in savagery—

Arab
Indian
dark woman
  (Williams, *Imaginations* 151)

The third and fourth stanzas again exhibit the Poundian eye for shading, presenting a rural variant upon "In a Station of the Metro." The blandness and imaginative poverty of the white crowds, as of the white daisy, are enlivened and enriched by the presence of the other shades, by the passing of the dark woman. Yet one wants to inquire of the poem, along with Alice Walker, when it shall arrive for the woman herself, rather than for the woman as thing. And what possible motivations, other than those of white rhetorical requirements, can justify the fact that it is always the darker color that is savage? As in these last two poems, blacks in the rest of Williams's verse seldom complete significant actions; their value is lodged in their merest presence. Black people do become objectified, with Williams deploying them as images. The black loafs about, waddles, and functions as a colorful but mute background. For Williams, it often seems, so much depends upon:

> . . . a little black boy
> in a doorway
> scratching his wrists
>
> the cap on his head
> is red and blue
> with a broad peak to it
>
> and his mouth
> is open, his tongue
> between his teeth
>> (*Imaginations* 236)

These tendencies become more pronounced in *Paterson,* where they combine with the avid sexual curiosity about blacks revealed in "The Colored Girls of Passenack." In the very earliest pages of *Paterson* Williams remembers having seen a photograph in the *National Geographic* which featured the nine wives of an African chief seated, seminaked, upon a log (*Paterson* 13–14), a sort of "ready-made" phallic device of the type Cummings had had to invent in *Him.* My point is not that such scenes have not occurred, but that this is all that Williams wants of Africa, witness the later passage in which the poet reproduces from an unidentified source an account of African Ibibio fertility rites and customs (143–44). Looking at the *National Geographic* photograph, Williams reads the women's figures as libidinal signs which he will speak into an American language:

> Caught motionless in a photograph, the chief's wives become hieroglyphs of a meaning that they cannot themselves articulate; rather the poet will go on, as he later does, to articulate it *for* them, or perhaps more accurately, to attribute it *to* them. Similarly, immobilized in a cellar to which the "Lady of the House" leads "Dr. Paterson," the beaten "Beautiful Thing" becomes the object of the poet's meditations (on, among other things, her function as an object of exchange among New Jersey gangs) rather than the subject of her own musings. (Gilbert 12)

Williams is after the "wild animal vitality," which he associates with the nonwhite, just as he was in "The Colored Girls of Passenack" when he claimed that "the American White girl today is shop-worn compared to the Negro girl—at her liveliest" (*Negro* 72). In a beach scene early in *Paterson,* Williams watches as:

3 colored girls, of age! stroll by
   their color flagrant,
     their voices vagrant
their laughter wild, flagellant, dissociated
from the fixed scene

(51)

while a white girl lies under the bush with her lover nearby. Even when the President for Life of Haiti finds his way into *Paterson*'s flow, it is not as an evidence of tyranny or of ambition. Williams is again primarily interested in Duvalier's own fertility symbols:

     the greyhaired President
(of Haiti), his women and children,
       at the water's edge,
sweating, leads off finally, after
delays, huzzahs, songs for pageant reasons
over the blue water
in a private plane
    with his blonde secretary.

(191)

As moving as the "Beautiful Thing" section of *Paterson* is at every reading, when read against this background it must be seen that Williams has done as much himself to make a "thing" of her as have those who "maled and femaled [her] jealously" (127). To see a black woman as "a flame, / black plush" (128) is, as Fred Miller had earlier suggested to Williams, in some sense to deny her her humanity.

There is but one passage in *Paterson* in which Williams seems to greet a black person on an equal footing, and that is a literary episode, a toast to the Afro-American poet Melvin Tolson, poet laureate of Liberia (the only American poet ever to be honored as the poet laureate of another nation), and author of the *Libretto for the Republic of Liberia*. But even in the process of saluting this black poet, Williams dilutes his praise by making Tolson share it:

     . . . to Tolson and to his ode
and to Liberia and to Allen Tate
(Give him credit)
and to the South generally
     Selah!

(*Paterson* 183)

Though each of these entities is worthy of praise for one or another accomplishment, it appears symptomatic that Williams will not allow Tolson to take his credits alone. He must share them with Allen Tate, who is being credited either with the courage required to help a little-known poet find a wider audience for his work or with the courage to have overcome his own substantial prejudices, and who wrote an introduction for Tolson's *Libretto* which, it shall be shown shortly, effectively encrypts Tolson's work within white discourse. Lastly, Williams widens his toast to include the South generally, and as much as it may be true that Tolson was a product of the southern experience, this cannot but lessen the significance of his accomplishment, just as Williams earlier subsumed the experience of the middle passage within the larger, whiter experience of immigration.

As *Paterson* nears its end (we cannot say it concludes), Williams reproduces a snippet from the jazz musician Mezz Mezzrow's autobiography, *Really the Blues,* in which Mezzrow declares that "any white man if he thought straight and studied hard, could sing and dance and play with the Negro. . . . you could dig the colored man's real message and get in there with him" (*Paterson* 221), a passage whose inclusion may be motivated by Williams's belief in a commonality of human imagination and an availability of experience. Williams's own writings, in contrast, show that he was not terribly concerned with thinking straight and studying hard about Afro-Americans. He would instead describe a black aesthetic of his own, severed from the historical facts of black experience in this country; he would rather use the nonwhite as local color in his poetic constructions than join in, as Mezzrow attempted, in the mutual improvisation of American art and culture.

Williams's inability to break through the received terminology of race and to improvise with the real contributions of black American culture is manifest in a reading of *Man Orchid,* the unfinished improvisatory novel he collaborated on with Fred Miller and Lydia Carlin. The poet had long evinced an interest in jazz and on several occasions wrote poems attempting to make use of jazz rhythms, of jazz as a subject matter, and of the language of the musicians themselves, poems such as "Ol' Bunk's Band" and "Shoot It Jimmy." If he sometimes seemed unaware of the ironies of his own efforts in this regard, as in the last lines of "Shoot It Jimmy," which, with their declaration that "They can't copy it" (*Earlier Poems* 269), appear to declare the impossibility of the very task they are undertaking, Williams nonetheless was inspired by the rhythms and energies of jazz and wanted them for his own. One of the great losses to our literature may have occurred when no one took Williams up on his suggestion of starting a determinedly interracial magazine, an idea that was born along with the idea of improvising *Man Orchid,* for the enterprise might well have altered the course of Williams's subsequent work and of American letters generally.

It is illuminating that the inception of *Man Orchid,* was based upon a racial misunderstanding, upon the kind of categorical error which has marked so much of the ambiguous trail of American racial history. The idea for writing *Man Orchid* came about as a result of a meeting in a jazz club between Williams and Bucklin Moon, a Doubleday editor whom Williams and Miller took to be a fair-skinned Negro, perhaps because he had written a novel, *The Darker Brother,* and edited an anthology of fiction about American blacks (Mariani, *New World* 513–14). Thus *Man Orchid,* an improvised novel with an imaginary black man for a central character, like so many other literary creations of blackness by whites, had its origin in the projection of white mythology into an imagined space of otherness. Williams was, as Paul Mariani has noted, "now projecting himself into a black persona" ("Black Novel" 70). That Williams is truly disseminating his own aesthetic interests through this jazz age figuration emerges in the pages of *Man Orchid* as the novel's authors' differing perceptions of race and blackness begin to battle within the text. For Williams from the outset, as in so many of his writings on blacks, *Man Orchid* was a repository for libidinal longings, a refuge from the worn restrictions of puritanism, and an opportunity to oppose what he saw as the pure American impulse of jazz, as represented in Bunk Johnson's music, to the agonized and Anglicized wasteland of Eliot. His coauthors did not always see it in quite the same light, and while Williams was innovative enough to understand that the tensions this open disagreement might bring to the text could produce a vibrant work, they contributed in the end to the project's demise.

"Under this vibrant sign of jazz—whose frivolity masked a secret nostalgia," Michel Leiris has written his memory as a white man encountering jazz (Leiris 109). Within the hieroglyphs of Williams's contributions to *Man Orchid* may be discerned his nostalgia for a sort of prelapsarian encounter with authenticity. Williams's black orchid begins in a nostalgic tropic, flaunting its "complex sexual devices. There it is again, the fluted and bulbous mechanism" (Williams, Carlin, and Miller 77). From there he moves to a reassertion of that Steinian (and Hegelian) ascription of nothingness to the black other, an existential blank out of which Williams believes the black improvises his own authenticity, his own unencumbered being: "What men are is purely brain stuff. Everybody knows it and rejects it. Everybody spends his whole life trying to prove he just doesn't exist. But only the soldier knows it, the soldier and the nigger" (102). Admittedly Williams sees this as a positive movement, but there appears to be an enormous price to pay if the black other is to accept this opportunity to achieve his primordial creativity. Also following Stein's example in *Melanctha*, Williams's protagonist would really rather be white. Speaking of the period following his college years he remarks, "From that time on I became a white man in my dreams" (104). Where Williams advances beyond Stein in this respect is in noting that this longing for whiteness is rooted in the social consequences of being black in a white world and is not an intrinsic feature of mixed blood.

Though Fred Miller shared Williams's enthusiasm for jazz and his initial excitement about writing a jazz text, his resistance to the direction of Williams's side of the project is registered forcefully: "Now returning to this novel, Man Orchid. Why the orchid?—to begin with. There's the old, tiresome and at bottom snobbish literary assumption that the Negro in America is an exotic bloom. Negro equals jungle. Despite the fact that he has been here longer than the second, third, even ninth generation Eurp European—Negro equals jungle. Then why doesn't the ofay bank president of German descent equal Black Forest? The Rutherford doctor of Welsh descent equal the Cromlechs? or Welsh rarebit?" (Williams, Carlin, and Miller 111). Williams does not rise to the bait of that final, personal provocation. Rather than respond to Miller's troublesome queries directly, in his next contribution to the novel Williams gives a textual shrug and turns back to his more aesthetic interests: "My reply to that is: we're establishing an identity if it takes the whole novel to do it and nothing else ever happens except a "beautiful woman" running along beside it talking to herself. Let her run along; she's beautiful, isn't she?" (111). Where Williams wants the energy and freedom of jazz for his own, to make a beautiful thing of words torn from blank blackness, Miller cannot bring himself entirely into the project without reflecting upon the status of his subject and the politics of that bringing. At one point Miller wrote to Williams about the obvious problem that might confront a white writer engaging such an effort: "I don't know enough about him and his special type, the colored intellectual (although I've been acquainted with and 've liked lots of ordinary Negro folk, laborers, musicians et al); AND I can't fake what I don't know. That last is bad. In jazz "faking" is a name for playing by ear or improvising. If I can't fake, what'm I doing trying to help out on a verbal improvisation?" (qtd. in Mariani, "Black Novel" 73). Again, Williams declined to meet these objections head on; his interest was in keeping the project going. The verbal construction itself was what mattered, and while it would certainly be missing a great deal to throw out all of Williams that is not politically agreeable, it is worthy of note that he is so resistant to having his attention directed to fundamental questions about the racial context of his endeavour. It becomes even more noteworthy in light of evidence that Williams himself valued such attention to context in other poets. Writing a review of Charles Henri Ford's *The Garden of Disorder,* Williams singled out just such an instance in that poet's lines: "I always look for such lines as these— 'I, Rainey Betha, 22, / from the top branch of race-hatred look at you.' That's hard material to handle. It tests every resource of a poet to do it well" (*Something to Say* 88).

Miller and Carlin, in their portions of *Man Orchid,* attempt to discover to the extent it is possible for them as white intellectuals the position of a black intellectual such as their main character. Miller, sounding a bit like Langston Hughes, is first to sound the issue: "Bad enough to be black, it was. Double trouble to be black and intellectual. But to be black and intellectual and over-size, all at the same time—that was the limit" (Williams, Carlin, and Miller 79). For Miller this troublesome double bind leads to a sensitivity to racial context, as in the scene in which the character wonders if the whites at a party are making a fool of him: "Am I being guyed? Being made sport of in the ofay lair?" (92). In turn, such heightened sensitivity to the perceptions and intentions of white society develops in the character a double consciousness of the type Ralph Ellison would later describe, an ability to see on both sides of the racial veil at once. At one point Miller's figure chides himself for stooping to the whites' level while at the same time conjecturing upon the assumptions of his white friends, assumptions that might be shared by his white authors and readers: "Shame on me (to himself). Indulging in white backbiting. We're supposed to be a people barbaric, that is, pure in heart, are we not?" (94). In passages such as these Miller shows that he has thrust himself into a sort of double consciousness of his own, which, if not quite a Melvillean deconstructive turn, at least affords him an opportunity to view himself *as if* he were in a position of otherness. Lydia Carlin's portion of the text exhibits the same doubled perspective, particularly the lengthy meditation on racial possibility in chapter 5 in which her narrator wonders what it would be like to be white. One passage is wonderfully ironic, occurring as it does in the midst of a "jazz" novel written by whites about blacks: "Then it came to me, what I'd rather do than anything else in the world. Play in a dance orchestra like that one in the pavilion. Play the piano, with a horn and a slap-bass and a drum. That would be as good as heaven, and I could stay up all night and sleep in the day time. I wondered if colored people could get jobs like that" (96). (That last sentence is a far better example of racial irony in white writing than any in Williams or H.D.) Like Miller too, Carlin gives her characters a sure sense of the expectations of whites, as in the reasoning offered to explain a decision not to reveal a theft committed by a white boy to his mother: "She'd much rather think you took the money. You see white folks expect the colored to do like that. In fact they're kind of disappointed if we don't because it looks like we act almost as good as they do" (96).

A chapter by Williams follows this sharp delineation of racial difference with a philosophical erasure of such difference, and while Williams in making his point again dissolves historical context, he comes closer here than anywhere else in his published works to a truly subversive tunneling through the language of race, and for that reason his response needs to be given at length:

> What I mean is that you don't explain anything, not to someone. You can only explain it to no one. Because no one understands. No one can possibly be two at once. No one can be black and white.
>
> Except me! What do you know about that? But quite philosophically obvious that isn't for one moment true. I am myself and I cannot for one moment, being myself, be black and white at the same time. It is philosophically impossible.
>
> Therefore—How can one even say therefore? Like that. Only white can say, "therefore." I should say only black can say "therefore." You see, obviously, nothing that borrows from both sides of a question can maintain a separate existence. (Williams, Carlin, and Miller 101)

Had Williams chosen to press on in this manner he might have done much to further the dismantling of the racist apparatus of American verse, but just as the novel itself was ultimately abandoned, Williams seems to have thrown up his hands and abandoned this line of thought: "Eureka. I am black. Therefore I am white. Black, white. White, black. Ampersand, quicksand: What's the difference?" (101). This last rhetorical question might well have served as a goad to further investigations. Instead of an overarching interest in exoticism out of context, an approach to the other that went little farther than a celebratory perusal of a waitingroom copy of *National Geographic,* Williams might have taken his language to a limit point at which racial difference folded back upon itself and race revealed itself as an imagined construction, a thing made with words that might be made up or made over. But, he did not.

Until recent years it was common to consider the poet H.D. (Hilda Doolittle) as either an apolitical imagist, or as tainted by the fascist leanings of some of her colleagues, Pound among them. Her publicly available writings evoked no overt interest in race at all, and those published pieces such as "Red Roses for Bronze" which subsequent scholarship reveals may have a racial context contain no direct reference to race and could be read by the most astute without raising any questions of race. But recent and long overdue attention to this important figure of American modernism, much of it focused by feminist scholars, has resituated our understanding of her works and has resulted in the publication at long last of works which had been available only in manuscript. It can now be seen that H.D. gave considerable thought to race and to the positions of Afro-Americans within European and American society, but in the process of recovering this material and recontextualizing it, some have made larger claims for H.D.'s presentation of race than the record will bear. While H.D. may be credited with working against the assignment of blacks to a position of social and aesthetic inferiority, most notably in her work on the film *Borderline,* her identification with blackness often carries the air of the imperial ego appropriating imagined qualities of otherness, and her work is not free of stereotyped imagery.

In her crucial examination of these issues, "Modernism of the 'Scattered Remnant': Race and Politics in the Development of H.D.'s Modernist Vision," Susan Stanford Friedman argues that "H.D.'s personal experience with the Harlem Renaissance played a key role in deepening and broadening her early feminism into a fully progressive modernism based on an identification with all the people who exist as 'the scattered remnant' at the fringes of culture" (94). Friedman's formulation raises two fundamental difficulties. In the first place, H.D. had no direct personal experience of the Harlem Renaissance to speak of. Indeed, Friedman herself acknowledges, on the page facing her statement of her thesis, that "H.D. appears to have missed the Harlem Renaissance, as well as the periodic disruptions against class and race privilege that disturbed the political and social surface of American life" (95). H.D. was an expatriate during the Harlem Renaissance, and, with the exception of Paul Robeson, seems not to have had any significant contact with any of the key black figures in that flowering of African-American arts. The fact is that most of H.D.'s contact with black arts was mediated by white activists such as Carl Van Vechten and Nancy Cunard, which indicates the second difficulty with Friedman's thesis. When judging the question of H.D.'s identification with blacks, it is crucial to note that she was largely identifying with a literary blackness transmitted by whites. As was so often the case with white modernist writers, H.D. sometimes projected her own white mythology onto the black other and then identified with that otherness.

This conflation of literary invention with material reality, this reification of the literary construct, is visible in H.D.'s report of her earliest experiences. In the first section of her memoir *The Gift,* titled "Dark Room," H.D. recalls a childhood visit to a production of *Uncle Tom's Cabin.* The adults present, apparently glossing the significance of the production for their children, set the process in motion by which the borderlines between historical constructions, literary figurations, and present day occurrence are blurred in the young girl's psyche: "They told us that the book was called *Uncle Tom's Cabin* and that the play we were going to be taken to see, in a real theater, on the other side of the river, was called *Uncle Tom's Cabin,* but it was the book that started it or it was the real story, in the beginning, that started it, because Uncle Tom was a real darky on a real plantation, *Way down upon the Sewanee river"* (H.D., *Gift* 13). Even at this early age H.D. can be seen to identify with these others upon a stage, but at this stage it is an identification which tends, under the urgings of the adults, to melt the distinctions of historical experience: "We were Americans and so were the darkies who were tied together and so was Simon Legree and so was Little Eva" (14). This was the first play that the narrator had ever seen, and it triggered aesthetic longings which were to have an important bearing on the adult artist's development. Looking to the future, the young poet thinks to herself, "there would be someone else who was myself, yet who was the child of the Lady who Played the Piano; then I would be Little Eva and I would have an Uncle Tom who was not really an uncle, but it was like that. It was called a play . . ." (19). It is just such an obscuring of roles and boundaries which accounts for what interest the film *Borderline* holds as drama, an interest which is often organized around the figure played by H.D., a clearly bigoted character who is set against the black characters with whom H.D. would clearly identify.

That sort of identification at the domestic meeting point between black and white might also be traced to H.D.'s youth, if we follow the poet's biographers in reading *HERmione* as an autobiographical novel. In the interplay between the protoganist Her, and her household's black servant, Mandy, we again see the youth aligning herself with a black figure, even to the point of adopting the older woman's speech patterns. "Her fell into the rhythm of Mandy's speech, the moment she began to speak to Mandy" (H.D., *HERmione* 26). Yet much later in the work, H.D. uses that same Afro-American speech as comic relief in the best, or worst, minstrel tradition: " 'Choriambics,' she said to herself, sustained against the bulk of a huge negress who pushed Her aside with a lumbering basket, who cried in high bull-bellow to the conductor, 'I done said 22nd street, I done tol' you when I paid you' " (149). That type of clichéd image makes it a bit difficult to accept some recent claims for H.D.'s presentations too quickly.

In that same scene in which the young Her fell into the maid's speech rhythms, it is Her who instructs the black woman in the errors of racial discrimination: "A gardener is a gardener, a black gardener is as good as a white gardener. There's no need *dis*-criminating" (H.D., *HERmione* 26). Friedman, who argues that H.D. has in this volume avoided the familiar stereotyped pattern of relationships between young white girls and the black servants they love (recall Benét's line: "But then they loved their mammies—there was that—"), acknowledges that episodes such as this could be read as patronizing but asserts that such a reading "does not take into account the subtle irony and humor that permeates the texture of *HER*" (Friedman 106). But such an argument assumes that it is not possible to be ironic while patronizing. H.D. does present her younger character with considerable irony, and her narrative is at its most humorous when the young girl is most deliberately ironic. During a dance Her sees "with ironic precision" a picture of a dumpy white woman who reminds her of a trinket owned by Mandy, the family servant: "That sort of thing's all right for Mandy; 'Well, I do see,' she found herself exclaiming, 'that sort of woman standing on a sea-shell sort of art is simply negroid.' She had said that 'that sort of woman standing on a sea-shell sort of art is simply negroid' and she was waiting for George to acclaim her, to say, bravissimo Bellissima . . ." (H.D., *HERmione* 136). Later in the same scene, Her sees Fayne Rabb crossing the room as a girl in a Greek tunic who "stood for one ironic moment before the negroid sort of art picture of a woman on a sea shell" (138). An irony of this level is hilarious, the more so for the adult author's allowing the character to be so self-consciously proud of her own irony. Such moments allow the artist to look back laughingly at her own earlier attitudes, while simultaneously lampooning the posturings of Ezra Pound, here represented by George, and perhaps even the pronouncements on art of Gertrude Stein. But even as H.D. rises above her own earlier prejudices, she seems to rise even further above Mandy, whose appreciation of her trinket is not ironic and is given no quarter. Readers need not feel that they are inadequately attuned to irony if they sense patronizing here; such scenes are patronizing. No matter the extent to which Her identifies with Mandy and takes her side against the prejudiced nonsense offered by Her's sister-in-law, Minnie, no matter how effectively H.D. pillories the prejudice which surrounded Her in her youth, there is no doubt that Mandy occupies a space of lesser aesthetic sensibility, and that is where she remains even though H.D. gives her the last word in Her's story.

This difficulty arises again in *Borderline*, the film in which H.D. appears along with Bryher (Annie Winifred Ellerman) and the Robesons. As H.D.'s biographer Barbara Guest has reported, the intention in making this experimental silent film was, among other things, to use the position of the African diaspora as a metaphor to limn borderline states of psyche and aesthetics. The characters Pete and Adah, played by Paul and Essie Robeson, according to H.D., "dwell on the cosmic racial borderline. They are black people among white people" (qtd. in Guest 196). The film is impressive for being ahead of its time in portraying an assertive black male character who struggles to maintain his dignity against the incursions of whites, even if it fails to impress much either as drama or as cinematic experiment. This is one of the rare films made by whites during this period which shows a black man physically challenging a white rival. And refreshingly it is the black characters who are shown as endangered by the moral decadence of the whites, rather than the other way around. Throughout, H.D. turns in a performance calculated to exhibit the ugliness of racism. Her character, Astrid, possessed by jealousy, resorts to the refuge of hatred when Thorne, played by Gavin Arthur, is attracted to the black woman, and calls him a "nigger lover."

Still, while *Borderline* offers one of the first compelling denunciations of racism in the history of American cinema, this collaborative endeavour in which H.D. was a contributing artist continues the elaboration of stereotyped, albeit positively, images of Africans in the West. It is the black female whose attraction to and for Thorne serves as the force which drives the drama, once again inscribing the historic suspicion of black female sexuality. That the woman is also clearly part white underscores the sense of danger and discord which is so often associated with racial amalgamation in American letters. (In a piece written during the filming of "Two Americans," H.D. shows herself to share some of Gertrude Stein's suspicions regarding the psychological proclivities of American mulattoes: "Paula Howard . . . thought more as white folks, consistently, being more than half-white . . ." (qtd. in Guest 199). Also, *Borderline* is further evidence of the tendency among white artists to associate persons of African descent with nature. The characters played by the Robesons are made veritable creatures of the natural environment in starkest contrast to the enervated and decadent whites whose bohemian goings-on go on indoors, surrounded by smoke and drink. Oddly enough, the environment in this film is a European mountain district; there is one curious scene in which the Robesons are shown at play in the outdoors, which suggests strongly that even in the snowy Alps the African is somehow closer to nature than the whites who live there.

It is true, as Susan Stanford Friedman remarks, that "H.D.'s attempt to oppose and transcend racism through identification came directly out of personal experience" (115). H.D. can be said perhaps more than William Carlos Williams, though she addressed race at much less length, to have attempted to demonstrate the vacuity of racism and to have had some understanding of the questionable status of her own feelings on the subject. But one need not look to the "covert racism in dealings with the Robesons" suggested by her private references to the "chocolate baby" (Friedman 102), nor to letters in which she refers, in ironic quotation marks, to the "darky" problem (qtd. in Friedman 96) in order to raise doubts about the extent to which she had transcended racism through identification. There are sufficient stereotypes, even in *Borderline,* and there is enough patronizing, even if ironic, in *HERmione* to question just how far "identification with Otherness rather than a perpetuation of it was . . . responsible for the sensitivity with which H.D. approached the subject of race" (Friedman 115). To identify with the qualities one has imagined and posited in the other does not serve to halt their perpetuation, quite to the contrary it gives them renewed vigor. A simple reversal of the values attached to the qualities of the subjugating subject and the other does not, as much as any one of us might wish it to, subvert the signifying system of racial dominance; rather it continues it at another, perhaps even more persistent level. It may be that identifying with the other by appropriating the imagined properties of others may be the last seal against the reality of their existence's impinging upon our consciousness.

Following Williams, the second wave of American modernism, represented most interestingly by the poets of objectivism, repeats these same images of racial discourse, sometimes countering their own political thrust, which was generally toward a leftist humanism. Among these poets, only Charles Reznikoff wrote at length in verse of the black experience in America. His longest poem, *Testimony: The United States (1885–1915), Recitative,* is divided up into sections according to geographical region and subject matter. Within these divisions, there is a repeating section entitled "Negroes," which is comprised of court testimony from cases involving blacks, rendered into verse patterns by the poet. These sections, taken as a whole, constitute the most substantial consideration given to black life by a white poet during the modernist period, and for once they let that life speak for itself, in the form of dispassionately reported depositions. One example shall have to serve:

Several white men went at night to the Negro's
house,
shot into it,
and set fire to his cotton on the gallery
his wife and children ran under the bed
and as the firing from guns and pistols went on

and the cotton blazed up, ran through a side door
into the woods.
The Negro himself, badly wounded, fled to the
house of a neighbor—
a white man—
and got inside.
He was followed,
and one of those who ran after him
put a shotgun against the white man's door
and shot a hole through it.
Justice, however, was not to be thwarted,
for five of the men who did this to the Negro
were tried:
for "unlawfully and maliciously
injuring and disfiguring"—
the white man's property.

                                    (*Testimony* 1:136–137)

Reznikoff allows the irony of America's racial injustices to foreground itself
in these pieces, as in this one, which makes no comment on the fact that there
were no charges for destroying a black man's property or for assaulting him
and his family. But despite the clear stance against injustice taken here and
elsewhere, as in his inclusion among his "found" poems of a description of a
slave sale gleaned from the autobiography of the Afro-American writer Solomon Northrup (*Poems* 204–206), Reznikoff, when he left the area of ready-
mades and began to write his own descriptions, as in the novel *The Manner
Music*, can be found to have invoked the same stereotypes of blacks used by
his predecessors in modernism. The effect of lines borrowed from Northrup
which condemn the slave trader for calling a black woman a "blubbering,
howling wench" (*Poems* 206) is somewhat mitigated by the novel's narrator's
description of the face of a young black man as having "the surly look of a
sleepy child. . . . His brows were drawn together in two lines that ran up the
bridge of the flat nose. Slowly he raised his hand to the back of his head and
scratched his kinky hair" (*Manner Music* 112). This image taken alone might
not count for much, but the novel includes others which establish a pattern of
such descriptions. The nonwhite in this objectivist fiction is marked by sloth
and ugliness. While riding on the street the narrator observes a "negress"
seated near him in the car: "very fat, broad nose, thick lips, half-shut eyes,
coming from some charring probably, because she carried a bundle with her
in which was, I suppose, an old dress and old shoes. And in her hand, held

idly, a spray of flowers, large white flowers with a reddish tinge at the heart" (*Manner Music* 58). This could as easily be Williams's character in "A Negro Woman," making her way home from an encounter with that poet, or any of innumerable other fat mammies who populate white writing. Reznikoff also exhibits in this novel the tendency shared with Pound to describe the black face in terms of a "primitivist" African artifact, as when his narrator spies "another waitress, with an ugly face, the sad ugly face of a negro idol that has seen many slain and heard much wailing, . . . swaying to the music" (*Manner Music* 47).

The sort of misunderstanding of African culture Reznikoff perpetuates in this passage appears again in a poem which Carl Rakosi wrote and submitted for inclusion in Nancy Cunard's *Negro* anthology, a poem entitled "The Black Crow." Here Rakosi revives all the stale white myths about the dark continent that were met with in Lindsay's "The Congo." In the Africa of "The Black Crow" even the four winds are "spooky" and, as Wallace Stevens's snow man requires a mind of winter, here "One must have sullen wits / to foot the jungle / like another darkness" (*Negro* 268). The effect becomes truly comic as Rakosi, generally a much more cautious deployer of imagery, manages to employ a surprising number of dead metaphors in a small literary space:

Now though one's black feet
straggle in the thrum
of oil palms, mumbo-jumbo
bangs a tom-tom.

The continent is waterbound
and one outside the singer
in the shack. And Sambo,
fat cigar in heaven, chucks the white dice
gravely with a black crow.

                    (*Negro* 268)

This is so close to Lindsay that it needs to be read as a parody, but the authorization for such a reading does not seem to inhere in the poem itself as clearly as it does in other, more clearly defined Rakosi parodies such as "So much depends" (*Ere-Voice* 18). As it happens, the curious later publication history of "The Black Crow" shows it to be a parody of Wallace Stevens, in at least one of its incarnations. In Rakosi's *Collected Poems,* a substantially revised version of the poem appears as the untitled third section of a longer piece, "Domination of Wallace Stevens." But readers of Cunard's *Negro* anthology would not have had that later context within which to judge the workings of "The Black Crow's" array of racist images. The status of that parodic context is itself called into question by the fact that a shorter version of "Domination of Wallace Stevens" appears as "Homage to Wallace Stevens" in the collection *Amulet* (74), without any sign of "The Black Crow." It might seem that Rakosi was unsure if his parodic measures would be read as such, and in at least one sense he would have been right to be uncertain. Just as Henry Taylor's "De Gustibus Ain't What Dey Used to Be" cannot be read, even as irony, without activating a vocabulary of racism, "The Black Crow" cannot be read parodically without giving privilege to the substance expressed in the style being parodied. If "The Black Crow" is a parody, it is one which leaves the original suppositions of its model intact, destroying only the form of Stevens's work while leaving its white mythology largely untouched. Fortunately, there are several insightful essays elsewhere in *Negro* which attempt to come near to the truth of the history of African civilizations and which do much to demolish the fictive ground upon which "The Black Crow" and "The Congo" are constructed.

Other, nonparodic poems by Rakosi appear to repeat Stevens's treatments of blacks uncritically. "Sylvia," which asks us to "Trot out the negro singers, ladies, clowns / and athletes to extol the morning" (*Collected Poems* 438), continues Stevens's use of blacks as poetic stagehands. "Blackbirds," identified as "street talk," perpetuates the link between blacks and gambling seen in the "Black Crow" and in Lindsay's work, with a nod to the minstrel tradition later taken up by John Berryman, and identifies Mr. Bones as "the black God" (Rakosi, *Collected Poems* 272). But if Rakosi seemed ahead of his time in this regard, he also, like several of his contemporaries, began to move to a deeper understanding of the dynamics of racial alignments, a less offensive pattern of imagery, and a less patronizing approach to black Americans.

His jazz poems, such as "The Adventures of Varese," are as effective in their manipulation of rhythm and register as those of Williams. His own "take" on the fatalism of the racially persecuted is surer than that of Williams, and, in its Old Testament–flavored ironic combination of resignation and optimism, is more akin to the spirit of the poets of the blues and Gospel than anything in Williams, as can be seen in the short poem "The Age:"

> I shall
>   not prevail.
> The heart
>   is my negritude.
> (Rakosi, *Collected Poems* 37)

(Note also Rakosi's duplication of the cadence of that Baptist hymn that became the anthem of the Civil Rights Movement in the 1960s.) Lastly, like
Faulkner, Rakosi exhibits admiration for the creative surge that rises from the
depths of Afro-American experience of slavery and self-recreation, for the
imaginative renewal:

> of Negro cabins
> > with the cotton picker's
> deep slave voice
> > imploding
> into warm hosannahs,
> the other Florida
> > of patient Africanus.
> > > (*Collected Poems* 86)

These more liberal verses do not lie comfortably next to the peculiar institution of parody in "The Black Crow," but they are testimony to the tension in
the minds of modernists such as Rakosi between democratic, even radical
political ideals and the too slowly shifting shades of racial metaphor during
the period of their careers. If the parodic gestures of "The Black Crow" strike
polite minds as dated, clumsy, and vulgar now, the lines of "Americana"
embody the sort of subtle irony the later Rakosi finds everywhere in the to-
pography of race in our country. Visiting Washington, D.C., Rakosi notes
that those central documents of American political history, the Declaration of
Independence and the Constitution, with its recognition of slavery in the form
of counting each black as a partial man, now lie two hundred years after their
adoption:

> . . . in a glass
> > and bronze
> case
> indecipherable
> > sealed
> in helium
> > under the eyes
> of a black
> > guard
> in the National
> > Archives
> > > (*Collected Poems* 319)

The tension between leftist pronouncements and the received structures of
racial discourse is most acute in the work of objectivism's chief theorist,

Louis Zukofsky, who early on in his career evinced both an interest in Marxism and a tendency to use racist epithets. A poem entitled "Poem" begins:

> How many
> Times round
>
> Deck, ladies?
> What says
> the nigger?
>
> "Fi' minutes
> After a
>
> Man's breath
> Leaves
>
> His body
> He knows—'
>
> Much 'bout
> Himself's
>
> Ten years
> befo' 'e
>
> Was bo'n"
>   (*All* 28)

That Zukofsky was on occasion sensitive to the emotional weight of the word "nigger" may be judged from the fact that the words "black man" were substituted for it in the version of this same poem that the poet published in Nancy Cunard's anthology, *Negro* (*Negro* 269). The piece also shows Zukofsky to have been as ready as his mentor, Ezra Pound, to resort to blackface dialect. He does this more curiously in his play, *Arise, arise,* which enjoyed an Off-Broadway production in the thirties, and which features two black characters who inexplicably switch back and forth between this minstrel style of speech, replete with "de's" and "dat's," and standard English and even standard French. This practice recurs, more effectively, in the eighth section of Zukofsky's long poem, "*A,*" where it is at least rendered more sensible by its appearance in a passage which is a cacophony of dialects playing against one another:

> I spec it will be all 'fiscated
> De massa run, ha! ha! De darkey stay, ho! ho!
> So distribution should undo excess—
>   (50)

Zukofsky's attraction to dialect and to puns converges with his early pro-
clivity for the use of racist epithet in *"A,"* section 7, in a romping passage
which begins with the poet's meditation upon a group of sawhorses outside a
window, then moves to his shouting, "See! For me these jiggers, these dancing bucks: Bum pump a-dum" (41). Barry Ahearn, in *Zukofsky's "A": An
Introduction,* rightly points out that "jigger" in these lines "refers not only to
street cars and dancers, but also to measures of Whiskey" (62). But interestingly, in pursuing this most polysemous of poets, Ahearn fails to note
that "jigger" is also a term of abuse for the black race, and Zukofsky's own
lines authorize a reading of the word that takes this into account by placing the
term in contiguity with "dancing bucks," another racist name which simultaneously intends finance, and one which is repeated several lines later in the
same section. This reading is reinforced by Zukofsky's use of such epithets in
other early sections of *"A,"* such as the very Poundian passage which recalls:

The time was Arcy Bell:
A nigger
Had a city and a country home
And a rabbit patch on which
    he "conveniently did shoot them"
                (29)

And further down the same page:

Arcy agin' the wall
Shoot high yaller
Agin the wall!

As was the case with *The Cantos,* *"A"* takes a firmly denunciatory stance
against slavery even in its earliest pages, but again the poet's own referential
apparatus tends to militate against his social positions; employing the terms of
racial otherness is the discourse's form of justifying the victim's victimiza-
tion. If, in *"A,"* section 8, Zukofsky can speak approvingly of "Negroes and
whites holding the doors / against night-riders" (99), then why, one wonders,
when he comes to speak against modern forms of racial oppression does he
revert to the use of the term "nigger," as in this segment from *"A,"* section
13:

Candy nigger babies and the beast Apartheider
Hind dependence of gold dust Africa
On slaviest business
            (265)

Similarly, Zukofsky's substitution of the spelling "nigritude" for the name of
the artistic and political movement known as "negritude" in the lines of "*A*,"
section 23, that describe "ebony Images whose 'nigritude offends" (562),
steals much of the force from the elegant closing of "*A*," section 15, which
combines a tribute to Williams with a plea for racial harmony:

> *negritude* no nearer or further
> than the African violet
> not deferred to
> or if white, Job
> white pods of *honesty*
> *satinflower*
>
> (375)

And again, when the possibility of black rebellion enters into the poem, in the
form of a quotation from an unidentified source, a stereotyped image embedded within the passage prejudices its reception:

> 'nobody not
> a hut
> standing, if
>
> a gang
> of *thick-lips*
> armed suddenly
>
> took to
> travelling on
> the road
>
> catching the
> white swine
> right and left
>
> I fancy
> every farm
> and cottage
> hereabouts would
> get empty
>
> (329)

The best that can be said for this is that, unlike other passages we have examined, this speaker holds both races in equal contempt.

But "*A*" is the poem of a lifetime, one into which the poet allowed the
events of his day, and one in which those events can be seen to contribute to

the development of the poet's thought as they occur. As *"A"* reaches the period of the great civil rights struggles of midcentury, his tone when speaking of blacks becomes less denigrating, and as a result his expressed political positions come to appear, to use a key term of objectivism, more sincere. Only a few pages after the passage just cited, Zukofsky speaks elegiacally and effectively of the tragedies that met the Congo and its independence leader, Patrice Lumumba (398–99). And he writes yet more powerfully in *"A,"* section 14, of the deaths of civil-rights workers and the horrible bombing of a church in Birmingham, Alabama, an act of terrorism that took the lives of four children. Still, though Zukofsky can be seen moving away from his early adoption of standard racial imagery, the poem that took him fifty years to write is read in much less time, and those early images will do battle in the reader's mind with the more temperate later stance.

Among those poets of objectivism who write of blackness at all, only Kenneth Rexroth and George Oppen seem, on the evidence of their so-far collected poems, to have never employed the more typical terms of disparagement. Most of Rexroth's work in this realm of discourse belongs more properly to the era of political liberalism to be discussed in a later chapter, but as he was identified with the objectivists early on in his career, he might be taken up here as an example of a left-leaning objectivist whose imagery did not seem as a rule to counter the sense of his statements. The nearest thing to such an occasion in his collected poems is found in a tribute to the people of Bordeaux who engaged in acts of resistance and sabotage against the Nazis, in which Rexroth notes the "best people in town / Were the black feline Negroes" (*Collected Longer Poems* 246). The insertion of the catty adjective is troublesome, even in a poem which is praising the "Negro workers" who "made Bordeaux industrially / Worthless to the Nazis" (247) after hearing of the atrocities committed by the Germans against the Jews in their city. Rexroth had an eye for the insincerity of many of his fellow leftists when it came to matters of race and once wrote wryly, in "The Dragon and the Unicorn":

The Stalinists always measure
The success of their meetings
By the number of Negroes,
Youth, and women they bring out
              (217)

And he is unique among objectivists (with whom, it is true, he may have been grouped simply because he did not write sonnets) in his ability to apply this

eye for the ironies of race and society humorously without descending to the
level of minstrelsy:

> In K.C. everyone, even
> The whores and an appreciable
> Number of Negroes, looks like
> Truman. I go out with a
> Black, deep bosomed, aquiline nosed
> Girl like a Sudanese—no
> Public place possible in
> Kansas City, so we go
> To the house of a friend, who
> Turns out to be my train porter,
> Drink beer and dance to records.
>
> (253)

There is no sense here that the poet in any way holds himself in a position of
superiority or power over these individuals, and no sense that they are in any
way congenitally inclined to be more fun-loving than he is. A significant
contrast is available here to the descriptions of blacks offered by Pound and by
Reznikoff. Pound, in the *Pisan Cantos,* compared a black man's face to an
African mask. Reznikoff, in *The Manner Music,* compared the face of a black
woman to the visage of an African idol. In Rexroth we find, possibly for the
first time in white modernism in America, the simple comparison of an Afro-
American woman's face to that of an African woman. The poet may have
literally arrived for the woman herself in this reminiscence, but what is of
greater interest is the fact that, alone among white objectivists writing of race,
he presents blacks and whites in this nation as having more elements of
culture in common than was traditionally thought by the intellectual mainstream. The fact that everybody looks like Truman in Kansas City highlights
the ludicrous nature of that city's segregation of public places.

If there is a serious criticism to be leveled at Rexroth with regard to his
writings on Afro-America, it is that he finds himself to have so much in
common with blacks that he occasionally presumes too much. He is the only
one of the objectivists to have published any sustained critical work on the
writings of black poets, and he devotes a chapter of his *American Poetry in
the Twentieth Century* to their history. In that chapter, though, when he comes
to a discussion of the poetry written by LeRoi Jones (Amiri Baraka) during the
period of cultural nationalism, Rexroth suddenly begins to play the white
man's game of deciding for the black person which black leader or writer
should be attended to. First, Rexroth claims that "one would judge from his

recent work . . . [Jones] heartily despises" Langston Hughes (158). None of this recent work is cited, however, and the remark remains puzzling in light of Baraka's several statements of admiration for that earlier author. Rexroth is apparently confusing a dispute over political and aesthetic tactics with a personal distaste. That same failure to cite a source plagues the chapter's most presumptuous remark. Rexroth says of Baraka's late work that it does not appeal much "to ordinary Negroes, who find his later poetry, like his remarkable plays, offensive because they 'portray the worst aspects of the race,' with, in every sense, a vengeance!" (158). (This is of course the same sort of charge brought against Hughes in the twenties and thirties.) Who is this "ordinary" Negro? The absence of an attribution for the critical judgment reported by Rexroth and attributed to an entire race is damning. It represents another episode in the history of white intellectuals' substituting the responses of a few like-minded blacks for the judgments of the people at large. If we leave aside the question of how many "ordinary" people of any color find any postmodern verse they read "appealing," we are still left with the conclusion that Rexroth is setting himself up as the possessor of a special knowledge of the thinking of blacks and as being able to speak on their behalf. Rexroth remains, for all that, one modernist writer who began to turn away from the image of the nonwhite as a lesser, exotic creature. In this same chapter on black verse he shows himself more aware of the "cultural continuity" of Africa than were any of the white American poets who contributed to the *Negro* anthology, and by 1971 he is able to claim, possibly still with a good deal of presumption, that "today everybody is aware that African accomplishments in music and sculpture are the equal of any in the world" (*American Poetry* 149).

A late poem from George Oppen's *This in Which* deserves mention in passing, alongside Rexroth's "The Dragon and the Unicorn." Oppen's "The Zulu Girl" appears to be a straightforward description of an African woman which, like the Rexroth piece, makes no savage comparisons to masks, idols, or beasts:

Her breasts
Naked, the soft
Small hollow in the flesh
Near the arm pit, the tendons
Presenting the gentle breasts
So boldly, tipped

With her intimate
Nerves

That touched, would touch her
Deeply—she stands
In the wild grasses.

(130)

It is a description as lovely as anything in Williams, and lacking that poet's occasional air of prurience. Oppen's heartfelt support for the great civil-rights movements of his time is evident in his powerful elegy for Mickey Schwerner, one of three civil-rights workers slain in Mississippi and the cousin of the poet Armand Schwerner (236–41). It remains a curiosity that the only identifiably black person described in Oppen's poetry is not an American but his anonymous African woman. Along with Alice Walker, one wonders too when Rexroth and Oppen are going to lift their eyes from these African breasts and give their readers the women whose presence they so boldly announce. Again, it is not that we would have poets give up writing of breasts, but their presence as images so prevalent against the absence of whole black people is indicative of a way of thinking of blackness by white people which denies the wholeness of black life.

Rexroth and Oppen were anomalies among the younger writers of modernism's second wave. The movement begun by Pound, Eliot, Stein, Stevens, and Williams was already being assimilated into academia and succeeded by American poets who viewed literary tradition in the Eliotic sense, expressed by "Tradition and the Individual Talent" and *After Strange Gods.* Despite the power of objectivist writing, the canon forming power over modernism was passing to the New Critics and to the poets influenced by the Fugitive group of Southern Agrarians, a group which had little room for the black woman herself and little regard for blackness in any of its human forms. Far more typical than Rexroth's are these lines from Laura Riding's "O Vocables of Love," which, like those of Eliot and Crane, turn to frozen metaphors from America's vocabulary of racial imagery to trope death and eternity. They could as easily have appeared in "The Dry Salvages," or in *The Bridge:*

. . . wing on wing folds in
The negro centuries of sleep
And the thick lips compress
Compendiums of silence—

(*Poems* 119)

The only other appearance of a black subject in *The Poems of Laura Riding* repeats this same deathly trope. In "The Life of the Dead," the morbid catalogue of equipment for "Mortjoy's Theater" includes "Ebony sticks, theater glasses, the massive negro's trumpet" (373), trumpeting Riding's own associations of black humanity with fatality. Allen Tate, who befriended Riding and mediated her entrance into the Fugitive group, wrote to Donald Davidson in the fall of 1925 to say: "There are two poets I'm betting on—Laura [Riding] and Hart Crane; if I'm wrong about them, I'm wrong about everything" (*Literary Correspondence* 146). While these lines may not represent the qualities that led Tate to bet so heavily, they do help explain one of the reasons Riding's works and Crane's were so resonant for Tate in ways that the poetry of black writers seldom was; all three white poets spoke a common language, a language that had expelled blackness.

Chapter 4

Two

Agrarians

We live in a society where the symbolism of the poetry I read, the Bible I read, everything is charged with the white man's values—God's white robes, the white light of hope—all these things are an affront to me. I find myself schooling myself to resist all this symbolism and invert it for myself.

—Avon Williams, quoted in Robert Penn Warren, *Who Speaks for the Negro*

If I have to this point given little specific attention to white poets from that region of the United States most closely identified with the history of slavery, it has been in part because high modernism did not belong to any particular region but primarily because it has been my thesis that the image structures of racism were distributed fairly evenly throughout the language of the nation, forming a sort of lingua franca of racial understanding. Thus the northerner, Cummings, and the former Baltimorean, Stein, could speak remarkably similar lines out of their divergent experiences. But the modernist era cannot be left behind without a consideration of major southern poets, because it was the group once known as Southern Agrarians who consolidated and disseminated the brand of modernism represented by Eliot and Crane most effectively. As exemplary of this grouping of poet-critics, Allen Tate and Robert Penn Warren will serve, both because they have been the most active and influential of the Southern Agrarians and because the development of their thoughts about black people and history over the period of their lengthy careers occurs over a divide that has its nascence shortly after the beginning of their cooperative efforts as Fugitive poets and thinkers. Some of their first works hint at a split in the solid southern front expressed by the anthology of essays titled *I'll Take My Stand*. That nascent split becomes visible as early as in the writing of the two biographies which the two poets undertook in their youth.

Allen Tate received the commission to recreate the life of Stonewall Jackson, of whom Tate could say as early as May of 1927: "I am already convinced that had Jackson been in chief command from the beginning we should now be a separate nation, and much better off than we are now; and that if Jackson hadn't been killed in 1865 the battle at Gettysburg would have been won. I think these things because I want to; yet I have a surprising weight of expert opinion, political and military, to support my prejudice" (Tate and Davidson, *Correspondence* 199–200). Tate's statement, made in a letter to Donald Davidson, is notable not so much for its special view of history as for the fashion in which it reveals the willfulness with which Tate approaches history and his marshaling of support for what he admits is a prejudice. Robert Penn Warren was engaged in a biographical enterprise of his own at the same time, eventually producing the volume *John Brown: The Making of a Martyr.* While Tate was contemplating an alternative outcome for the Civil War, Warren was contemplating the forces that led to abolitionist fervor, examining the development of a man who had early on asked himself to reflect upon "the wretched, hopeless condition of fatherless and motherless slave children," and from that reflection determined himself upon a course of "eternal war with slavery" (*John Brown* 19). Warren's endeavor was one which would inevitably lead him to reexamine many of the social positions which he had begun by sharing with Tate. Though Tate's opinions on matters of race and society show little substantive change over the course of his career, Warren's work is often marked by a considerable ambiguity which arises from his constant struggle with the attitudes he had adopted in youth. Warren may have begun as an apologist for the South's special mode of social organization, and he may end having moved no farther than to a stage of radical uncertainty, but he can be seen to have interrogated his own thought formations in a manner that was not so characteristic for his colleague Tate. Where Allen Tate would seek expert opinion to support his prejudice, Warren's project is typified by his response when Dr. Walker of the Southern Christian Leadership Conference asked him why he had set out upon the investigations that make up his book *Who Speaks for the Negro?* Warren told him: "I wanted to find out about things, including my own feelings" (*Who Speaks* 232).

In Allen Tate's contribution to the *Partisan Review*'s Pound symposium, he says: "I consider any special attitude toward Jews, in so far as they may be identified as individuals or a group, a historical calamity; and it is not less calamitous when the attitude is their own. I consider antisemitism to be both cowardly and dishonorable" (512–22). So dishonorable does he find it that he pronounces himself prepared to fight a duel with anyone who might accuse him of it. But this has the self-serving ring of Eliot's assurances to his public that, being a Christian, he could not be an anti-Semite. There is a most tendentious sense to Tate's fourth clause that the victim's own attitude has contributed to the calamitous history he has suffered, and this solecistic mode of reasoning typifies Tate's approach to the nonwhite, about which he had his own special attitude.

That special attitude is already apparent in Tate's earliest writings, and it is the attitude which Robert Davis, in his contribution to the Pound symposium, identified cogently in his chiding of "Southern Regionalists." Tate's biography of Stonewall Jackson, published in 1928, advances an irrational defense of the "positive good" argument for the maintenance of slavery, a defense remarkably similar to Eliot's comments in *After Strange Gods,* and one based on Tate's nostalgia for an agrarian society of the type he would like to see reestablished: "The institution of slavery was a positive good only in the sense that Calhoun had argued that it was: it had become a necessary element in a stable society. He had argued justly that only in a society of fixed classes can men be free. Only men who are socially as well as economically secure can preserve the historical sense of obligation. This historical sense of obligation implied a certain freedom to do right" (*Jackson* 39–40). This freedom to do right was obtained, of course, at the expense of a class of kidnapped Africans fixed into bondage by a massive system of murder, rape, and degradation, the peculiar institution that was followed by the institution of "Jim Crow" laws following Reconstruction. Having spoken sympathetically of the "positive good" of the peculiar institution, Tate later, in *I'll Take My Stand,* exhibits a similar attitude toward the special system that came after. In the progress of his "Remarks on the Southern Religion," this poet who thought the South would be better off as a separate nation complains that "the South shows signs of defeat, and this is due to its lack of a religion which would make her special secular system the inevitable and permanently valuable one" (168). Tate is after the same homogeneity of race and religion which Eliot's conception of culture and tradition demands, and the secular system he wants this religion to invest with permanent value is one which includes segregation.

Allen Tate's prose fictions are historical fictions, and the characters who animate their pages also animate the prejudices of their periods. The narrator of "The Migration," whose span of life overlaps that of his fellow Virginian, Thomas Jefferson, recalls his childhood belief that when a "Guinea Nigger" passes by carrying a child, "he was taking the child to some hidden place to devour it. A Guinea Nigger liked nothing better to eat than babies" (*Fathers* 328). His childhood belief in the inherent savagery of the nonwhite informs his later recollection that: "No one paid much attention to the morality of Negroes in those days, though my mother, and I think most Methodists, believed that they had souls which must be saved. I have never been able to make up my mind about this. It is true that in the last fifty years the Negro race has improved, and religion has done them much good" (*Fathers* 330). Lacy Buchan, the narrator of Tate's only novel, *The Fathers,* belongs to a later era, and the events he speaks of occur during the antebellum and Civil War periods. When he tells the story, he is a retired doctor, age sixty-five, living in Georgetown, looking back at the events of his youth. The children Lacy Buchan grew up among may no longer have believed that blacks literally were cannibals, but the adult racial beliefs expressed by Lacy and the other characters in the novel show that little had changed since the time of "The Migration." "The perpetual fear of women," according to this male narrator, was still "Negro Men" (245). And racial amalgamation, common practice among slave owners, was yet held to yield disastrous progeny, as is evident in Lacy's summary of the character of "Yellow Jim": "Except for Coriolanus I think he was the best Negro I ever saw; he was the most refined Negro, a gentleman in every instinct. But he was a Negro, and I am not sure that he would have been as good as he was if his white blood, which everybody knew about, had not been good. But since there is a difference of opinion on this question, I had better say that white blood may have ruined poor Yellow Jim in the end. He knew what his blood was and he had many of the feelings of a white man that he could never express" (205). In the fictions of real life this was the same congeries of attitudes which led social scientists of the early twentieth century to attribute the black intelligence they had measured to the presence of white blood. In the fiction of *The Fathers* Yellow Jim lives out the expectations of these clashing beliefs by fulfilling the perpetual fear of women, by attacking a white woman, albeit at the instigation of one of the other white female characters of the book.

The discourse of *The Fathers* is confined within the system of racial belief that Lacy Buchan embodies; there are no serious dissenting voices raised within the fiction. There are, though, scenes in which Tate contrives to disconcert the self-assured narrator, as on the occasion when Lacy Buchan confronts a free black landowner. Lacy, seeing no house on the property the man has been plowing, inquires as to whose land it is: " 'It ain't nobody's.' He spat, and I thought there was a trace of insolence in his gesture. He glared at me. 'It ain't nobody's. It's mine, that's whose. I's free. I's free born.' He waved his pipe in the air, and gave me a sly look" (188). And later in the novel, as the white characters impel Yellow Jim along his path to destruction, Lacy comes to an ironic realization for one who is a defender of slavery, that all of the white characters have "used" Yellow Jim. Further, he finds himself asking, "What had we done to Yellow Jim more than we were, minute by minute, doing to ourselves?" (245). It is a question whose rhetorical nature is underscored when Jim is shot dead.

Some of the articles of the southern faith expounded by Tate's narrators in his prose fictions are also spoken by the voices of his verse, along with the epithets which white speech uses as a sort of shorthand. For example, in

"Message from Abroad" a man's shadow is described as "a long nigger / gliding at his feet" (*Poems* 11), an image which replicates Crane's, Eliot's, and Riding's associations between black people and mortality and looks forward to later works by Randall Jarrell and Michael Blumenthal. An idiot in Tate's poem of the same name is placed "in the long sunset where impatient sound / Strips niggers to a multiple of backs" (*Poems* 157). "More Sonnets at Christmas" asks that you:

> . . . pray most fixedly
> For the cold martial progress of your star,
> With thoughts of commerce and society,
> Well-milked Chinese, Negroes who cannot sing,
> The Huns gelded and feeding in a ring.
>
> (*Poems* 53)

This poem, whose date, 1942, might help to explain the presence of its final image, is strikingly like the moment in the *Pisan Cantos* which recalls Pound's bemusement at finding a man of color with positively no musical talent. Both poems require a prior agreement on the part of the reader that black people may be said to be inherently superior singers. To pray for "Negroes who cannot sing," even if your intention is to indicate your own impatience with the stereotype, is to declare yourself presently bound by it and to assume that you are surrounded by Negroes who can sing.

Tate's poems also provide moments which, like Lacy Buchan's confrontation with the freedman, should trouble the self-assurance of white discourse, but these moments are usually problematized in ways that deflect that thrust. "Sonnets at Christmas" encompasses the following confession: "When I was ten I told a stinking lie / That got a black boy whipped" (*Poems* 51), a confession which demonstrates that white privilege extends to relations among children. The lie haunts the adult, and the speaker finds himself now "punished by crimes of which [he] would be quit." A like moment of conscience occurs in part 4 of "Sonnets of the Blood," in which Tate gives us a Virginian

> Who took himself to be brute nature's law,
>
> . . . .
>
> Who meditated calmly what he saw
> Until he freed his Negroes, lest he be
> Too strict with nature and than them less free.
>
> (*Poems* 168)

The same poem asks earlier, "Why do you make a fuss / For privilege when there's no law of form?" But both the adult confession of childish abuse and the Virginian's act of manumission presume the existence of white privilege. The argument in these poems is against the abuse of the privilege, not against its power. And there is a strange logical dissonance in Tate's thought on such matters. Having argued that the South's special secular system is necessary to the development of the social and economic security which makes possible a "historical sense of obligation," which is the foundation of the "freedom to do right," Tate then shows the Virginian doing right by freeing his slaves, who have formed the material basis for his economic and social security. Tate shows no awareness of this inconsistency.

"The Swimmers" (*Poems* 175–79), an unabashedly autobiographical poem, presents the reader with more of these inconsistencies and seems to be a furthering of the confessional spirit of "Sonnets at Christmas." Tate is portrayed for us in "The Swimmers" in the innocence of preadolescence, in a stage of life at which he has little knowledge of the past of slavery or the present of racism and segregation. He indicates his adult discomfort with that earlier stage of innocence when, while naming his swimming companions, the nickname "Nigger" is applied to his friend, Layne. The epithet is set in quotation marks in the text. This use of the citation form may be taken to indicate that the name was applied in childhood innocence, while simultaneously demonstrating Tate's awareness that this act of naming might be read as demonstrating complicity in the context of the racist scene that follows. Tate's initiation into knowledge of the South's special secular system is accomplished through his witnessing of the ritual act of lynching carried out by the males of his community, the ultimate scapegoating of the radically other. This initiation brings Tate into an awareness of the secret that is shared openly by his society, and the poem's final stanza shows him recognizing the fact that he too is now a secret sharer in the knowledge guarded by this communal silence:

> . . . Alone in the public clearing
> This private thing was owned by all the town,
> Though never claimed by us within my hearing.

In the public clearing of the poem, the poet finally breaks the silence within which the enforcers of white privilege guard their operations. But the last three words give evidence that as a knowing adult the poet has, until this instant of our reading, maintained the silence. His speaking at last of the private thing owned communally appears to be a confession of the type seen in "Sonnets at Christmas," but the terms of the confession contrive to lessen the speaker's own level of responsibility. There is a sense throughout *The*

Fathers that the characters are playing out the fate of postlapsarian man, that their sufferings are required to expiate the sins of the fathers, and that same sense pervades "The Swimmers." Warren, writing in *The Legacy of the Civil War,* notes that this attitude is symptomatic of the post–Civil War South. "The race problem," according to this point of view, "is the doom defined by history. . . . Since the situation is given by history, the Southerner therefore is guiltless; is in fact an innocent victim of a cosmic conspiracy" (Warren, *Legacy* 55–56). The limited guilt to which Tate admits in his poem is a sort of original sin that has been thrust upon him without his having done anything more damning than having been a witness. But even before he assumes the weight of the communal secret of the lynching, he has assumed the language that makes the lynching possible. As harmless seeming an act as using the name "Nigger" as a nickname for a friend immures a speaker in a system of repressing language; it is an act which cannot be sanitized later, and responsibility cannot be easily fenced off by the citation form. Nowhere in his work does Tate show a sensitivity to the possibility that his own special attitude toward the nonwhite might redound calamitously.

Allen Tate's writings afford his readers an opportunity to gauge the extent to which such special attitudes have exercised their influence over the entry of the poetry of the nonwhite into American letters, for Tate has had occasion to write critically of black poets. Like Thomas Jefferson before him, Tate sometimes gives the impression that blackness lies outside the realm of poetry and that black poets may enter into the canon only by being poetically nonblack, whatever that may finally mean to the white critic. In reviewing *An Anthology of Negro Poetry,* published in 1924, Tate applauds the volume as "the first significant attempt on the part of white critics to do justice to Negro literature in America" (*Poetry Reviews* 21). But when it becomes clear what Tate means by "doing justice" to black letters, it also becomes clear that he is allowing his special attitudes about the nonwhite to operate as critical criteria. He praises the anthology's editors for having sharply curtailed the number of poets in this historical record: "It is perhaps just as well that the entirety of poetry in this field of American literature isn't generally available, for, as the editors of this book say, it is on the whole pretty worthless" (21). It would appear that doing justice to Negro verse includes the adopting of a belief that blacks write badly in general, without providing evidence or explanations to support the assumption that they should write any more badly than any other portion of the population at large. If Tate feels that most poetry written, not just most Negro poetry, is worthless, he does not say so. In summarizing and approving the conclusions offered in the editors' introduction, Tate reports that "the complete assimilation of American culture will equip the Negro with the 'refinement' and 'taste' requisite to writing in a tradition utterly alien to his temperament" (22), the same tack Tate will take many years later when introducing the poetry of Melvin B. Tolson. Again, Tate offers no explanation of why the tradition should be alien to an entire race of people whose presence in this nation extends as far back in time as that of white people. Nor does Tate recognize that he has confused a culture's rendering itself alien to the outsider with the outsider's ability to comprehend that culture. Of special interest is Tate's claim to knowledge of Negro temperament, a claim which he repeats momentarily: "It is therefore not difficult to see why the editors of this book place Dunbar and Braithwaite (who is only Negro by accident of blood and has as little of the Negro temperament as Longfellow) above Claude McKay. Repeated reference is made to the 'finish' of those writers" (22). Tate states that Braithwaite is Negro only by accident of blood, as if there were some other way to become a Negro and despite the knowledge that the presence of any black blood at all has historically been sufficient to meet America's definition of the nonwhite, no matter how white an individual might appear. The statement further denies whatever Braithwaite, the voluntary Negro, may have volunteered for when he determined that he would not "pass." Tate knows what the Negro temperament is and pronounces it alien to Braithwaite (although his linking of Braithwaite to Longfellow probably would have done little to raise Braithwaite in the estimation of Pound or Frost). It is also significant that Tate is establishing a hierarchy of refinement, with blackness, represented by McKay, at one end and "finish" at the other. Tate concludes his review with remarks about Jean Toomer, whom he had come to know personally through Hart Crane and who was not represented in the anthology under review. Tate attributes Toomer's great artistic success, expressed best in *Cane,* to the fact that Toomer "is interested in the interior of Negro life, not in the pressure of American culture on the Negro" (22). One might expect such a remark from any of the New Critics who argued against what they viewed as sociological literature, but there is a political program in this criticism as well, one which Tate will still be found pursuing years later. For Tate appears to believe, judged on the basis of this conclusion, that the successful black artist will present characters stripped of their most immediate concerns. This same man who wrote that "the essences [of the South] are not magnolias, niggers and cotton fields" (Tate and Davidson 192) could praise a book about the South by an Afro-American author which prominently features black characters and cotton fields only by considering the work an abstract artifact divorced from the pressures of American culture that account for much of its power. Just as "The Swimmers" presents a lynching apart from the history of racism, closer in kind to a sanitized crucifixion scene hung in a niche than to the realities of racial oppression, so he wants black art to arrive cleansed of its history of white oppressions.

Braithwaite, whom I have not yet permitted to speak for himself, seems to have taken most of the remarks made about him by whites with a certain equanimity. Some thirty years after this review of Tate's, he writes to Melvin Tolson on the occasion of the preface Tolson had solicited from Tate for his *Libretto for the Republic of Liberia:* "This is a different Tate than I knew twenty-five years or thirty years ago who did not accept the Negro artist on the higher level of excellence. It is, apart from anything else, a great achievement to have converted this critical authority to the single standard by which all artists irrespective of race or color should be judged" (qtd. in Farnsworth 306). In point of fact though, Tate's attitudes had changed little in the intervening years, and his acceptance of Tolson's late work was based upon criteria similar to those upon which he based his championing of Toomer, who had to all intents and purposes stopped publishing in the interim. Braithwaite was probably simply pleased that Tate had undertaken a commendatory preface for Tolson at all. The short essay Tate provided six months after agreeing to the task has been more accurately characterized by Tolson's biographer, Robert M. Farnsworth: "Tate's attempt to subsume the 'Negro' characteristics of the poet and the poem under a high compliment to their art represents the blandly patronizing tone of white critics that many black writers and critics during the fifties resented and rebelled against with increasing assertiveness" (142).

There are numerous ironies and missed opportunities reported in the account Farnsworth has put together of the relationship between Tolson and Tate. Tolson had submitted work to Tate when the white poet was editor of the *Sewanee Review.* Tate had returned the manuscript with a note that he would like another look at the work later, but he left the *Review* not long after that. Many years earlier, the two poets as young students had attended college in the same city. In later life, Farnsworth reports, "Tolson noted with whimsical regret that he attended Fisk University while the Fugitives were arguing out their poetic and cultural credo at Vanderbilt only a short distance away. If he could have participated in these discussions, he often implied, his development as a modernist poet might well have begun years earlier. It is at least as interesting to speculate on what difference it would have made to the program of the Fugitives if Tolson had been a participant. Because of the color line it did not happen" (24). There were, of course, no black writers among the

Fugitives, not just because they would not have been allowed at Vanderbilt, but also because the Fugitives, in arguing out their cultural credo, began to produce a strengthened discourse in defense of the South's secular system, a discourse which eventually solidified in the volume *I'll Take My Stand* and in Tate's call for a religious underpinning for the inevitability of segregation.

Still, Tolson asked Tate in the winter of 1949 to undertake a preface for the *Libretto,* modestly advancing his justifiable claim to have "initiated the modernist movement among Negro poets" (qtd. in Farnsworth 140), and Tate at length produced the essay we now have. In that essay, Tate finds the *Libretto's* climax to be a rhetorical success while a poetic failure but concludes all the same that the *Libretto* is a work of major significance. His reasons for its significance reveal once more the operations of his special critical attitude with regard to black writing. Having noted the sheer intelligence evidenced in the poem, Tate goes on to claim Tolson as the first Negro poet to have fully assimilated the poetic language of his time, a reflection of Tolson's own claim for his work. Further, though, Tate claims that Tolson's success is also attributable to his having been the first Negro poet to have assimilated fully "the language of the Anglo-American tradition" (Preface 11), an assertion which suddenly casts the claim in a way which Tolson had decidedly not intended. This further claim ignores the history of other black poets who had previously assimilated Anglo-American modes, going back as far as Phillis Wheatley, and makes a value claim for that tradition over others, reasserting the privileged position of white discourse and fulfilling the prophecy Tate had made in the twenties about Negro poets' assimilating American culture. Tolson is not to be judged only for his contemporaneity but for the extent to which he is able to assume the Anglo-American idiom convincingly, for his willingness to steal back into the traditional order from which his people have been banned. Tate, to give him credit where it is due, does not believe that black poets have been incapable of assuming this idiom, just that they have resisted it. But it remains clear that one of his critical criteria is the adept assumption of white tradition. Karl Shapiro took note of this phenomenon in an article he wrote for the *Wilson Library Bulletin* some years later:

Mr. Tate is a confederate of the old school who has no use for Negroes but who will salute an exception to the race. He sees Tolson as an exception. . . . Mr. Tate invites Mr. Tolson to join his country club. . . . But in trying to assert that Tolson has been assimilated by the Anglo-American tradition, he puts Tolson in quarantine and destroys the value of the poem—possibly this critic's conscious intention.

> The refusal to see that Tolson's significance lies in his language, Negro, and that only that language can express the poetic sensibility of the Negro at the door of freedom, is a final desperate maneuver to contain the Negro within the traditional culture. And for that it is too late. The tradition is already ante bellum. (Qtd. in Farnsworth 171–72)

There is much that is problematic about this response from a poet who took a position opposed to Tate's in the *Partisan Review*'s Pound symposium, as he opposed Tate on so many matters, particularly in his imputation of intention on Tate's behalf and his odd notions about what it means to "speak Negro." Most interestingly, Shapiro has reversed the terms of Tate's proposition that Tolson had assimilated Anglo-American tradition and claims that Tate claims Tolson has been assimilated. This move's interest lies in the fact that while it is incorrect, it anticipates the effect of Tate's preface. Tate's critical maneuver has the effect of bringing about that assimilation, of making the radical other over into something that resembles oneself.

Tate goes on to argue in his preface that the sole distinguishing feature of "Negro poetry" is its subject matter, which, he believes, is generally the plight of the segregated black consciousness, the story of the pressures of American culture upon the Negro. He further warns that attempts to exploit uniquely black folk language or to develop a black linguistic aesthetic may produce good poems (he mentions the works of Langston Hughes and Gwendolyn Brooks) but will not be very different from what white poets "can" write. This is indeed a conundrum, for Tate is putting forward the critical theory that a black poet who masters the Afro-American traditions and idioms will not be distinguishably black because white poets can accomplish the same thing as well; the only recourse then is in learning to sound like those same white poets (who sometimes write "black") and speak in the Anglo-American idiom. If this task is not accomplished, according to Tate's analysis, the black poet will be limited "to a provincial mediocrity in which one's feelings about one's difficulties become more important than the poetry itself" (Preface 11). Tate has gotten his cart in front of somebody else's horse here, and he leads himself to the conclusion that the aggressive spirit of modern black writers will offer no greater poetic possibilities than the "resigned pathos" of Paul Laurence Dunbar, a misjudgment whose enormity can be indicated simply by listing names such as Robert Hayden, Owen Dodson, Henry Dumas, Amiri Baraka, Jay Wright, Audre Lorde, Michael Harper, and Al Young.

Tate comes to the same sort of conclusion about Tolson that he had come to with regard to Toomer. Tolson succeeds, he says, because "by becoming more intensely Negro he seems . . . to dismiss the entire problem, so far as poetry is concerned, by putting it in its properly subordinate place" (Preface 12). Again, Tate is claiming to recognize "the interior of Negro life" separated from the forces that form it. Tolson did not ignore the pressures of American culture on black life, and those pressures are clearly visible both in the *Libretto* and in the later *Harlem Gallery*. The black poet was not as willing to subsume "the entire problem" as Tate would have him be, and he foregrounds that problem in the poem "Chi," speaking of:

> The white and not-white dichotomy,
> the Afro-American dilemma in the arts—
> the dialectic of
> to be or not to be
> a Negro
> (Tolson 146)

Surely there is nothing any less universal in the poet's contemplation of these cultural pressures, embodied as Tate wants "in a rich and complex language, and realized in terms of the poetic imagination" (Preface 12), than in Tate's own contemplation amidst the symbolism of white Christianity of some of these same pressures at the close of "The Swimmers." And it should be evident that another of those cultural pressures applied to blacks in America has been the force of this kind of white criticism.

At the time he was commissioned to produce an essay on race relations in the South for the Agrarians' manifesto, *I'll Take My Stand,* Robert Penn Warren's political beliefs differed little from those of Allen Tate's, and Warren's essay calls for no more than modest amelioration of the black man's position within a segregated society. He had not yet begun to ask himself the question later used in the title *Who Speaks for the Negro?* He had rather decided on the Negro's behalf that his spokesman was to be Booker T. Washington, and Warren's plea to "let the negro sit beneath his own vine and fig tree" ("Briar Patch" 264) is much like the metaphors constructed by Washington in his Atlanta speech to describe the separate economic and social development he envisioned for Afro-America. It is certainly no surprise that a Southern Agrarian should argue for an agrarian way of life as the best route for black economic growth, but Warren, in advancing that belief, makes the same kind of claim to a special knowledge of the temperament of the nonwhite as that which we encounter in Tate: "In the past the Southern negro has always been a creature of the small town and farm. That is where he still chiefly belongs, by temperament and capacity; there he has less the character of a 'problem' and more the status of a human being who is likely to find in agricultural and domestic pursuits the happiness that his good nature and easy ways incline him to as an ordinary function of his being" ("Briar Patch" 260–61). The nonwhite is conceived of as having inherently easy ways, and this conception is linked to Warren's belief that blacks, as a class, are marked by what he terms a "genial irresponsibility" ("Briar Patch" 264), which it is his hope the development of a rooted, productive community might displace. Warren seems to know, though, that such a way of speaking forms the basis for continued separation of the races, and that such separation invariably protracts inequality. But he finds himself in a position somewhat like that of the antebellum intellectual he describes in *The Legacy of the Civil War,* when "the only function left open to intellect in the South was apologetics for the closed society, not criticism of it; and in these apologetics there was little space for the breath of life, no recognition of the need for fluidity, growth, and change which life is" (39).

It was a position which Warren was not capable of occupying for very long, one which his intellect soon forced him to abandon. In a deeply felt passage of self-criticism at the beginning of *Who Speaks for the Negro?* Warren recalls that he never read the essay defending segregation after its publication because it made him uncomfortable (10–11). His recollection of his motivation at the time he wrote it is that he wanted to fashion a defense of a humane segregation, but he acknowledges that the self-consciousness of the essay "indicated an awareness that in the real world . . . there existed a segregation that was not humane" (*Who Speaks* 11). A defense of segregation requires a system of belief in the difference of the other and entails necessarily a defense of the force required to sustain segregation. Looking back thirty-five years after *I'll Take My Stand,* Warren admits that he "uncomfortably suspected . . . that no segregation was, in the end, humane. But it never crossed [his] mind that anybody could do anything about it" (*Who Speaks* 12), a statement which offers further confirmation of the existence within white discourse of an agreement that the lesser position of the black person is inevitable and unalterable. This sort of lingering discomfort is to be found in all Warren's later writings on race; it is the discomfort attendant upon one who recognizes the serious error of a past position that is still public. When Dr. Walker of the Southern Christian Leadership Conference tells Warren that it is courageous of him to use *Who Speaks for the Negro?* as a means of inquiry into his own feelings, Warren at first experiences a sense of rage: *"At the condescension—moral condescension. The Negro movement is fueled by a sense of moral superiority. No wonder that some splashes over on the white bystander as condescension. The only effective payment for all the other kinds of condescension visited on black men over the years"* (*Who Speaks* 232, emphasis in the original).

Warren's poetry reflects this transition from a clearly defined position of racism, even if a racism the author hoped was benign, to an uncomfortable moral questioning of the white poet's part in the racial discourse. It is the fact that Warren seems at all points in his poetry to be in the middle of this transition that accounts for much of the difficulty a reader has in assessing the manner in which the nonwhite appears in his verse. Both early and late, his poetry includes many of the standard racial stereotypes, but those stereotypes themselves often appear to be undergoing some form of poetic interrogation even as they are presented. There is a considerable degree of self-consciousness in Warren's inscription of these standard images; the poems sometimes display an awareness that they are repeating racist representations. We have available a number of statements from Warren which indicate his own awareness of the fluidity of the racial image. There are scenes in both *Who Speaks for the Negro?* (52) and *Segregation* in which the author observes as a stereotype literally dissolves before his eyes. In *Segregation* he reports the disappointment among the white personnel of a southern television station when a black man who has been invited in for an interview precisely because he is a stereotypical Uncle Tom suddenly steps out of character: "Things aren't promising too well. Uncle Tom is doing a disappearing act, Old Black Joe is evaporating, the handkerchief head, most inconveniently, isn't there" (39). And we can locate in Warren's comments on Ralph Ellison and William Faulkner an explanation of what Warren himself may think he is after in his use of ready-made racial images: "we may remark that Ellison's great admiration for Faulkner stems, in part, from the impulse that made Faulkner more willing perhaps than any other artist to start with the stereotype of the Negro, accept it as true, and then seek out the human truth which it hides" (*Who Speaks* 333–34).

In autobiographical musings on his experiences with his father, Robert Penn Warren has said that "if one of the children in our house had used the word *nigger,* the roof would have fallen" (*Who Speaks* 10–11), but the adult Warren shows little hesitation in his use of the name in his poetry, nor do his repetitions of many of the images used by Tate and others always appear to seek the human truth that such images ordinarily hide. "Ballad between the Boxcars" contains a disturbing simile in the speaker's description of a man who "would slide in slick, like a knife in a nigger" (*Selected Poems* 213). In "Tale of Time," the poem's persona describes nightfall over a Southern ghetto:

> that light
> Lay gold on the roofs of Squiggtown, and the
>   niggers
> Were under the roofs, and
> The room smelled of ur̓ne
>   (*Selected Poems* 145)

Like poems by Eliot, Crane, Riding, and others, Warren's poems sometimes associate blackness with time and mortality, as in part 4 of "Tale of Time":

> Whom we now sought was old. Was
> Sick. Was dying. Was
> Black. Was.
> *Was:*
>   (*Selected Poems* 144)

Again following Tate's example, and looking forward to a poem by Michael Blumenthal, Warren will take these associations of blackness and mortality and find their vehicle in shadow, as in part 3 of "Penological Study: Southern Exposure," with its description of the light cast by a lamp "on the table already lighted, and shadows / Bigger than people and blacker than niggers . . ." (*Selected Poems* 121). Warren's tendency to use racist epithets seems most marked when he is in the ballad mode, as in "Pondy Woods," which tells the story of the hunted Big Jim Todd, who "was a slick black buck" (*Selected Poems* 322). Yet, if we remember the ballad form's roots in folk expression, we may begin to look here for Warren's effort to discover the human truth behind the veil of racist speech. As the voice of a ballad is presumed to be the voice of the folk, a southern ballad spoken by a white person might be expected to represent blackness in just this way, and we might begin to look to the poem for signals that its author is trying to get to the reality behind that voice's representations. What might it mean, for instance, that much of the plainly racist speech directed at Big Jim Todd as he hides from his pursuers is spoken to him in the ballad by a buzzard? Who might the buzzard speak for when he admonishes Todd, saying "Nigger, your breed ain't metaphysical" (*Selected Poems* 324)? This poem predates the English translations of the works of Derrida by nearly three decades, but it may prove useful to recall Derrida's identification of metaphysics as white mythology. The buzzard may then be seen as the carrier of the ostracizing power of white discourse, the trope which declares the otherness of the black and the disjunction between black and white time:

> . . . we maintain our ancient rite,
> Eat the gods by day and prophesy by night.
> We swing against the sky and wait
> You seize the hour, more passionate
> Than strong, and strive with time to die—
> With time, the beaked tribe's astute ally.
> *(Selected Poems* 323)

The buzzard pronounces white belief; that blacks are more passionate and live for the moment; they are marked by Warren's "genial irresponsibility." But the use of the buzzard as spokesman for this mythology sets up a disturbance within the discourse, for it is a spokesman with whom few readers will readily identify.

This marks a turning in Warren's representation of the nonwhite which, if never completed, is still significant. In "Tale of Time," after identifying blackness with pastness, Warren inscribes a similar turn away from the noth-ingness which Stein and others ascribed to the condition of the nonwhite:

> That blackness which she is, is
> Not deficiency like cave-blackness, but is
> Substance
> *(Selected Poems* 146)

In "Forever O'Clock," Warren can include among those things "that are not important but simply are . . . / A little two-year-old Negro girl baby" *(Se-lected Poems* 43), and in "Internal Injuries," he can offer, like a dictionary definition, an explication of *"Nigger"* (emphasis in the original) which doesn't so much seek out the human truth hidden by the term as it confirms, with its portrayal of an old black woman who steals from her employers *(Se-lected Poems* 127–28), discourse agreements regarding the morality of blacks. But he can also write a poem late in life which metaphorically exam-ines the manner in which these very stereotypes impede the progress of human happiness. The persona who speaks to us out of the poem "Old Nigger on One-Mule Cart Encountered Late at Night When Driving Home from Party in the Back Country," has had, on his way home from a night of dancing, a nearly fatal confrontation with what might best be considered as an image from his own vocabulary:

> There it is: death trap
> On the fool-nigger, ass-hole wrong side of
> The road, naturally: . . .
> . . . .
> Man-eyes, not blazing, white bulging
> In black face, in black night, and man-mouth
> Wide open, the shape of an O, for the scream
> That does not come. . . .
>
> (*Selected Poems* 14–15)

This is the consequence of the radical other's leaving its appointed position; near collision which leaves the white speaker in a ditch. Alone at night on a stretch of Louisiana roadway, the creation of white discourse, the "nigger," comes head on out of the darkness of white imagining into the path of the white man. It is not just the presence of the man on the "fool-nigger" wrong side of the road which is nearly fatal but also the speed at which the white man hurtles through the darkness toward his destiny. The poem carries the suggestion that no matter what destiny the white man may have charted for himself, he will sooner or later run across this hauler of his own junk rumbling in the wrong direction out of the darkness. The experience of this accident marks the white man as indelibly as the stain of original sin. He senses that this term returning out of his past is his future. He interrogates his image of the "old nigger," asking rhetorically:

> Brother, Rebuker, my Philosopher past all
> Casuistry, will you be with me when
> I arrive and leave my own cart of junk
> Unfended from the storm of starlight and
> The howl, like wind, of the world's monstrous blessedness,
> To enter, by a bare field, a shack unlit?
>
> (*Selected Poems* 17)

Nowhere in his writing does Warren consider the "doom defined by history" more thoroughly than in the first version of his long dramatic poem for voices, *Brother to Dragons,* a poem that takes as its occasion the tragedy acted out by Thomas Jefferson's nephews, Lilburn and Isham Lewis. Racism is not the subject matter of *Brother to Dragons.* It is rather symptomatic of the

evil that is in men and that has entered into American history to await expia-
tion by later generations. Warren depicts avarice, jealousy, and hatred as
having come into time as original sin, fathered by the founders of the tribe,
and as having stained the heritage of democracy. He sees this even in those
shrines we have established for the worship of the democratic ideal:

> to build Monticello,
> That domed dream of our liberties floating
> High on its mountain, like a cloud, demanded
> A certain amount of black sweat.
>
> (*Brother* 109)

The eventual self-destruction of the Lewis family appears not only as the
immediate result of the misguided passions of Lilburn Lewis, but equally and
inevitably as the working out of the nation's unpaid debt.

In the playing out of this tragedy, Warren shows himself sharply aware of
the extent to which the Founding Fathers' discourse was a system of language
devised and determined to make easier the abuse of other human beings. His
verses ably demonstrate the manner in which the builders of America, while
telling the world of their rational, egalitarian ideals, also told themsleves
things which made it possible to view slavery with equanimity, things which
led to that deafening of the ears and hardening of the heart to black suffering
which Crèvecoeur took note of. In recalling the construction of the Lewises'
carriage road, Warren's voice slips into an ironic resounding of that ancient
discourse:

> The black hands had grabbled and the black sweat dropped.
> But niggers don't mind heat. At least not much.
> And sure, somebody's got to build the road.
>
> (31)

These lines repeat claims heard as long ago as in Las Casas's proposals to shift
labor in America from the backs of Indians to those of imported Africans. And
the white characters of *Brother to Dragons* repeat all the images agreed upon
within white discourse about blackness. Laetitia Lewis, Lilburn's wife, believes that colored folks are "just like children. / Be nice to them and they'll be
nice to you" (52). She also believes that "when a nigger bleeds, the blood is
bright, / Brighter than white folks' blood" (82). Both Laetitia and her brother-
in-law, Isham, seem to be particularly disturbed by the way "nigger eyes will
roll" (55), and this somehow has the effect of making it easier for Isham to bear

an unreasoning hatred for the slave George, whose murder will lead to the dissolution of the Lewis clan:

> I never hated George.
> Before, I mean. Him just another nigger.
> But now to see him standing there so weak,
> And frail to fall, and how his eyes were rolling
> Like one more nigger sick and nigh to gone,
> It looked to me there wasn't a thing but hate
> Inside me, and to hate that nigger George
> For being so God-damn mean-weak was nothing
> But sweet joy.
>
> (125)

It is this irrational hatred and abuse of those without power that Warren places at the heart of this American tragedy, and it is this hatred which white discourse agreements were constructed to enable. When a person can, like Laetitia's brother, criticize a woman for being "too clean to be a nigger" (147), he has irreversibly denied the humanity of the other and established the rationale for her enslavement.

There are other passages in *Brother to Dragons* in which Warren engages in his program to illuminate the human reality hidden by the discourse spoken by the white characters, passages in which he attempts to show how black slaves may have acted within the confines of their status to exercise power where they could. Most of these passages have to do with the black mammy of the piece, Aunt Cat, who, according to the poet, "knew the simple classic formula: / Divide the white folks and sit back and wait" (57). The one area of power relationships within which a house slave such as Aunt Cat might contend was within the structures of family affection, and Warren takes Cat's tactics within that area as exemplary:

> Now anybody raised down home—down South—
> Will know in his bones what the situation was.
> For all those years Aunt Cat had fought in silence
> For Lilburn's love, for possession of her Chile,
> With the enemy, the rival, Lucy Lewis.
> The rival had the armament and power:
> The natural mother, warm and kind—and white.
> The rival whose most effective armament
> Is the bland assumption that there is no struggle—
> Nor can be—between white love and the black.

It is a struggle, dark, ferocious, in the dark,
For power—for power empty and abstract.
                    (91–92)

There is another tragedy for Aunt Cat here, though. Not only is the white family structure the only scene in which she can struggle to exercise power, but, as the system of slavery so often denied to the black slave the opportunity for the natural expression of familial love, the white family came to be, in white eyes, the "proper" area for Cat's expression of her humanity. Warren is cognizant of the ironies of this situation, as he so often is. He perceives two human realities behind the stereotype of the devoted slave; one is the tendency observed by Franz Fanon of the oppressed to adopt the oppressor; the other is the real affection felt by black men and women for their fellow human beings:

                    . . . if the word *love*
          Sounds too much like old Thomas Nelson Page
          To sit easy on our stomachs salivated with modernity,
          Then we can say that in the scale of subordination,
          The black, that victim of an obsolescent
          Labor system (we can't, you see, just say
          "Immoral labor system," as I'd near done,
          For that wouldn't be modern, except for people
          Who want things both ways)—well, to start again:
          The victims of the obsolescent labor system
          Had been conditioned, by appeals to the ego,
          To identify themselves with the representative
          Of the superordinate group, i.e., the mistress—
          In other words, they liked her "tol-bul well."
          .   .   .   .
          In other words, the humanity of the poor slave
          Could rise above the system's corrupting arrangement,
          Ignorance, resentment, slyness, sloth, despair,
          The limen of anguish and the bar of rage,
          To recognize the human hope of another person
          And if that is not love, then it's something better.
                              (105–106)

This is the nearest Warren comes to truly arriving at the reality of the humanity as it moves behind the signifiers of race propagated by the likes of Thomas Page in books like his *The Old South* and accepted as true, and there certainly are no like moments to be found in the poetry of Warren's associate, Allen Tate.

But there remain elements of the narration of *Brother to Dragons* which problematize the reader's acceptance of Warren's attempts to turn racial metaphor inside out in this fashion. One of the voices in the poem is identified as belonging to "R.P.W.: The writer of this poem," and it is that voice which, on occasions such as the description of the building of the Lewises' carriage road, repeats with clearly ironic intent the racist assumptions of white slaveholders. That same voice, however, makes other comments which are not so evidently to be read as irony. In the opening of the poem, R.P.W. is heard describing the current appearance of the town of Smithland:

> It looks the sort of town Sam Clemens might
> Grow up in now and not be much worse off.
> River and Catfish, nigger in the shade
>
> (18)

This repetition of the image of the black as an element of nature might be read as a dig at Clemens, but such a reading appears forced in light of other, similar remarks made by R.P.W. in the course of his commentary, and in light of that voice's apparently unmotivated switching back and forth between the use of the epithet "nigger" and the noun, "Negro"; the two names are synonymous for R.P.W. in a way that they had not been for Melville in the preceding century.

Still, *Brother to Dragons* is the only work of its kind to emerge from among the Southern Agrarians, and it serves as a mapping of Warren's continued battle with the system of racial imagery he found himself operating within, a battle which he has not yet completed. In this work he puts those inherited racial images under erasure, as it were, demonstrating their usefulness to an oppressive social system and their uselessness as descriptions of the actual anguish and motivations of the people to whom they were applied. At the end of *Brother to Dragons* Warren can be found emitting rhetorical questions into white discourse of a type Tate never seems to ask:

> . . . What if
> We know the names of the niggers by the wall,
> Who hunkered there and moaned? Yes, we know each name,
> The age, and sex, and price, from the executor
> Who listed all to satisfy the court:
> .   .   .   .
> We know that much, but what is any knowledge
> Without the intrinsic mediation of the heart?
>
> (212)

Chapter 5

The Poetry of

Race and

Liberalism

Now I must take up our quarrel:
never dangerous with women
though touched by their nectared hair,
you wrote in that needful black idiom
offending me, for only your inner voices
spoke such tongues, your father's soft prayers
in an all black town in Oklahoma, your ear lied.
That slave in you was white blood forced to
    derision.

Michael Harper, *Images of Kin*

Among the generation which followed that
of Allen Tate and Robert Penn Warren, a generation which came to maturity
contemporaneously with the modernist canonization of T. S. Eliot and the
installation of New Criticism in the academy, the readiness to adopt the aesthetic practices of the ruling elders was matched by an unwillingness to accept
the sometimes avowedly reactionary political programs of those same elders.
While some of the younger poets, such as Randall Jarrell, might be accurately
described as social conservatives, few could be found with any patience for
the fascism of Pound or with much interest in the agrarian nostalgia of Tate
and the other Fugitives. The liberalism of Roosevelt's New Deal democracy
was far more attractive to the next generation, and their general adherence to a
liberal humanism led to a shift in poetic discourse on matters of race. Even
those who professed political conservatism were chastened by the outcome of
racially based political movements in Europe. In *Race: The History of an Idea
in America,* Thomas Gossett summarizes the response of American intellectuals of the thirties and forties to the theories that gave impetus to the rise of
nazism and fascism:

> The racist mouthings of Hitler, Goering, Goebbels, and their racist philosopher
> Alfred Rosenberg, were a compound of horror and absurdity. Americans realized
> with a shock, especially after World War II, that the Nazis had meant exactly
> what they said—that they were perfectly willing to carry out their beliefs by a
> program of genocide—by killing literally millions of Jews and other peoples they
> regarded as inferior. The recognition that race prejudice is not merely regrettable
> but also highly dangerous was no longer limited to the minorities who suffered
> from discrimination or to the students of racism. (445)

The example of the Holocaust was chastening to many in the American body politic, and it may even account for such phenomena as the virtual disappearance of racist imagery from the published verse of Wallace Stevens in the postwar period. A significant number of the male poets under discussion in this chapter served in the armed forces during the war, and in later years wrote political poems of moral suasion emphasizing the democratic ideals of equality and national unity that had been the focal points of the American war effort.

Also, the solidification of anthropology and sociology as discrete academic disciplines contributed to a general trend that was already visible in realistic and naturalistic fiction, a trend toward the examination of man's situation in his world as a means of explaining his moral and cultural attributes, and away from more narrow, hereditary accountings of the type prevalent in the twenties. As Gossett says of this era, "more and more, the attempt would be made to explain human societies not upon the basis of their biological inheritance but upon social processes, a method of study which amounted to an emphasis upon environment" (416). This shift in emphasis in American thought, which had been building through the last several decades, combined with the reaction to the racism and genocide in Europe and the wide dissemination of Roosevelt's New Deal politics and found expression in numerous poems by white writers which emphasize the common aspirations and humanity of all races and which argue against racist injustice. But just as environmental explanations of society did not immediately supplant hereditary explanations (witness the continuing controversy over race and intelligence in the sixties and seventies), neither did the liberal discourse fully succeed in controverting the tradition of racist discourse, in part because white liberal poets argued most often the political issues and matters of conscience and less often attempted the sort of direct confrontation with racist imagery mounted by Melville. There is nothing in the poetry of the twentieth-century white liberal which attacks that system of imagery on its own ground in quite the way that "Benito Cereno" did, save Robert Lowell's rewriting of "Benito Cereno" itself. The humanist project undertaken in certain of the poems of this period is primarily argumentative, and as effective as this argument may have been, it has not been able to deconstruct wholly the language of race in America, the system of naming the radically other.

Randall Jarrell offers an example of the partial success of the argument with racism. Jarrell mounts a modest foray against the cosmology of the Southern Agrarians from within the realm of southern writing by whites. Speaking specifically of the poetry of Robert Penn Warren, Jarrell offers a critique of the sense of the presence of evil in history that is to be found in the works of both Tate and Warren, the sense that there is a social original sin carried through history and visited upon later generations, an ineluctable burden never entirely expiated. Jarrell detects an element of guilt in the writings of the Southern Agrarians, guilt about not engaging in the difficult act of doing something directly about the evil in society: "The only excuse you can find for doing nothing is to say that the world is essentially evil and incurable, that anything you did would only be a silly palliation to hide from yourself the final evil of existence; and so you believe in Original Sin, and dislike progress, science, and humanitarianism, and go in for religion and the Middle Ages, and so on. *This* reason for Red's [Warren] poems being what they are is the same one you find in thousands of others (Allen's, for instance)" (*Letters* 108). This is strikingly similar to the charge Warren was later to level at those earlier southern writers who saw themselves as victimized by the doom defined by history.

Jarrell also notes presciently the link in the writings of the Southern Agrarians between that historical sin and the nonwhite. When Jarrell seeks an analogy for Warren's obsessive pursuit of historical evil in his poems, he not at all fortuitously turns to the problem of racial representation: "It's like solving the Negro problem by sending all the Negroes to Africa and then maintaining in all your dreams and writings that they're pure Evil and that the world is Africa—and they never contradict you, because the real mixed-grey ones aren't here anymore, and the pure Blacks of your imagination were formed to confirm you: so your theory is a nightmare" (*Letters* 108). Jarrell shows an awareness foreign to Tate that the image of the nonwhite propagated in white discourse is purely fictive and exists to confirm the white in the status of subject and privilege. It is in this sense that the theory is a nightmare, because it propounds a blackness, an Africa, which is the locus of all the evil that the white subject wishes to be shut of.

There is yet a sense in which Jarrell has not entirely disentangled himself from the nightmarish veil he so adequately describes, as is indicated by his speaking of "the Negro problem," as if it were the existence of the black other which constituted a problem rather than the white response to that existence. Jarrell's poems seem free of the kind of personal prejudice we have detected in some of his predecessors, but there is still this lingering of traditional ways of speaking of the nonwhite. This is most apparent in Jarrell's continuation of the traditional associations of blackness with morbidity and eternity. Nearly all of the black people who figure prominently in his poems, admittedly a small group, are associated with death, and the only times that the word "nigger" appears are when death is spoken of. In "Lady Bates," one of the finest of Jarrell's early works, he addresses the deceased young girl whose name supplies the poem's title directly, telling her:

Day and night met in the twilight by your tomb
And shot craps for you and Day said, pointing to your soul,
"This *bad* young colored lady,"
And Night said, "Poor little nigger girl."

(*Poems* 26–27)

In addition to the use of Christian symbolism in these lines (and the inevitable crapshoot), it might be supposed that "Night's" speaking of the deathly signifier, "nigger," might have some of the same effect as the buzzard's similar role in Warren's "Pondy Woods." In "The Dead in Melanesia," the poet speaks of the black islands' man-god who "Fell to the schooners cruising here for niggers" (Jarrell, *Poems* 187), an ironized repetition of historical fact. Jarrell, like the earlier Southern Agrarians, seems always to find connotations of death when he thinks blackness, but he has reached a stage where he recognizes that these are the images of white thinking and that they are not representative of the actualities of black life in America. When, in a poem from *Blood for a Stranger,* he images "the Negro sitting in the ashes, / Staring, humming to the cat" (*Poems* 374), he goes on to identify those images plainly as "the inhabitants of the country of the mind."

Though possessing neither the influence nor the audience that Allen Tate was able to command, Muriel Rukeyser is paradigmatic of another strand of modernism which coexisted with the New Critics and seemed, with its open embrace of political and sociological thematic materials, to offer an ongoing critique of the view of history offered by Tate and his associates. A poem like Rukeyser's "The Lynchings of Jesus" might be laid alongside Tate's "The Swimmers" as an example of the sort of approach taken by the more left-leaning of the humanist writers of the period. Both poems appeal to a structure of Christian symbolism, and specifically to the crucifixion, but Rukeyser, whether wisely or not, is the more overt in her manipulations of these symbols, foregrounding her analogy between the black victims of lynchings and the sacrifice of Christ. Likewise, where Tate presents a lynching perceived in innocence and stripped of history, Rukeyser is at pains to establish connections between previous victims and the Scottsboro Boys on trial, and further to others in her political martyrology such as Sacco and Vanzetti. What her poem may lack in subtlety, it attempts to make up by being comprehensive. This strategy does have the effect of restoring the context of twentieth-century lynchings that Tate had left behind. Before coming to the Scottsboro court-room, then, Rukeyser gives her reader:

> . . . the case of one Hilliard, a native of Texas,
> in the year of our Lord 1897, a freeman.
> Report . . . Hilliard's power of endurance seems to be
> the most wonderful thing on record.   His lower limbs
> burned off a while before he became unconscious
> and his body looked to be burned to the hollow.
> Was it decreed (oh coyly coyly) by an avenging God
> as well as an avenging people that he suffer so?
>
> (27)

The reader is thus prepared to read the prosecution of the Scottsboro defen-dants as another in a chain of such depredations. And the defendants are not seen simply as victims. They become revolutionaries for Rukeyser: "John Brown, Nat Turner, Toussaint stand in this courtroom" (28).

Elsewhere in her work Rukeyser is as adamant in her pursuit of the human-ist's goal of establishing the commonality of human experience as Tate was in his definition of the otherness of black life. She handles this program most effectively in poems such as those collected in *U.S. 1*, which portray black and white workers faced with a common tragedy. Several of the poems in this volume concern the building of the Hawk's Nest tunnel through Gauley Mountain in West Virginia. The tunnel, intended to divert water from the New River to a hydroelectric plant, was drilled through rock that was nearly pure silica, a fact which was known to officials of the companies involved in the construction. The event is no longer widely remembered, and the tunnel itself is invisible under water, but at the time Rukeyser wrote her verses the construction's effect upon the men who labored at it was known to be one of the worst industrial disasters in American history. (Ironically, the tunnel was planned and commissioned by Union Carbide, the company more recently associated with the worst industrial disaster in the history of India.)

The depression-era segregation in West Virginia proves to be the source of comic relief in Rukeyser's retelling of the incident. In "George Robinson: Blues," we are told plainly enough:

> Gauley Bridge is a good town for Negroes; they let us stand
>   around, they let us stand
> around on the sidewalks if we're black or brown.
> Vanetta's over the trestle, and that's our town.
>
> (84)

If West Virginia's black people are segregated into their own townships, the demands of modern industrialism yet require their integration into the work force, and it is this requirement and the sharing of labors and losses incumbent upon it which provide the circumstance Rukeyser uses in her poem to emphasize the shared humanity of black and white. Both groups of workers are equally susceptible to the disease that George Robinson, for want of a proper diagnosis from the company doctors, calls "tunnelitis." And the silica the workers drill through together, the cause of the tunnelitis, erases the racial distinctions which have been so crucial above ground. Rukeyser, through Robinson, turns this deadly chemical into a symbol:

> As dark as I am, when I came out at morning after the tunnel at night,
> with a white man, nobody could have told which man was white.
> The dust had covered us both, and the dust was white.
>
> (85)

The note struck in these last lines is part of a motif which recurs in all of Rukeyser's works; one of her major projects, expressed in such poems as "The Soul and Body of John Brown." "Despisals," "Martin Luther King, Malcolm X," and so many others, is the overt denunciation of racial injustice and the search for images that convey the extent to which black and white destinies are bound together in this nation. When she says, in "Secrets of American Civilization," that "Slave and slaveholder . . . are chained together" (514), she strives for a trope that encompasses all her political beliefs in social justice and her belief in the essential equality of human aspirations.

Though Muriel Rukeyser was avowedly to the left politically of most of the other widely appreciated poets of her day, her assertion in her verses of an egalitarian humanism was something she had in common even with more centrist writers. The same spirit that informs her poem "The Soul and Body of John Brown" may be found in Stanley Kunitz's "To a Slave Named Job," which commemorates the figure of an Indian carved from a log by a black slave:

> . . . aloof and bold,
> with his raised feet poised
> for the oppressor's neck.
> The cigars he offers
> are not for sale.
> They fit his hand
> as though they were a gun.
>
> (8)

Kunitz's poem may also be read as a continuation of the liberal humanists' desire to identify the struggle of the Afro-American for his rightful place in society with the struggles of other oppressed peoples, in this instance with those of the native Americans. That approach can be located as well in these lines from William Everson's "The Masculine Dead," which emphasize the commonality of the black laborer's efforts with those of later, voluntary immigrants:

> Negroes staggering under their loads,
> They can break on their arms the back of a ram;
> Tall golden Swedes whose nostrils suck the smell of the sea.
> They try their muscle against the earth,
> But strong as they are the earth beats them.
>
> (69)

Rukeyser's poems memorializing those whose lives have been ruined or taken in the racial clashes of America's history also find their correlatives in the writings of her liberal contemporaries. David Ignatow, whose career nearly coincides with hers, wrote a short elegy for the slain civil-rights worker Medgar Evers in which, speaking in Evers's voice, he considers specifically the symbolic import with which the white discourse of radical otherness has invested the nonwhite:

> They're afraid of me
> because I remind them of the ground.
> The harder they step on me
> the closer I am pressed to earth,
> and hard, hard they step,
> growing more frightened
> and vicious.
>
> (233)

The poem has the effect of quietly underscoring the self-confirming and self-defeating nature of the discourse's assertion of otherness. Each time that the assertion is made, Antaeus-like it acquires greater symbolic strength and comes to confirm the threat that it has posited. The discourse describes the savagery of the other and then must take steps to protect itself against that savagery.

Anthony Hecht, in his "Black Boy in the Dark," also concerns himself with the white mind's use of the black other. In the midst of the symbols of our nation's tearing at itself, a Civil War memorial, the assassination of Presi-

dent Kennedy, the escalating war against Viet Nam, Hecht finds a black youth
to be a sort of symbolic measure:

> An eighteen-year-old black boy clocks the nation,
> Reading a comic book in a busted chair.
>
> Our solitary guardian of the law
> Of diminishing returns?
>
> (6)

The boy observed daydreams, like many young Americans, about sitting in
the White House or achieving commerical success, and Hecht suggests, in
keeping with a liberal political stance, that the extent to which these dreams
are impossible of attainment is a measure of how far our democracy has still to
go. The poem closes with an image that forms an interesting contrast to
Crane's "nigger cupids," an image which Hecht uses, as Ignatow had used
the voice of Medgar Evers, to reveal the operations of racial discourse, to
gloss the symbols that discourse uses to keep itself in a position of primacy:

> But what, after all, has he to complain about,
> This expendable St. Michael we employ
> To stay awake and keep the darkness out?
>
> (7)

This process of looking at the way the white mind operates in the language
of darkness marks one departure these writers made from the discourse of the
modernist fathers. In some ways the New Critical way of looking at poetics,
while it steadfastly resisted such sociological subject matter, lent itself well to
the examination of racial language. A poetics of ambiguity and irony should
have been superbly equipped to approach an area as laden with ironies as is
the racial discourse. And the poets of liberalism were prepared to turn their
attention to the ironies of liberal actions. William Meredith, for one, in his
poem "Do not embrace your mind's new Negro friend," attends, with more
subtlety than Frost had managed to muster, to the fashion in which some
liberals have rushed to friendship with the black race without reflection upon
the depth of that friendship or upon the terms they choose as its foundation:

> Do not embrace your mind's new Negro friend
> Or embarrass the blackballed Jew with memberships:
> There must be years of atonement first, and even then
> You may still be the blundering raconteur
> With the wrong story, and they may still be free.
>
> (41)

In mid-admonition Meredith includes a remark that demonstrates his own knowledge of the extent to which the "Negro" is a construct of white language, a rubric actual black people have been expected to live under as victims of language "Who have been convinced by the repeated names / That they are Jews or Negroes or some dark thing" (41).

Other poems that participate in this argument of ironies seem almost to call across the years to precursor poems written within the traditional discourse on race. Howard Nemerov's "A Negro Cemetery Next to a White One" attacks both the practice and the terminology of racism while offering a sort of corrective to the title of Wallace Stevens's "Like Decorations in a Nigger Cemetery." Where Stevens ignores the question of the segregation of the society of the dead, Nemerov takes it as his point of departure for an examination of the ironies of the speech acts of racial separation. Beginning by imagining himself a deceased black person turned away at the gate by a "dark blonde angel holding up a plaque / that said White only" (372), the poet proceeds to a consideration of the oddities implicit in such a situation:

> Some ghosts are black and some darknesses white.
>
> But since they failed to integrate the earth,
> It's white of them to give what tantamounts
> To it, making us all, for what that's worth,
> Separate but equal where it counts.
>
> (372)

These lines neatly point up the inadequacies of the law laid down by the Supreme Court in *Plessy vs. Ferguson,* demonstrating just how much promises of equality in separation were worth, while ironically emphasizing the natural equality of human corpses. They also undermine archly the terms of the compliment white people pay to one another, as in the lines excised from Eliot's *The Waste Land* which repeat it. It *is* white of white people to behave in such a fashion, to extend their system of separating the other into the other world.

A poem its author, James Wright, inscribes to the Afro-American poet Etheridge Knight, "On a Phrase from Southern Ohio," bears a relationship to such works of Allen Tate's as "Sonnets at Christmas" and "The Swimmers." The immediate situation of the poem is much like that of "The Swimmers." The poet portrays himself as a young boy out on a lark with several companions, identified specifically by name and by nickname, playing in wilderness and water. The poem also uses a symbolic apparatus as resonant as the Christian motifs of Tate's work; Wright and his playmates literally make their way across a boundary, the watery line between West Virginia and Ohio, while figuratively transgressing a borderline of race and experience. In opposition to the passive "fall" into knowledge of "The Swimmers," though, Wright's characters do not appear to share in any prelapsarian innocence. Indeed, when the boys cross the river on a skiff, they are "lazy and thieving," a description which prepares the reader for what is to follow.

Arrived upon the opposing shore, the boys scale a scarred mountain, where strip mining has torn away the face of a foothill. Their sense of themselves is revealed as they make their way up the naked face; they are said to have "Climbed / Straight up / And white" (35). Wright is clearly working toward the creation of some ritual experience here, and that sense is heightened by the diction in the descriptions of the beauty that remains atop the denuded peak: "a vicious secret / Of trilliums, the dark purple silk sliding its hands deep / down." When it comes time for Wright to speak of the paradigmatic act at the center of his poem, he momentarily abandons the somewhat mystical language of such descriptions in favor of a colloquial, narrative tone:

> Well, we found two black boys up there
> In the wild of the garden.
> Well, we beat the hell out of one
> And chased out the other.
>
> (35)

This differs from Tate's confession in "Sonnets at Christmas" in that it depicts a primal enactment of white privilege through force by children who are clearly responsible for their act. Wright does not see himself as having benefited from something which creates and maintains the state of affairs. This poem inscribes the constitution of whiteness, and the expulsion of blackness from a newly claimed paradisal territory. It is self-questioning, wondering what it is in us that causes us to expel the other, closely resembling the descriptions of the rock fights between white and black boys that appear in Richard Wright's *Black Boy*. The damnation of this primal episode is not an inherited sin but the damnation of not being able to account for ourselves. James Wright, writing as an adult, is haunted by his own past actions and the question of what they may portend:

> What were those purple shadows doing
> Under the ear
> Of the woman who was weeping along the Ohio
> River the woman?

Damned if you know;
I don't.

                    (35)

Wright does not see himself as punished by a crime of which he would be quit. Rather, he is concerned with his own implication in the crime.

Robert Lowell, for many the epitome of the liberal poet of midcentury, was somewhat unusual in that he apprenticed himself to both Allen Tate and William Carlos Williams. Certainly some of the distinction of his style derives from this amalgamation, and his uses of history share some of the same distinctions. In his obsessions with the fate of the nation and the effort to locate that fate's origins in the acts of the people who established it he is close to Tate, but in his willingness to allow the current to enter his verse directly he is much nearer to Williams. The poems gathered into his collection *Notebook*, like the later parts of Zukofsky's "*A*," span the period of the great civil-rights movement and the subsequent Black Power movements of the 1960s, and this fact is reflected in the poems along with Lowell's ruminations on other political issues of the time. These reflections produce a poetic discussion of race which differs considerably from that of his two teachers.

In "Coleridge and King Richard," Lowell's portrait of the earlier poet and the King includes these lines directed against that agreement among white speakers that blacks are more given to endurance than others:

it was a comforting fancy that only blacks
could cherish enslavement for two hundred years
most negroes in London had onwardlooking thoughts
by 1800, moved farther from the jungle
and reveries of kings, than Coleridge
                    (*Notebook* 169–70)

This attack upon the position that comforted Las Casas and Jefferson in their enslavement of Africans, an attack which appears to observe the romantics' distinction between fancy, wit, and imagination, is indicative of Lowell's general stance. Elsewhere he writes sympathetically of those blacks who acted against white domination, as in "Piano Practice," a poem dedicated to Lowell's fellow poet Adrienne Rich, with its lines:

        We've robbed the arsenal
to feed the needy, Toussaint, Fanon, Malcolm,
the Revolution's *mutiles de guerre,*
shirtless ones dying, killing on the rooftops . . .
                    (*Notebook* 195)

But as we saw in reading Zukofsky, a liberal political position does not of itself force a rupture in white discourse. The same Lowell who writes against the assumption that blacks are constitutionally more enduring than other races may hold to a few misconceptions still, as in his description, in "Out of the Picture," of one who "plucked all the flowers, deflowered all the girls / with the exaggeration of a Negro, / with too many words" (*Notebook* 257).

As the political attitudes discovered in *Notebook* suggest, Lowell had natural affinities for Herman Melville's project in "Benito Cereno" of undoing, within the reader, the knots of racist imagery produced by white discourse. Lowell rewrote Melville's novella as a verse play, which premiered in November of 1964 with Roscoe Lee Browne in the role of Babu, and which Lowell included with his dramatization of stories by Hawthorne, with whom Melville had many disagreements over the politics of race and slavery, in the volume of historical plays, *The Old Glory*. Melville's high drama was an obvious choice for staging, and in Lowell's version the discord between the racial imagery held in the mind of Captain Delano and the actuality of the events in which he becomes enmeshed is maintained.

A stage production tends to lose the effect of Melville's narrator's access to the thought of his main character, a tendency which Lowell counters by having Delano give voice to more of his prejudices than he does in Melville's original. Lowell's other major departure from his source is his ending of the story. The original was either too difficult or too ghoulish for staging, so Lowell has eliminated the final image of Babu's staring, decapitated visage. In most other respects, the dramatic version follows Melville quite closely but does not appear to have as much force, perhaps because Lowell's handling of the dramatic form does not allow for as much subtlety in the process of the audience's discovery of the true nature of the events.

Melville's narration has created a character in Delano with whom the reader sympathizes, despite his holding a number of reprehensible ideas, because he comes across as a hapless naïf. This impression does not come across as effectively in the play because Lowell's device of having the Captain speak more of his prejudices openly tends to prejudice the audience against the character. Delano, as presented by Lowell, seems to hold violent biases against anyone who is not a white American democrat of the Jeffersonian order, and he links many other nationalities to the nonwhite. He says of the French that "they're like the rest of the Latins, / They're hardly white people" (*Old Glory* 142), and of the Spaniards, "Spaniards? The name gets you down, / you think their sultry faces and language / make them Zulus" (146). Delano even makes distinctions among the blacks, preferring American blacks to Africans. His sidekick, seaman Perkins, shares this prejudice, complaining of Babu, "Why doesn't he talk with a Southern accent / Like Mr. Jefferson" (154), which remark brings up a feature that does not appear in the original. Both Delanos, Melville's and Lowell's, have strong feelings about racial amalgamation, but in the play, responding to Perkins's repetition of the rumor that Jefferson had fathered illegitimate children by his slaves, Delano swears, "that's the quickest way / to raise the blacks to our level" (142). Melville's Delano was a man of such naive simplicity as to be impervious to irony, and it was this that kept him from understanding what passed before his eyes. Lowell's Delano seems, though still annoyingly simple, to have a positive delight in irony. This is revealed cogently in a speech he addresses to Perkins early on:

In a civilized country, Perkins,
everyone disbelieves in slavery,
everyone disbelieves in slavery and wants slaves.
We have the perfect uneasy answer
in the North, we don't have them and want them;
Mr. Jefferson has them and fears them.

(144)

And where Melville allowed other characters to carry the major burden of indicating ironies to the reader, Lowell assigns some of these tasks to Delano, as when he has Delano remark to Babu, "I see you have a feeling for symbols of power" (169).

Lowell does make full use of the opportunities for dramatic irony which this tale affords to comment upon the emptiness of the agreements about race within white discourse. At one point Cereno tells his visitor that "A captain is a servant, almost a slave, Sir" (*Old Glory* 151), a line which Delano reads figuratively but which the audience takes literally as a description of Cereno's present state. In a later discussion between Babu and Delano, Babu responds to Delano's pronouncements with the remark that "the United States must be a paradise for people like Babu" (167). And Delano's constant claims for the superiority of American democracy, like some of Jefferson's, often contradict the many statements he makes regarding the innate inferiority of blacks. At one point Delano claims "no one has an inferior mind in America" (188), despite his belief in the inferiority of the black intellect. At another point, while lining the Africans up for rations, he boasts, "Each man shall have his share. / That's how we run things in the states— / to each man equally, no matter what his claims" (190), a boast that ignores the unequal status of the black slave as thoroughly as did the Declaration of Independence. Lowell carries over from the novella its major scenes of dramatic irony and embellishes them with his own touches. The scene in which a Spanish seaman tosses a knot to Delano, a knot "for someone to untie" (177), is repeated, but in a version that is sharply abbreviated to make time for some of Lowell's symbolic stage business, of which there is much. The scene in which Babu reenacts the ritual shaving of his master, Cereno, is also repeated, amidst symbol-laden scenery, not all of which is derived from Melville. For example, the seat taken by Cereno for his shaving is "a broken throne-like and gilded chair" (184). This innovation is symptomatic of Lowell's alterations of these scenes. He does not seem to trust his audience to "get" the irony, so he adds touches guaranteed to drive the irony home. In Melville's version the chair is a "large, misshapen arm chair [of malacca], which, furnished with a rude barber's crotch at the back, working with a screw, seemed some grotesque engine of torment" (151). This would appear sufficiently laden with ironic import without Lowell's transformation of it into a gilded throne.

It is Lowell's repetition of Melville's deconstruction of white mythology that accounts for what powers his play exercises over us. Lowell's "Benito Cereno" is the only work of its kind to appear under the pen of a poet of his generation and political leanings, and many of its words had previously appeared under another pen. And yet Lowell's version is to some extent a diminution of Melville's breakthrough. In his adaptations for the stage, Lowell has rendered Delano so unlikable, and the action so obvious, that Melville's technique of letting the white image system overturn itself in the minds of the audience is lost. The play's conclusion is but one instance of this larger problem. Where Melville ends with the larger society's destruction of Babu, the brains behind the rebellion, and the image of his disembodied head staring in warning out over the countryside, into the readers' eyes as it were, Lowell closes with an act of individual murder which confirms white power. Babu, after the revolt has been put down, attempts to surrender to Delano. "Holding a white handkerchief and raising both his hands" (*Old Glory* 214), Babu advances toward Delano, calling out "Yankee Master understand me. The future is with us," a line in keeping with Melville's ending. Lowell, however, gives Delano the last word. The Yankee master shouts out, "This is your future," and shoots Babu as the stage lights go down. Melville's trope for the future was the image of the Spanish captain following his leader to his death. Lowell's is the white American dispatching the black revolutionary into the darkness. The endings are alike only in that both include the unwillingness of the white speaker to understand the black other. Lowell's handling of this material may be seen as an advance over Tate's manipulations of history and race, but it is in fact no advance over what Melville had already accomplished in the preceding century.

Karl Shapiro, whose disagreements with Allen Tate, Ezra Pound, and T. S. Eliot over matters both political and aesthetic are probably too numerous to be counted, is most vocal in his disagreements on matters of the representations of race. Unlike Tate, Shapiro opposed the award of the Bollingen prize to Pound, on the basis of Pound's anti-Semitism, thus mingling sociopolitical and artistic judgments. That act is characteristic of Shapiro's willingness to mix aesthetics and politics, to reject art which expresses opinions he finds abhorrent no matter the significance of its merit as art, and to use his own art as a platform for airing his social beliefs. But Shapiro also serves as one more example of one whose personal commitment to the equality of all races does not instantaneously set him free from the agreements entered into by those who enter white discourse. Though he wrote often in opposition to racism, Shapiro's work shows him to have harbored a few special attitudes of his own about Afro-Americans.

Shapiro's writing on matters of race goes back to his earliest published poems. In "University," he complains that "To hurt the Negro and avoid the Jew / Is the curriculum" (*Collected Poems* 10), and another poem from the same period, "The Snob," chides those who join college fraternities, "Where it is weakly sworn by smiles to cow / Unequals, niggers, or just Methodists" (30). Recognizing the real dangers presented by people possessed of such attitudes, Shapiro says of the snob that "he is not funny and not unimportant." Shapiro moves on from these attacks upon the genteel, and Gentile, practice of prejudice to a more sophisticated critique of the special view of history promulgated within white discourse during his time, particularly by Eliot and Tate. "Conscription Camp" addresses the Commonwealth of Virginia in the second person, deriding the ellipses within official histories of the South and within the Southern Agrarian view of history:

> You manufacture history like jute—
> Labor is cheap, Virginia, for high deeds,
> But in your British dream of reputation
> The black man is your conscience and your cost.
>
> (47)

As this quotation indicates, Shapiro shares Lowell's interest in recovering American history, as he shares Lowell's tendency to overexplain, though nowhere with as much verbal facility as Lowell. He also adopts simultaneously with Lowell and the other liberal voices of his era the device of centering poems upon the acutest ironies of the history of a slaveholding democracy. "Jefferson's Greeting" could well have been one of the speeches of Captain Delano in Lowell's rendering of "Benito Cereno," and it is also strongly reminiscent of the passage in Warren's *Brother to Dragons* which contemplates the construction of the carriage road leading to the home of Jefferson's kinfolks, the Lewises. Shapiro depicts the return to Monticello of the author of our Declaration of Independence:

> When suddenly there burst from every side
> The blacks, who pull the horses from the shafts
> And haul him like a chariot up the drive,
> Cheering, dancing, crying his return,
> Lifting the master bodily
> Up the steps and over the threshold,
> Kissing his hands and feet, even the ground
> He passes over, the great Virginian, home
> Whose wilderness he carved into decorum.
>
>   (301)

The seemingly irresolvable dissonance in the situation of one who holds the belief that all men are created equal and who also holds slaves and considers them lesser and other than white men is heightened by the fact that the joy expressed by the welcome offered by the blacks in this passage is probably genuine. It is a replication of Warren's examination of the image of the devoted slave in *Brother to Dragons*.

There is a sort of dissonance too in Shapiro's argument with racist discourse. One poem, "Nigger," appears to be an attempt to explode the complex of images connoted by that epithet. Shapiro addresses the "nigger," the stereotype, directly and wonders that the image endures "When you boxed that hun, when you raped that trash that you didn't rape, / . . . / When you felt that loop and you took that boot from a KKK" (*Collected Poems* 65). He wonders as well at the origins of the image of the African in American writing:

> With a swatch of the baboon's crimson bottom cut for a lip,
> And a brace of elephant ivories hung for a tusky smile,
> With the muscles as level and lazy and long as the lifting Nile,
> And a penis as loaded and supple and limp as the slaver's whip.
>
>   (65)

It is when Shapiro turns to address the contemporary, urban stereotype that the poem begins to turn against itself. The stanzas on Africa questioned the origins of the image. The later passages, however, with their diction and their mode of address, seem to accept the legitimacy of the image they describe and thus lend it a substance the poet may not even believe it has:

> Are you beautiful still when you walk downtown in a knife-cut coat
> And your yellow shoes dance at the corner curb like a brand new car,
> And the buck with the arching pick looks over the new-laid tar
> As you cock your eye like a cuckoo bird on a twelve-o'clock note?
>
> (65)

Intentional criticism might save these lines from themselves. If the reader is an idealist he or she might assume, with no textual evidence, that Shapiro's images have simply gotten beyond his control and taken on a life he planned to deny them. But the quatrain contains an element of romanticized noble savagery, and there is another poem, "Jazz," which indicates that the poet is at least partially behind the veil of that particular portion of racial discourse. "Jazz" offers a description in prose stanzas of a "Negro street" in Baltimore, a description which we are to read as portraying the spirit and source of jazz music in the daily life of Afro-America. But the "negress" who walks through the poem's second stanza is indistinguishable from the negress of Cummings's *Him* or from Stein's *Melanctha*. She is no more than a frozen metaphor for the racial other paraded through the white poet's imagination: "a teeming Negress crowds at the perfume counter, big arms like haunches and bosom practically bare. She laughs with her friends above the cut-glass bottles with Frenchified names and recently invented colors. She purchases a sizeable vial of some green scent, pays green dry money, unstoppers the bottle and dumps the entire load between her breasts! O glorious act of laughter in the highly serious bazaar of the Jew-Store!" (185). Shapiro's sincere dedication to the elimination of racism and its social consequences is unquestioned. And his championing of many black poets from his various positions of editorial and institutional power has been unstinting. But when he leaves the abstractions of his argument against antidemocratic policies to create a portrait of an individual black person, he finds himself repeating the tropes of exoticism used by earlier white poets.

This repetition is attributable to the fact that Shapiro views the nonwhite as a representative of difference in a society that has betrayed its commitment to the celebration of pluralism. When Karl Shapiro praises a black poet in his criticism, as he praises his friend, Melvin B. Tolson, in his preface to Tolson's *Harlem Gallery,* it is as an element of difference. As noted in the preceding chapter, Shapiro took sharp exception to what he saw as Tate's assimilation of Tolson into the Anglo-American tradition. In his own preface to Tolson's later volume, Shapiro again appropriates Tolson for his argument with Tate. Here Shapiro declares: "It is one thing to accept an artist on the grounds of his art (regardless of race and creed) as long as the artist can adjust to the ruling 'Graeco-Judaic-Christian' culture. It is another to accept an artist who contravenes that culture. Tolson belongs to the second category; he is in effect the enemy of the dominant culture of our time and place" (12). It may be as incorrect to say of a black poet who prides himself on having brought modernism to Afro-American verse that he has contravened the culture of his time as it was to say that his success was founded upon his assimilation of Anglo-American tradition. It is not clear that a poet who, as Shapiro says of Tolson, outpounds Pound, has contravened the dominant literary culture.

Where Tate had virtually expelled the elements of Afro-American culture from his consideration of Tolson's *Libretto for the Republic of Liberia,* Shapiro enshrines what he thinks are the earmarks of black culture. Shapiro advances his belief that "Tolson writes and thinks in Negro, which is to say, a possible American language" (Preface 13). Since Tolson is black, it is probably safe to say that he thinks as a black. But it is not at all evident what Shapiro thinks it is to think in Negro. It is much more evident that Shapiro's real interest lies in his contest with Eliot's and Tate's ideas about the tradition of language and poetry. For Shapiro, Tolson performs "the primary poetic rite for our literature. Instead of purifying the tongue, which is the business of the Academy, he is complicating it, giving it the gift of tongues" (13). Tolson truly does complicate the language of our time, but in what sense it can be said of a poem with what Shapiro calls a "baroque surface" (14) that it is written in Negro, Shapiro neglects to spell out. His assertion has been angrily contested by a number of black critics, most notably Sarah Webster Fabio in her essay, "Who Speaks Negro?" and it has complicated the wider reception of Tolson's poem. Tolson's later works are as allusive as anything of Pound's or Eliot's. They do, as Tolson submits, take their organizing principles from high modernism. One might object that the "Negro" they speak, if that is what they do, is considerably different from that spoken by Langston Hughes or Gwendolyn Brooks. Black poets may be different in some regards from whites; they also differ significantly from one another, a point to which Shapiro would no doubt agree. But Shapiro's claim that Tolson's work is written in Negro subsumes the difference between black poets beneath a much larger and consuming difference. For Tate to accept Tolson into the country club he had to erase much of Tolson's difference. Shapiro finds himself driven, in his battle against Tate, to exaggerate Tolson's difference to a point where it is the whole point; Tolson's language has value for Shapiro to the extent that it is other than traditional white language. For Tolson's poetry to have the effect Shapiro wants it to have, it must come to us as radically different. As a result, Shapiro's version of the liberal imperative has the unanticipated effect of reinforcing white discourse declarations of the otherness of the nonwhite.

The Dream Songs of John Berryman offer additional unanticipated results. In those poems, Berryman commits the white man's version of "writing in Negro"; he is one of those poets who talks black in the way that Tate warned black poets about when he advised them not to use black folk idioms as the basis for their work. It is this writing in Negro of Berryman's that is the source of the objection lodged against him by Michael Harper in the verses that form the epigraph for this discussion. What has offended Harper is that on no fewer than seventeen occasions in the course of *The Dream Songs,* Berryman speaks at length in the same sort of minstrel dialect encountered in the poetry of Pound and Cummings, the white man's mimickry that proceeds from an ear that lies. This begins with the second poem of the volume, when Henry, the central character of Berryman's sequence, avers:

> Arrive a time when all coons lose dere grip,
> but is he come? Le's do a hoedown, gal,
> one blue, one shuffle,
> if them is all you seem to require.

(4)

Such speech is offensive, and Harper is right to deny the validity of it as a representation of black speech acts. But Berryman differs from Pound and Cummings in that he is not attempting to represent black speech. What is going on here is indicated by Harper's observation that "only your inner voices / spoke such tongues." *The Dream Songs* are the not wholly conscious imaginings of Henry, the white man, and this dialect is an enactment of the white mind playing at blackness within its system of stereotypes. Henry "blacks up" and acts in an oneiric minstrel show. He plays the traditional role of Mr. Bones to his mind's Negro friend, the Interlocutor. When this occurs, *The Dream Songs* represent the dream life of white discourse.

Thus when Berryman's Henry begins to play out a "coon show," it should be clear that this is a white performance with a white audience representing that audience's traditional representations of the nonwhite; it is not Berryman's own attempt to portray blackness. This technique allows the poet to overturn certain agreements of white discourse, as Melville had, within the white mind. For example, white discourse has long held that the ideal human status is to be free, white, and twenty-one, but Henry Whiteman, when he puts on his dream's burnt cork, dreams himself "free, black & forty-one" (44). Henry in his cups uses blackness as a liberating device. When he is Mr. Bones he feels himself freed from the strictures of white society. He tells himself at one point, "Better get white or you' get whacked, / or keep so-called *black* / & raise hell" (136). One way that blacked Henry raises hell is to argue for the extension of civil rights to real black people. In one of his conversations with Interlocutor the issue of integration is taken up from an identifiably liberal point of view:

After eights years, be less dan eight percent,
distinguish' friend, of coloured wif de whites
in de School, in de Souf.
—Is colored gobs, is colored officers,
Mr. Bones. Dat's nuffin?—Uncle Tom,
sweep shut yo mouf,

is million blocking from de proper job
de fairest houses & de churches eben.
                                                    (67)

Elsewhere Henry uses the same method to exhort blacks to rebellion, punning on Marx and Engels in a way that simultaneously blasts the white agreements about black intelligence:

Negroes, ignite! You have nothing to use but your brains,
which let bust out.—What was that again, Mr. Bones?
De body have abuse
but is one, too.—One-two, the old thrones
topple, dead sober. The decanter, pal!
                                                    (251)

There is a difficulty with such an approach. It is difficult to speak in this dialect to a white audience without activating the entire racial image structure of our language. This may be a representation of white speech acts, but it is not handled in such a way as to contravene entirely the referential impulse. It is not possible to forget that this refers to black speech at some misguided level, and so some readers will either be offended or agree that black people really do speak as Henry has them. This practice has a residual effect upon the liberal argument put forward in *The Dream Songs*. How seriously can readers take an argument for the recognition of the rights of Afro-Americans when that argument is couched in derisive terms and made in the course of an oneiric "coon show"?

The fact is that dreaming Henry preaches a liberal course while dreaming racist representations; in the words of a folk saying, the drunk man speaks the sober man's thoughts. His subconscious, as constructed by Berryman, lampoons the very people whose cause he advocates. In this sense Berryman, like Shapiro, reasserts the discourse's marking of the otherness of the nonwhite, even while attempting to argue on the other's behalf. It is in just this respect that the moral suasion of liberal poetry has sometimes been unable to complete its program. Liberal poets of midcentury have argued more forcefully and frequently than at any time since Reconstruction for racial justice, but they not only failed to deconstruct the discourse of racism within the American language, they sometimes spoke in its image.

Chapter 6

Recent Poetry

and the Racial

Other

There is no worthier subject for poetry in our
time
Than the fear that the races should rise and rend
each other.

Nathaniel Tarn, *The Beautiful Contradictions*

A comprehensive reading of recent verse turns up no discernible overriding trend in racial discourse to compare to the romantic racism of much high modernism or the nostalgic plantation mentality of early Southern Agrarianism, this despite the enormous flow of writings on race from all sides during the first decades of the century's second half. While the struggle for racial justice was developing new strategies and meeting with unparalleled successes, the discourse on race among white poets continued to follow the patterns it had set for itself earlier in the century. Poets of a liberal or radical persuasion continued to argue as their elders had, no matter which of their elders they had chosen to follow in matters of aesthetic philosophy. And, partly because the moral suasion of earlier liberal poets had not been able to prevail completely against racist images in language, other poets repeated those same frozen metaphors of racial alienation. A Melvillian rupture within the discourse is still lacking, and as a result, the images found in recent poems are as familiar as the "old darky mowing the lawn" in the epigraph to Henry Taylor's "De Gustibus Ain't What Dey Used to Be." When we read poetry like Adrienne Rich's "From an Old House in America," in which the poet identifies herself, as an American woman, with the slave women giving birth while chained between the decks of the slave ship (*Doorframe* 215), it is difficult not to recall Pound's similar comparison of his position in the army detention center to the same hellish slave ships, and difficult as well to avoid the thought that both poets, born to white privilege, presume too much. Rich, as we shall see, later came to be troubled by this kind of presumptive identification, but she has never completely freed herself from it, and other poets have made little attempt to move away from the echoes of our literature's racist past. Such resonance is to be found everywhere that blackness appears in recent verse by white Americans. Michael

Blumenthal's recently published volume, *Days We Would Rather Know,* for example, contains a poem titled "Twice Born Matches" in which the poet sits by the sea and sees his own shadow:

> Suddenly,
> a large black man
> emerges from the ocean and walks
> Toward me. He is the man I have
> been dreaming of for years, the man
> who stands beside the dead bodies
> of my family, without flinching,
> and drinks from the blood that remains
> in their veins.
>
> (44)

Shadows have of course intimated mortality throughout the history of English-language verse, but more particularly, in American verse black people have been associated both with shades and with death and time in just this way. One has but to remind oneself of Allen Tate's image of a man's shadow, "a long nigger / gliding at his feet" (*Poems* 11), or of Warren's description of "shadows / Bigger than people and blacker than niggers" (*Selected Poems* 121), to see that Blumenthal's progression from his own shadow to the threatening black presence is no more than white discourse's reinscription of its traditional tropes in the verse of a new generation. The patterns to be identified in the poetry of the century's second half as it touches on race are the same as those already identified.

The liberal imperative was brought into postmodernism by Charles Olson, a poet whose date of birth places him more aptly with the poets discussed in the preceding chapter, but who is considered here because of the lateness of his first publications, because of the sharp break he makes with those other liberal poets aesthetically, and because of his immense and direct impact upon the younger poets of postmodernism, most of whom are still publishing. Olson was not just influenced by the ideals of Rooseveltian democracy, he served in the Roosevelt administration and worked in the campaigns. But his interest in the discourse on race has a much earlier and more literary antecedent, identified in one of his earliest poems, "Letter for Melville 1951," which speaks of a "Captain / 25, part Negro, part American Indian and perhaps / a little of a certain Cereno" (*Archeologist*), and goes on to remark of him "(How much light / the black & white man threw—Orestes!—on / democracy!)." Like Lowell, Olson concerned himself considerably with the formation of our imperfect democracy and with the contributions, acknowledged and unacknowledged, made to that formation even by those excluded from democracy's processes. At one point prior to the composition of *The Maximus Poems,* Olson had contemplated the writing of a book to be called *Red, White, and Black,* which would present "the differing ways the Indian, white and Negro found out how to shape a human society in the West" (qtd. in Butterick xxi). Like Lowell also, Olson had a close relationship with Williams, who with Pound constitutes Olson's primary poetic influence. But Olson kept himself free of the racial ideologies of both Pound and Williams, believing as he did that "No man can attack a race and remain useful to anyone as an artist" (*Encounter* 15).

Among the things Olson did take from Pound was the work of Leo Frobenius, which Olson works into *Maximus* as Pound had worked it into *The Cantos,* witness Olson's reinvocation of the legend of Gassir's lute (*Complete Maximus* 509) in a fashion similar to Pound's. But Olson went beyond Pound and Frobenius in his African researches, and *Maximus* considers the possibilities of African contributions to early civilization that had not occurred to Frobenius:

There may be East African
—and again What about Libyan?
movements to the center
of the 2nd millenium
      (*Complete Maximus* 274)

Here Olson is repeating Graves's hypothesis in *Greek Myths* that the Canaanites may have originated in Uganda and come up through lower Egypt (Butterick 392–93). Both Pound and Frobenius prefer to believe that cultural influence traveled in the opposite direction.

Olson's major contribution to the racial discourse in poetry, however, is in his use of historical materials regarding the slave trade, an aspect of history which the student of Gloucester could not very well ignore. It is common practice in *The Maximus Poems* for Olson to make his attack upon racism through the deployment of historical records demonstrating the monstrosity of the slave trade and praising those who opposed it, and *Maximus* is free of the complicating notes of personal prejudice which counteract the effects of similar strategies in Pound. One of the finest examples of this is to be found in Olson's rewriting of Richard Saltonstall's legal actions against slave traders in 1645:

Saltonstall cried Havoc here
when Guinea ship

came Boston with
two natives roared
unto the court you *shall*
return these men,
right back, and see
they get to their own
homes, you'll sell
no human flesh, alive or
dead, in Boston
   (*Complete Maximus* 530)

The moral fervor of Saltonstall's action appeals to Olson as much as the moral
rightness of his position. Olson is generally fond of such clear moral demarca-
tions and proudly proposes to advance the recognition after the fact of those
who resisted the easy riches of the slave trade. In the first volume of *Maximus*
he favors William Hawkins, who traded fairly with the Africans, over his son,
John, who kidnapped them and was subsequently honored by the English
crown:

He [William] paid goods
for goods,
he did not grab them,
as his son did, trading
on his father's welcome

It was the son
was knighted, the father
I restore. It was the son
for a crest:
"a demi-Moor
proper,
in chains."
   (*Complete Maximus* 67)

Olson additionally views the slave trade as a disruptive force in the emergence
of American enterprise; he complains somewhat bitterly that the slavers
"would keep you off the sea, would keep you local, / My Nova Scotians"
(*Complete Maximus* 16), thus isolating the New Englanders and making them
slaves to the triangular trade.

   Olson does not confine his historical researches to the slave trade itself; he
also commemorates the black woman, Maria, who was burned alive at the
stake on Boston Common in 1681 (*Complete Maximus* 98). An early *Maximus* letter which was not included in the original published volume moves
from an homage to an African slave, Aba 'Ougi by name, to a transcription of

a Negro spiritual, "He Never Said a Mumberlin' Word." The poem begins with 'Ougi's capture on the Ivory Coast, and follows him to the specific white family that purchased him "for labor and for stud" ("Letter 24," 7). Olson, in aligning the spiritual with the historic facts of a specific case is out to draw the connection, as others have, between the specifics of suffering and the triumph of a people's poetry. With the purchase of 'Ougi:

> What they also got, was a voice. And they killed
> him, in the end,
> 25 white men beat him to death because of
> his voice (who sang, on a windy morning, Green
>
> > > trees
> > > a-bending,
> > > poor sinner
> > > stands a-trembling,
>
> Christianity, carried by Northern missionaries,
> frightened plantation owners, and "Charles",
> the Christian name they gave him, made musical signals
> to announce the return of preachers
> to the pine woods (on a stormy morning, My Lordy
>
> > > calls me,
> > > by the thunder
> > > ("Letter 24," 7)

In one of many acts of heroism by slaves recorded in Olson's verses, 'Ougi uses his voice, singing the folk compositions of his faith, to lure the hunting whites and their dogs away from the place where the other slaves are meeting. His voice, his enunciation of the poetry of Afro-America, was literally his end, and in moving to the transcription of the song 'Ougi sings, Olson makes him a type of the Christ figure, dying for others by saying their grace: "He bowed his head and died / And he never said a mumberlin' word" ("Letter 24," 8).

As a poet, Olson is drawn to this forceful example of the cost of song, and of its worldly powers, and he presents 'Ougi throughout as a human like many others, tested in the fires of persecution, finding salvation in the soul's ability to wrench song out of suffering and to keep clean the language that proceeds from one's own experience.

Olson does not restrict his interest in racial justice to the distant past. Just as the slave trade had debilitating consequences for the early American community, Olson believes modern prejudices have also served to impede human development. Late in *The Maximus Poems* he thinks of his father's work in the postal service, and of how successive waves of immigrants have had their labors exploited in this country:

>   my father a Swedish
> wave of
> migration after
> Irish?   like Negroes
> now like Leroy [*sic*] and Malcolm
> X   The final wave
> of wash upon this
> desperate
> ugly
> cruel
> land this nation
> which never
> lets anyone
> come to
> shore
>   (*Complete Maximus* 496–97)

This passage takes on yet greater resonance when we recall that the father of LeRoi Jones, the black poet and friend of Olson named in these lines (Jones appears in more poems by white writers than any other black poet in the history of American literature), was like Olson's own father a career postal employee battling prejudice in the workplace.

These passages from Olson's major work constitute one of his most carefully thought out themes, and they succeed in linking the humanism of liberal politics to the historical tradition of New England abolitionist thought and to the poetics of modernism. Olson also serves as the bridge into postmodernism, and these same themes are taken up by many of the younger poets who embraced Olson's methodology and interests.

"There are thousands, millions of whites in this country," notes Olson's close associate, Robert Creeley, "who have committed themselves not to look at the condition of the Negro" (175), echoing the discovery made by Crèvecoeur centuries earlier. A significant number of the white poets of our time never do look at Afro-America, but many others, some of them operating within the same postmodernist aesthetics as Olson, determined that they would look at the conditions of black Americans, as best they could working within their language. Their coming of age as poets coincident with the major movements of the civil-rights struggle gives added impetus to their determination. The fifties and sixties were a time when the drive for simple common rights under law met with violent opposition, a time in which, as Armand Schwerner said in a poem written in memory of his cousin, Mickey, who was brutally slain by Klansmen in Mississippi and buried in an earthen dam, "belief in the poem / [required] a major transplant every morning" (50). Part of that transplant which made new poetry possible involved the replacement of traditional modes of white thought, as represented in the historical verse of Tate and Warren. For Schwerner, "remission of sins is not in question / Jefferson is not in question / fear is in question 10:30 is in question hunger is in question" (49).

This sense of fear is one of the new notes in the poetry on race of this era. Earlier poets, whether they participated in traditional racial agreements or sought to undo them, wrote from a position of white safety. Now, as Schwerner's poem, which was prepared to be read at a benefit for the defense fund for LeRoi Jones following his arrest in the late sixties, demonstrates, the poet who spoke against the strictures of racism placed his person in peril. This fear is presented overtly in one of Paul Blackburn's journal poems, from the fall of 1967, which recounts a trip through Memphis, Tennessee, a trip Blackburn remembers as:

> . . . scary as shit
> mean white mouths and steel eyes out
> gunning for my beard and long hair and tight jeans
> The eyes say it loud and hard NIGGUHLOVUH! and
> I surely am, all the beautiful faces I see downtown
> are black   .   a pleasure to take bus back
>   to the ghetto.
>
>   (16)

Also in Blackburn's poems we begin to find reflections of the increasing interchange between black and white poets, interchange that continued even through the period which saw the peak of black separatist writing. While earlier white poets had remarked the presence of black poets, as did Williams in *Paterson,* we begin to see an actual exchange among poets in the poetry, as in Blackburn's several poems written after attending poetry conferences. One in particular takes Blackburn's experience of a reading by Sonia Sanchez as an occasion for figuratively clearing the decks of the accumulations of white imagery:

> All that sweet, warm
> blackness going down
>   what do be more dream

than real, sometime, it
  bein this grey boy talkin, after
all that hard sweet
blackness softening up his heart, seems I
trudge uphill thru the snowfall
thru the trees and lights and havto
spend the next two hours shovelin
sidewalk and driveway clear
of all this white shit   .

(105)

Such thoughts were unheard of, or at least unwritten of, among the poets of high modernism, even among those who did have intellectual contacts among black writers, and even among those who thought that blacks were by nature sweet. Blackburn's brief assumption of a black dialect and his praise of "hard, sweet / blackness" carry a suggestion of exoticism, of which more later, and the self-effacing tone may be troublesome, but the mere fact of a white poet's visibly taking inspiration from the public reading of black poets is something new in white letters.

Blackburn's continuation of the modernist and postmodernist historical methodology is equally in evidence in his journal poems. Like Olson, he followed Pound through the thicket of Frobenius's researches, later widening his inquiry to encompass the complex interrelationships between ancient African cultures, modern Africa, and African-American history. A journal poem titled "Fire" develops from a consideration of the urban unrest of the 1960s and the assassinations of the Kennedys, Malcolm X, and Martin Luther King, Jr., to a formation of spiritual and cultural forces which is opened with a repetition of the reference to the tale of Gassir's lute as reported by Frobenius and used to good measure by both Pound and Olson:

Gassir's lute
  the light
  shining on Oshun's face
  is not easy to behold.   to be held.
Do you think you can put your hat on your head
and walk away with him? Down that hill?
  But Haarlem is a Dutch name
    and the Dutch have forgotten us. Deutsch?
The destroyer? What did you think Oshun meant?

(60)

Blackburn has taken the tale from Frobenius's archive and placed it alongside the cosmology, represented by Oshun, of the Yoruba people, who form the majority of the population in the region now known as Nigeria. Into the mix he then brings the culture of the Dutch colonists, who gave the name to a part of Manhattan whose population today consists primarily of persons of African descent, many of Yoruba background, and many of whom will be more familiar with that Dutch name than with the African deities. That irony is not Blackburn's sole concern, though. He also wants to establish the continuous richness of African culture in history, and thus he notes that "the epic Dausi goes back to 500 perhaps BC, at / which time Homer" (60). This note serves to call to mind the fact that the Western tradition with which we are most familiar is not the only one available to us, nor should it be the only one attended to, since others have reckoned in its formation. Blackburn closes this segment of his poem with a simple acknowledgment of the sources that set him off on these studies: "Thank you, Leo Frobenius / —to feed the song" (61).

George Economou is another whose poetry shows the direct influence of Olson in its use of historical materials. As Olson was interested first in documents pertaining to the New England sea trades, Economou seeks out specifically documentation of the experience of immigrants to America from Eastern Europe and the Mediterranean. He makes use of such documents, as Olson did, to restore to history the memory of those who opposed slavery in the early days of our nation; names such as that of Thaddeus Kosciuszko, who left a testament "in his own good English" declaring:

> . . . should I make no other
> testamentary disposition of my property in
> the United States [I] thereby authorize my
> friend Thomas Jefferson to employ the whole
> thereof in purchasing negroes from among his own
> as any others and giving them liberty in my name,
> in giving them an education in trades or otherwise,
> and in having them instructed for their new condition . . .
>
> (80–81)

In this way the engineer who is now little more than a name in history books created an opportunity for a few of Jefferson's slaves to enjoy manumission without having to await the deaths of Jefferson and his wife.

Economou also repeats the sort of references to the Middle Passage that are encountered in *The Cantos* and in *The Maximus Poems*. He again brings his particular interests to bear on this aspect of our history, and he draws parallels between the forced migration of blacks between decks, the voluntary migration of white labor in steerage, and the final solution the Nazis arrived at for moving their own slave labor. Economou then echoes a line carved on the Statue of Liberty to bring out the ironies it must hold for Afro-Americans:

> On the frontier of new profits
> and faced with similar problems
> similar minds arrive at similar
> solutions:
> > cattle cars
> > > steerage class (down
> in the cargo hold)
> > > and slave ships
> > > > to carry
> profitable cargoes
> > > 452 black asses
> *your tired your poor your huddled*
> > > > (6)

This passage also recalls Olson's similar denunciations of the immoral actions that proceed from decisions based primarily on the profit interests of capital. Both poets seek to identify the enormity of human cost exacted to provide for the comforts of a privileged class of white entrepreneurs, and both find in the conception of human beings as profitable cargo an origin for later ills of our commerce.

This critique of capitalism's involvement with racism recurs among some of the poets associated with the Beat movement, who were also influenced mightily by Pound, Olson, and particularly, Williams, but who followed different aesthetic principles from most of the poets aligned with the Black Mountain group. Allen Ginsberg, whose *Howl* resounds in "Negro streets," complained loudly that "Social Demos have made a White Xtian dictatorship" (146) of the labor movement in this country, thus widening the area of critique to include the managerial levels of organized labor. Ginsberg generally finds racism to be a virulent aspect of a much larger social malaise, a cultural vapidity which is symbolized for him by the person of President Eisenhower. "Eisenhower is anti-negro," Ginsberg says, "because all those colored people are not prepared to sit in schools in Little Rock until they become invisible like Ralph Ellison" (146).

There are many passages in Ginsberg's work where he can be found straining at the strictures of racial imagery, where he is on the verge of breaking through traditional descriptive modes. But he never seems entirely to free himself from that descriptive veil which causes us to see only what we have told ourselves is to be seen. In one instance, Ginsberg is thinking of a woman he saw on a bus in East Harlem in the late forties, a woman of mixed ancestry, and his description of her lacks most of the white dread of racial amalgamation so familiar in our literature. But it is not free from the trope of exoticism our language forces the nonwhite to inhabit. The woman on the bus is

> a mulatto or negress, with a perfect oval face, without makeup of any kind, and exotic and beautiful features. . . . The extremity of the oval, the extremity of her mulatto beauty. . . . —a middle or lower class type but so lifted out of social context by her physical appearance I couldn't figure what she was doing on the bus, or in Harlem life. Expression not of arrogance or sexuality but of angelic coolness. . . .
>
> How can such people exist unnoticed without being made heroes by the first passerby? (21)

The spirit that animates these lines, and more specifically the rhetorical question with which they end, will be instantly recognizable to readers of William Carlos Williams. In this passage Ginsberg has removed the obsessively sexual interest that marks so many of Williams's observations of Afro-American women. There is still a note of exoticism here, though, and the fact that the exoticism is not simply an attribute of this individual woman but rather of Ginsberg's general representation of the nonwhite is attested to by the frequency with which exoticism appears as an aspect of blackness in his writings, as in his dream piece which speaks of "talking to Nigger Prophetess in her junkheap car—" (116).

That element of exoticism may prove to be the most persistent element of the traditional structure of racial imagery in American verse; it appears in the poetry of every decade of the twentieth century, and in the poetry of writers of all political persuasions. Robert Duncan, associated with both the Black Mountain and Beat camps and father figure to the New American poetry in the San Francisco Bay area, though far from being a political conservative, still writes poems containing the same images of exoticism and primitivism found in Vachel Lindsay and Wallace Stevens. Duncan's "An African Elegy" differs very little from Lindsay's "The Congo," and differs from Stevens's "The Greenest Continent" only in that Duncan identifies himself with that primitivism. "I know," he writes, "no other continent of Africa more dark than this / dark continent of my breast" (33–35). For Duncan, as for Conrad, Lindsay, Eliot, Crane, and Stevens, Africa remains an area of darkness inhabited by exotic primitives and ruled over by death. Duncan draws an analogy between the marvelous creatures that stalk this region and those of "the mind's / natural jungle," establishing Africa as the trope for the most primitive, subconscious, libidinal areas of the psyche. His description of the peoples of Africa could have been lifted entire from Lindsay:

> The wives of the Congo
> distil there their red and the husbands
> hunt lion with spear and paint death-spore
> on their shields, wear his teeth, claws and hair
> on ordinary occasions.
>
> (33)

Duncan's poem reestablishes the identification of death with the nonwhite that we have seen in the works of both the modernists and the Agrarians. For Duncan, "Death is the dog-headed man zebra striped / and surrounded by silence who walks like a lion, / who is black" (33), and the arrival of that black death is presaged by the jungle's talking drums, the same "boom boom boom" that punctuates Lindsay's poem. Duncan implores us to "Hear in the coiled and secretive ear / the drums that I hear beat" (35). Without a history of the poetry of race in America, these might be read as Duncan's own surreal inventions. However, it is apparent that he has not created these tropes fortuitously; he has selected them from a vocabulary of symbols supplied by a racist discourse. It is not an accident that the symbolic presence of the nonwhite accompanies death in this poem.

Duncan's elegy is unlike "The Greenest Continent" of Stevens insofar as Duncan sees this death-ridden wilderness not as something to be ordered by a missionary imagination but as something to be embraced. Duncan does not wish to expel this black death from civilization, he wants to make love to it:

> Then it was I, Death singing,
> who bewildered the forest. I thot him
> my lover like a hound of great purity
> disturbing the shadow and flesh of the jungle.
>
> (35)

That same desire to embrace the exotic and primitive, as portrayed in the person of the nonwhite, figures in the poems of Frank O'Hara, a central writer of the New York School of poets. O'Hara's "The Poet in the Attic" is frankly autobiographical and names O'Hara himself as the poet of whom it is said "what a dog he is for the exotic" (*Retrieved* 43). The form which the exotic takes for him, in this poem written in 1951, is identical to the form it took for Duncan in his African elegy nine years earlier:

> And as Nubian niggers rub
> their bellies against his open lips
> he fashions a constrictor
> out of a dead feather boa
> (Retrieved 43)

Again we find that the exoticism of blackness leads to connotations of death. As Duncan had done, O'Hara not only presents blackness as sensual to a degree quintessentially foreign (like Williams's, O'Hara's immediate inspiration for this is a *National Geographic*), he wants to kiss this representative of the otherness of primitivism, to fondle it in the privacy of his imagination's attic.

This conflation of imagery is typical of early O'Hara and is indicative of his wholesale adoption of the stereotypes found in so much of high modernism; indicative also of a willingness to think of the mass of black people as an abstraction to be acted upon. That attitude produces additional images which are dangerous. Crane's and Eliot's images of rivers swollen with the corpses of the nameless nonwhite find their echo in O'Hara's description of cluttered rooftops "with holes for hanging niggers" (*Retrieved* 64) in his poem "A Darkened Palette." The tragedy of decades of lynchings is thus transmuted into a patch of color for O'Hara's verbal field of composition, and the human referent is left to its suffering in some other area, outside the poem. O'Hara's symbols in these poems are self-consciously surreal, but again and again we find that the image of the black is assigned the same deadly, exotic tasks. In "Easter," the poet evokes "the big nigger of noon," an image similar in its effects to Laura Riding's thick-lipped Negro centuries, and goes on, piling up images of genitalia and blackness, as in the lines "O sins of sex and kisses of birds at the end of the penis / cry of a black princess whose mouth founders in the Sun" (*Collected Poems* 98–99), or the later "Black bastard black prick black pirate" (*Collected Poems* 99). O'Hara is simply making more overt the standard attribution of genital centeredness that white discourse makes to the nonwhite. O'Hara continues into his later poems the practice of identifying with the radically other which he has constructed in his mind. He even claims blackness for himself, in "Answer to Voznesensky & Evtushenko," when he tells the two Soviet poets "we are tired of your tiresome imitations of Mayakovsky / we are tired / of your dreary tourist ideas of our Negro selves" (*Collected Poems* 468). Interestingly, when O'Hara does speak of individual blacks, most specifically of black writers he knew or whose works he read, much of the more offensive imagery disappears. But even then there is still to be observed the constitution of the self and the demarcation of the other on the basis of color, a basis which O'Hara goes so far as to make a poetics. In "Ode: Salute to the French Negro Poets," he addresses himself to the West Indian surrealist poet Aime Cesaire and offers as a poetic philosophy "race which is the poetic ground on which we rear our smiles" (*Collected Poems* 305), as if O'Hara were seeking some white equivalent of Cesaire's poetics of "negritude," forgetting for the moment that negritude arises in history in response to the white man's having first declared it as an organizing principle.

That identification with an idealized and romanticized sense of blackness appears among many of the poets of the fifties and sixties. Lew Welch, for one, offers a three-line ethics of "Comportment":

Think Jew
Dance nigger
Dress and drive Oakie
          (205)

Welch, like so many of his contemporaries, is animated by a sort of hip racism and seems to be yearning for the status of Norman Mailer's "White Negro." He and other poets of his time feel that they are outside of the mass culture, and whether they are properly "hipsters" or not, they attempt to appropriate for themselves the status of the radically other that they and their society have assigned to the nonwhite. Poets like Welch and John Wieners accept many of the white assertions about blackness as being adequate referential descriptions and then want those same descriptions to apply to themselves. They want to become "niggers," to step into the image structure of the farthest outsider. In Wieners's "A Poem for Cocksuckers" we see the homosexual artist, surely an outsider in 1958 when the piece was written, attempting to join his status to that of the nonwhite. In gay bars, Wieners says:

We may sing our songs
of love like the black mama
on the juke box, after all
what have we got left.
          (30)

What he has left is the bar and the social scene it represents, where he forms part of an insiders' group of outsiders, and the poem, where he will sing like the woman on the jukebox. He feels at home in both circumstances because in these places "it's a nigger's world," though that might be news indeed to the masses of black people trying to make their own worlds for themselves. Even while identifying himself with blackness, Wieners will follow white tradition in identifying that same blackness with morbidity. He writes in another poem:

> Some black man looms in my life, larger than life.
> Some white man hovers there too, but I am through with him.
> Some wild man dreams through my day, smelling of heroin.
> Some dead man dies in my arms every night.
>
> (96)

The black man who looms in Wieners's life is clearly the same one that loomed in the earlier poetry of Tate and Warren, and looms again on the beach before the persona of Michael Blumenthal's "Twice-Born Matches" years later.

The presence of such images in contemporary verse attests to the tenacity of discursive formations. The racial stereotype persists as a functioning sememe in the speech acts of white people. In a recent review of William L. Van Deburg's *Slavery and Race in American Popular Culture,* Hammet Worth-ington-Smith takes note of this phenomenon as it appears in the popular culture of the period we have been examining in this essay: "An anomaly which continues to manifest itself in American culture is one that perpetuates images of the African-American which are questionable. In spite of the aboli-tionist movement, the Harlem Renaissance, and the Civil Rights Movement of the 1960s, the quest to eradicate stereotypes in American culture detrimen-tal to the image of the African-American necessarily continues" (181). In fact, though, there is nothing anomalous about it. The questionable images of the Afro-American in white American language are the norm, so much so that they form the basis for all our discussions subsequently. They constitute the Afro-American other for the whites, and white culture cannot see blackness outside of the veil of descriptive terms it has evolved. It is not only the poets of society's margins who see blackness as abstracted otherness; poets of the mainstream such as Henry Taylor, Michael Blumenthal, and Daniel Halpern see the same things. When Halpern attends a party in a poem, he finds, not waiters, but "soft Negroes carrying / silver trays" (16). When he walks on his street, it is not an individuated musician who plays his music outside, but "a Negro with white shoes" (23). One of the things that makes Halpern's experience in "Central Park" a pleasant one of a Sunday is that "There was a Negro with white shoes who played / that Sunday" (24). Is this the same man playing in both poems, or is he simply a generic minstrel from the other world of the nonwhite? And when we are told that "the Negro tapped his foot / till the shade inched from his bench" the lines must be read in light of the ever-repeating shades cast by the nonwhite other over the white psyche in American poetry. Lines like these, when read in the company of all other American verse of this century, can be seen to fit into a massive signifying structure which constricts the poet, indicating to him and to his readers what it is possible to say about the nonwhite.

There is no sense in which contemporary American verse can be found to essay the eradication of the image of deadly otherness. There is not even any sense in which today's poets can be seen as essaying the sort of project represented by Melville's "Benito Cereno." While it is surely improper to demand such a project of our poets, its continued absence is significant and should not go unremarked. American poetry has, as I have shown, taken the image structures identified in the course of this study as adequate descriptions of the nonwhite. If white poets are to assume responsibility, not for political action, but for the real realm of their own activity, for the creation of their own discourse, they cannot simply repeat the tropes of the past and pretend to have said nothing political. What we do find in the works of avowedly radical white poets, such as earlier poems by Adrienne Rich, is instead an argument which, like those of the liberals of midcentury, does little against the prevailing system of imagery. In "Ghazals: Homage to Ghalib," Rich calls out to the poet LeRoi Jones and the black activist (now turned evangelist) Eldridge Cleaver, in a sort of self-condemning plea: "LeRoi! Eldridge! Listen to us, we are ghosts / condemned to haunt the cities where you want to be at home" (*Doorframe* 107). This poem serves to maintain the division between whiteness and otherness. It accepts the construction of whiteness rather than seeking some other ground for the creation of the self. And it offers no reason for the black other to listen. If you see yourself as a ghost haunting somebody else's home, you might expect nothing more or less than exorcism.

It is one of her few similarities to Robert Penn Warren that Adrienne Rich's discourse on race in her poetry and her prose seems always in transition; as her radical politics alter with reflection and changing circumstance, her understanding of the racial others and her relationships to them alters as well. Even as she made the self-effacing bow to the revolutionary icons of 1968, she understood the power of racist images. She was able then to ask, "Were you free then all along, Jim, free at last / of everything but the white boy's fantasies?" (*Doorframe* 108). Still, even though she had a clear enough conception of the appropriative power of white boys' fantasies, she was in the grip of a few white girls' fantasies of her own. In the 1976 volume *Of Woman Born,* speaking of her childhood relationship to a black nurse, she was able to declare quite matter-of-factly, "I had from birth not only a white, but a black mother" (253), and exercising the authority of one who cannot be contradicted by the now absent other, she asserted of this black woman that, " 'childless' herself, she *was* a mother" (254). In her zeal to wrest the power to define motherhood from the male-centered language she had grown up in, as the disparaging quotation marks around the word "childless" indicate, she feels free to name herself a child of this voiceless woman. This move reminds one a good deal of similar figures in H.D.'s *HERmione,* in which a white woman unilaterally identifies with what she knows of black womanhood. ("But then they loved their mammies—there was that—" [Benét].) Entering a confessional mode, Rich uses this relationship to describe the process by which she became aware of prejudice. She describes how, as she grew older, she mysteriously learned that this love and identification was somehow unseemly. The way she explains how she learned this sounds like a matter of inhalation: "It was simply 'the way things were,' and we tried to repress the confusion and the shame" (*Of Woman Born* 254). But when it comes to an explanation of how this black mother was adopted, there is an unusual shift of responsibility signaled by Rich's syntax: "For years, she had drifted out of reach, in my searches backward through time, exactly as the double silence of sexism and racism intended her to do. She was meant to be utterly annihilated" (*Of Woman Born* 254–55). This seems an untoward way to speak of a woman one has claimed as a mother. Rich presents her younger self as helplessly in the sway of these twin evils but somehow acting, or not acting, apart from them. It is this kind of maneuver that several black feminist critics have complained of in Rich's works. To Michelle Wallace, Rich's "gospel of pluralism seems narrow and earnestness is its greatest flaw" (18). In her most recent collection of essays Rich records one black woman's outraged complaint about the sort of convenient identifications performed by H.D. and Rich: "*But you don't know us!*" (*Blood* x). In the years since 1976 Rich has learned that such facile claims as her adoption of her black mother do not always hold up; her experiences of criticism from other writers and her own laudable process of self-criticism have revealed to her much of what she had earlier elided. As part of the introduction to the tenth-anniversary edition of *Of Woman Born,* she concedes that "in writing . . . of having been cared for by a Black nurse, [she] tried to blur that relationship into the mother-daughter relationship. But a personalized 'understanding' did not prevent [her] from gliding over the concrete system within which Black women have had to nurture the oppressor's children" (*Of Woman Born* xxv). Appending a note to that earlier description of her relationship to her nurse, she shows that she is now aware that "whatever the white child has received both in care and caring, the Black woman has given under enormous constraints" (*Of Woman Born* n255). These are powerful insights, not at all to be dismissed, but it is interesting that Rich does not press farther in her exploration of the means by which she was initially able to lay the claims of identification in appropriating this second mother, and in later letting go of her. If she has come to understand better than many the intersection of class and race in the economy of black-white child care, she does not yet appear willing to examine more deeply the status of her own descriptions of the experience.

That combination of earnest self-examination, radical witnessing, and odd blind spots continues in Rich's more recent poetry. In "Education of a Novelist" she has drawn lines from Ellen Glasgow's autobiography into a poem interspersed with her own commentary. In looking to the relationship between Glasgow and her mammy, Rich perceives the type of her relationship to her nurse, and she rejects the easy temptation to condemn the earlier writer for her confessed failures to fulfill her promises to the older woman:

> It's not enough
> using your words to damn you, Ellen:
> they could have been my own:
> > this criss-cross
> map of kept and broken promises
> > > (*Doorframe* 317)

Rich goes farther toward inspecting the ground upon which she once declared her nurse to be her mother here than she does in her critique of her earlier position in *Of Woman Born,* though she does not quite come to the point of the politics of identification with the other. She does, in "The Spirit of Place," a poem dedicated to the novelist Michelle Cliff, inscribe her recognition of the extent to which the language of mastery taints the consciousness of even the most progressive:

> it was not enough to be for abolition
> while the spirit of the masters
> flickered in the abolitionist's heart
>
> it was not enough to name ourselves anew
> while the spirit of the masters
> calls the freedwoman to forget the slave
> > (*Doorframe* 298)

It may be in her bearing witness to the history of racism that Rich has made her most important contributions, and in this she resembles somewhat Charles Olson. In part 27 of "Contradictions" she marks the fact, as did Olson, that "the Afro-American slaves / knew this: you could be killed / for teaching people to read and write" (*Native Land* 109). "Yom Kippur 1984" makes use of a contemporary incident to illustrate the continued presence of racism as brute, physical fact: "young scholar shot at the university gates on a summer evening / walk, his prizes and studies nothing, nothing / availing his blackness" (*Native Land* 77). "Virginia 1906" gives shape to Rich's handling of history, drawing a lesson from the patterns she discerns there:

This woman I have been and recognize
must know that beneath that quilt of whiteness lies
a hated nation, hers,
earth whose wet places call to mind
still open wounds: her country,
Do we love purity? Where do we turn for power?

(*Native Land* 41)

It cannot really be said that Rich has transformed the racial imagery of American letters, because in her discursive verse she seldom describes black people at all; they are named, their stories are told, and the poet is their witness. While she has done much to affect thinking about race, particularly about the interlocking relationships of race, gender, and economic class, her poems sometimes leave uneasy questions unasked about the position of their speakers. In "Frame," a poem which recounts a vicious assault upon a woman that took place in Boston in 1979, Rich has cast her bearing of witness in a form that has a perhaps unanticipated rhetorical effect. Most of the poem is a straightforward narration of this racist incident, with italicized interventions from outside the narrative frame offered by the poem's persona. This persona is present to prevent the event from being shrouded in the silence which sexism and racism intend for the assault upon a black woman by a white man. "I am not supposed to be / there," she repeats again and again as she views the action, "and I understand at once / it is meant to be in silence that this happens" (*Doorframe* 304). But this persona seems blind to a question that remains even as she breaks the power of that silence. She ends the poem with a direct address to the reader:

What I am telling you
is told by a white woman who they will say
was never there. I say I am there

(305)

This is testimony of great emotional force, and considerable courage, but by placing her persona in view of this violent act, Rich's poem calls the question of further intervention. A reader might feel that the silence should have been broken sooner. The poem, effective as it is, arrives too late to help the victim. At some point, others might wonder, is the oppressed to become more than the object of our identification and the subject of our witness? Why, finally, does the persona not *do* something? Rich has done, and continues to do, a great deal; she has long been an activist poet. But her poetry, and her prose, seem too often to frame the American story of the races in just this way.

In his *Truth and Method,* Hans-Georg Gadamer asks, as the title to his second supplement, "To What Extent Does Language Preform Thought?" a question which temporarily sidesteps, in its English translation, the conundrum of whether it is at all possible in learning to think in a language to avoid having our thought directed by the language of those from whom we learn. Gadamer holds before us:

> the fundamental doubt about the possibility of our escaping from the sphere of influence of our education which is linguistic and of our thought which is transmitted through language, as well as the doubt about our capacity for openness to a reality which does not correspond to our opinions, our fabrications, our previous expectations. . . .
>
> So, with increasing urgency, we are led to ask, whether there may not be hidden in our experience of the world a primordial falsity; whether, in our linguistically transmitted experience, we may not be prey to prejudices or, worse still, to necessities which have their source in the linguistic structuring of our first experience of the world and which would force us to run with open eyes, as it were, down a path whence there is no other issue than destruction. (491)

Gadamer is, of course, speaking of much larger issues than of race and poetry, but the doubt that he raises has serious consequences in the face of the often-repeated assertion within white discourse that the status it assigns to the nonwhite is inevitable, and irremediable, and in fact a property of the object under description.

Even in the silence about race that several of our major living poets observe, even in the critical silence that often surrounds the appearance of the racial discourse in American poetry, the discourse continues to speak itself to those of us who read American poetry. When we read that body of work, if not well before, we learn to read race; we learn what to expect to hear; we learn how native speech has sounded, and we learn what is expected of us as readers. We find ourselves, often, in the position of someone at a party who is expected to both get and appreciate his host's ethnic jokes. This makes it difficult in the extreme to think or to speak ourselves without repeating the disastrous error committed to paper by Las Casas and Jefferson and replicated through the centuries of New World writing, the error that allows us to think of another so unlike ourselves as to remain an object of description to be acted upon. That error, once made, forces us to speak thereafter in its own terms if we are to speak of it at all. It has not been possible, for example, to speak as I have here of the problems of white discourse without working within the initial dialectic that discourse sets up, without giving that discourse primacy, if only in the hope that someone might strike it down. This is because, as Gadamer notes elsewhere, "understanding always involves upholding the opinion that is to be understood against the power of the meaning dispositions that rule the interpreter" (qtd. in Hoy 68).

Our position as readers is much as Gadamer describes. We begin to doubt that there is any exit from this linguistic prison, that there may be any end to the possibility that the races might one day rise and rend each other as the result of the most willful of misprisions and the failure to speak a common language. The problems of racial discourse in America may be symptomatic of larger problems of the language of description, and efforts to effect consciously the evolution of languages have not in the past proven to be invariably efficacious. The problem is as Jean-François Lyotard has stated it in his *Discours, Figure,* "any attempt to reform language comes up against the circle that it is our tool, the only tool we possess, for the purpose of transforming it" (qtd. in Dews 41). It is as if our final image were to be that of the white jailer standing outside the door behind which Toussaint L'Ouverture, and blackness, are encrypted. But if there is a hopeful image on which to close, it is the highly abstract image of a man thinking, of Herman Melville at his desk rethinking our readings of race. Racism is in large part a linguistic phenomenon and demands, somewhat haughtily, to be approached as such. When we reread the poetry of America, a rethinking of our reception of its language is called for; we should become W. E. B. DuBois's double-conscious dreamer, able to view both sides of the veil of language at once. Questionable descriptions cannot be eradicated, as Hammett Worthington-Smith and most humanists would have them be, until they have been submitted to question. In order that we might see as clearly as any creature that sees symbolically can, in order that we might at the very least see our own signifiers clearly, the primordial falsity of white mythology has continually to be uncovered.

Works Cited

Ahearn, Barry. *Zukofsky's "A": An Introduction*. Berkeley: University of California Press, 1982.

Anderson, Sherwood. *Dark Laughter*. New York: Liveright, 1970.

Anderson, Wallace L. *Edwin Arlington Robinson: A Critical Introduction*. New York: Houghton Mifflin, 1967.

Bacigalupo, Massimo. *The Formed Trace: The Later Poetry of Ezra Pound*. New York: Columbia University Press, 1980.

Bakhtin, Mikhail Mikhailovich. *The Dialogic Imagination*. Ed. Michael Holquist. Trans. Caryl Emerson and Michael Holquist. Austin: University of Texas Press, 1981.

Baldwin, James. "Interview with Julius Lester." *New York Times Book Review* 27 May 1984, p. 24.

Benét, Stephen Vincent. Foreword. *For My People*. Margaret Walker. New Haven: Yale University Press, 1942. 7–9.

———. *John Brown's Body*. New York: Rinehart, 1954.

Berryman, John. *The Dream Songs*. New York: Farrar, Straus and Giroux, 1969.

Blackburn, Paul. *The Journals*. Ed. Robert Kelley. Santa Barbara, CA: Black Sparrow Press, 1977.

Blumenthal, Michael. *Days We Would Rather Know*. New York: Viking, 1984.

Brown, Richard Harvey. "Dialectical Irony." *Poetics Today* 4 (1983): 543–64.

Brown, Sterling. *"Negro Poetry and Drama," and "The Negro in American Fiction."* New York: Atheneum, 1969.

Butterick, George F. *A Guide to the Maximus Poems of Charles Olson*. Berkeley: University of California Press, 1980.

Casillo, Robert. "Pound and Fascist Ideology." Session on Ezra Pound's Fascism, MLA Convention, Washington, D.C., 29 December 1984.

Cohen, Milton A. "Black Brutes and Mullatto Saints: The Racial Hierarchy of Stein's 'Melanctha.'" *Black American Literature Forum* 18 (1984): 119–21.

Crane, Hart. *The Complete Poems and Selected Letters and Prose*. Ed. Brom Weber. New York: Anchor Books, 1966.

———. *Letters of Hart Crane and His Family*. Ed. Thomas S. W. Lewis. New York: Columbia University Press, 1974.

Creeley, Robert. *Contexts of Poetry: Interviews, 1961–1971*. Ed. Donald Allen. Bolinas, CA: Four Seasons Foundation, 1973.

Crèvecoeur, J. Hector St. John de. *Letters from an American Farmer*. New York: Dutton, 1957.

Cullen, Countee. "Incident" and "Heritage." *The Poetry of Black America: Anthology of the Twentieth Century*. Ed. Arnold Adoff. New York: Harper and Row, 1973.

Cummings, E. E. *Complete Poems, 1913–1962*. New York: Harcourt Brace Jovanovich, 1972.

———. *Him*. New York: Liveright, 1970.

Cunard, Nancy. *These Were the Hours: Memories of My Hours Press, Réanville and Paris, 1928–1931*. Carbondale: Southern Illinois University Press, 1969.

Davis, David Brion. *The Problem of Slavery in Western Culture*. Ithaca, NY: Cornell University Press, 1970.

Davis, Robert Gorham. "The *Partisan Review* Symposium." Giruetz and Ross 87–88.

De Certeau, Michel. *Heterologies: Discourse on the Other*. Minneapolis: University of Minnesota Press, 1986.

Dendinger, Lloyd N., ed. *E. E. Cummings: The Critical Reception*. New York: Burt Franklin, 1981.

Derrida, Jacques. *Glas*. Trans. John P. Leavey and Richard Rand. Lincoln: University of Nebraska Press, 1986.

Dews, Peter. "The Letter and the Line: Discourse and Its Other in Lyotard." *Diacritics* 14 (1984): 40–49.

Doolittle, Hilda. See H.D.

Duncan, Robert. *The Years As Catches*. Berkeley, CA: Oyez, 1966.

Economou, George. *Ameriki: Book One and Selected Earlier Poems*. New York: Sun Press, 1977.

Eliot, Thomas Stearns. *The Complete Poems and Plays 1909–1950*. New York: Harcourt Brace and World, 1952.

———. *The Waste Land: A Facsimile and Transcript of the Original Drafts, Including the Annotations of Ezra Pound*. Ed. Valerie Eliot. New York: Harcourt Brace Jovanovich, 1971.

Everson, William. *The Residual Years: Poems 1934–1948*. New York: New Directions, 1968.

Fabio, Sarah Webster. "Who Speaks Negro?" *Negro Digest* 16 (1966): 54–58.

Farnsworth, Robert M. *Melvin B. Tolson 1898–1966: Plain Talk and Poetic Prophecy*. Columbia: University of Missouri Press, 1984.

Fish, Stanley. *Is There a Text in This Class?* Cambridge, MA: Harvard University Press, 1980.

Frederickson, George M. *The Black Image in the White Mind: The Debate on Afro-American Character and Destiny, 1817–1914*. New York: Harper and Row, 1971.

Friedman, Susan Stanford. "Modernism of the 'Scattered Remnant': Race and Politics in the Development of H.D.'s Modernist Vision." *H.D.: Woman and Poet.* Ed. Michael King. Orono, ME: National Poetry Foundation, 1986. 91–116.

Frost, Robert. *The Poetry of Robert Frost.* New York: Holt, Rinehart and Winston, 1974.

Gadamer, Hans-Georg. *Truth and Method.* Ed. Garrett Barden and John Cumming. New York: Crossroad Publishing, 1982.

Gilbert, Sandra M. "Purloined Letters: William Carlos Williams and 'Cress.'" *William Carlos Williams Review* 11.2 (1985): 5–15.

Ginsberg, Allen. *Journals: Early Fifties, Early Sixties.* Ed. Gordon Ball. New York: Grove Press, 1977.

Giruetz, Harry, and Ralph Ross, eds. *Literature and the Arts: The Moral Issues.* Belmont, CA: Wadsworth Publishing, 1971.

Gossett, Thomas F. *Race: The History of an Idea in America.* Dallas, TX: Southern Methodist University Press, 1963.

Guattari, Felix. *Molecular Revolution: Psychiatry and Politics.* Trans. Rosemary Sheed. Harmondsworth, England: Penguin, 1984.

Guest, Barbara. *Herself Defined: The Poet H.D. and Her World.* New York: Doubleday, 1984.

Halpern, Daniel. *Traveling on Credit.* New York: Viking, 1972.

Harper, Michael S. *Images of Kin: New and Selected Poems.* Chicago: University of Chicago Press, 1977.

H.D. (Hilda Doolittle). *The Gift.* New York: New Directions, 1982.

———. *HERmione.* New York: New Directions, 1981.

Hecht, Anthony. *Millions of Strange Shadows.* New York: Atheneum, 1980.

Hegel, Georg Wilhelm Friedrich. *The Philosophy of History.* Trans. J. Sibree. New York: Colonial Press, 1900.

Heidegger, Martin. *Being and Time.* Trans. John Macquarrie and Edward Robinson. New York: Harper and Row, 1962.

Herskovits, Melville J. "The Dilemma of Social Pattern." *Survey Graphic* 6 March 1925: 676–78. Rpt. Baltimore, MD: Black Classics Press, 1980.

Homer. *The Iliad.* Trans. Richmond Lattimore. Chicago: University of Chicago Press, 1967.

Howard, Richard. Rev. of *Operas and Plays,* by Gertrude Stein. *New York Times Book Review* 24 May 1987: 9.

Hoy, David Couzens. *The Critical Circle: Literature, History, and Philosophical Hermeneutics.* Berkeley: University of California Press, 1978.

Ignatow, David. *Poems: 1934–1969.* Middletown, CT: Wesleyan University Press, 1970.

I'll Take My Stand: The South and the Agrarian Tradition. By Donald Davidson et al. New York: Harper and Brothers, 1930. Rpt. Baton Rouge: Louisiana State University Press, 1983.

James, C. L. R. *The Black Jacobins: Toussaint L'Ouverture and the San Domingo Revolution*. New York: Vintage Books, 1963.

JanMohamed, Abdul R. "The Economy of Manichean Allegory: The Function of Racial Difference." *"Race," Writing, and Difference*. Ed. Henry Louis Gates, Jr. Chicago: University of Chicago Press, 1986. 78–106.

Jarrell, Randall. *The Complete Poems*. New York: Farrar, Straus and Giroux, 1969.

———. *Poetry and the Age*. New York: Farrar, Straus and Giroux, 1953.

———. *Randall Jarrell's Letters: An Autobiographical and Literary Selection*. Ed. Mary Jarrell. Boston: Houghton Mifflin, 1985.

Jauss, Hans Robert. *Aesthetic Experience and Literary Hermeneutics*. Trans. Michael Shaw. Minneapolis: University of Minnesota Press, 1982.

Jefferson, Thomas. *Notes on the State of Virginia*. New York: Harper and Row, 1964.

Karcher, Carolyn L. *Shadow over the Promised Land: Slavery, Race, and Violence in Melville's America*. Baton Rouge: Louisiana State University Press, 1980.

Kirk, Russell. *Eliot and His Age: T. S. Eliot's Moral Imagination in the Twentieth Century*. New York: Random House, 1971.

Kunitz, Stanley. *The Poems of Stanley Kunitz, 1928–1978*. Boston: Atlantic Monthly Press, 1979.

Lacan, Jacques. *The Four Fundamental Concepts of Psycho-Analysis*. Ed. Jacques Alain Miller. Trans. Alan Sheridan. New York: Norton, 1981.

Le Guin, Ursula K. "American SF and the Other." *The Language of the Night: Essays on Fantasy and Science Fiction*. Ed. Susan Wood. New York: Putnam, 1979. Rpr. in *The Harper and Row Reader*. Ed. Wayne C. Booth and Marshall W. Gregory. New York: Harper and Row, 1984.

Leiris, Michel. *Manhood*. Trans. Richard Howard. New York: Grossman, 1963.

Lentricchia, Frank. *Criticism and Social Change*. Chicago: University of Chicago Press, 1983.

Lindsay, Vachel. *Collected Poems of Vachel Lindsay*. New York: Macmillan, 1925.

Lowell, Robert. *Notebook*. New York: Farrar, Straus and Giroux, 1971.

———. *The Old Glory*. New York: Farrar, Straus and Giroux, 1968.

McKay, Claude. *A Long Way from Home*. New York: Harcourt, Brace and World, 1970.

Mariani, Paul. *William Carlos Williams: A New World Naked*. New York: McGraw-Hill, 1982.

———. "Williams' Black Novel." *Massachusetts Review* 14 (1973): 67–75.

Marshall, Paule. "Characterizations of Black Women in the American Novel." *In the Memory and Spirit of Frances, Zora, and Lorraine: Essays and Interviews on Black Women and Writing*. Ed. Juliette Bowles. Washington, D.C.: Howard University Press, 1979.

Massa, Ann. *Vachel Lindsay: Fieldworker for the American Dream*. Bloomington: Indiana University Press, 1970.

Masters, Edgar Lee. *Vachel Lindsay: A Poet in America*. New York: Scribner's, 1935.

Matthews, T. S. *Great Tom: Notes toward the Definition of T. S. Eliot.* New York: Harper and Row, 1974.

Melville, Herman. *Battle Pieces and Aspects of the War.* Ed. Sidney Kaplan. Amherst: University of Massachusetts Press, 1972.

———. "Benito Cereno." *Four Short Novels.* New York: Bantam Books, 1963.

———. *White Jacket; or, The World in a Man-of-War.* New York: Grove Press, 1950.

Meredith, William. *Earth Walk: New and Selected Poems.* New York: Knopf, 1976.

Miller, Christopher L. *Blank Darkness: Africanist Discourse in French.* Chicago: University of Chicago Press, 1985.

———. "Theories of Africans: The Question of Literary Anthropology." *"Race," Writing, and Difference.* Ed. Henry Louis Gates, Jr. Chicago: University of Chicago Press, 1986. 281–300.

Miller, Eugene E. "Richard Wright and Gertrude Stein." *Black American Literature Forum* 16 (1982): 107–12.

Nay, Joan. "William Carlos Williams and the Singular Woman." *William Carlos Williams Review.* 11.2 (1985): 45–54.

Negro: An Anthology. Ed. Nancy Cunard. London: Wishart, 1934. Ed. and abridged by Hugh Ford. New York: Ungar, 1970.

Nemerov, Howard. *The Collected Poems of Howard Nemerov.* Chicago: University of Chicago Press, 1977.

O'Hara, Frank. *The Collected Poems of Frank O'Hara.* Ed. Donald Allen. New York: Knopf, 1971.

———. *Poems Retrieved.* Ed. Donald Allen. Bolinas, CA: Grey Fox Press, 1977.

Olson, Charles. *Archeologist of Morning.* New York: Grossman, 1971. N. pag.

———. *Charles Olson and Ezra Pound: An Encounter at St. Elizabeth's.* Ed. Catherine Seelye. New York: Grossman/Viking, 1975.

———. *The Complete Maximus Poems.* Ed. George Butterick. Berkeley: University of California Press, 1984.

———. *Maximus.* Letter No. 24. *Olson: The Journal of the Charles Olson Archives* 6 (Fall 1976): 7–8.

Oppen, George. *Collected Poems.* New York: New Directions, 1974.

Poe, Edgar Allan. "The System of Doctor Tarr and Professor Feather." *Complete Stories and Poems of Edgar Allan Poe.* New York: Doubleday, 1966.

Pound, Ezra. *The Cantos.* New York: New Directions, 1970.

———. *Guide to Kulchur.* New York: New Directions, 1970.

———. *Selected Letters, 1907–1941.* Ed. D. D. Paige. New York: New Directions, 1950.

Rakosi, Carl. *Amulet.* New York: New Directions, 1967.

———. *The Collected Poems of Carl Rakosi.* Orono, ME: National Poetry Foundation, 1986.

———. *Ere-Voice.* New York: New Directions, 1971.

Rexroth, Kenneth. *American Poetry in the Twentieth Century.* New York: Herder and Herder, 1971.

———. *The Collected Longer Poems of Kenneth Rexroth.* New York: New Directions, 1968.

Reznikoff, Charles. *The Manner Music.* Santa Barbara, CA: Black Sparrow Press, 1977.

———. *Poems, 1937–1975.* Vol. 2 of *The Complete Poems of Charles Reznikoff.* Ed. Seamus Cooney. Santa Barbara, CA: Black Sparrow Press, 1977.

———. *Testimony: The United States (1885–1915), Recitative.* 2 vols. Santa Barbara, CA: Black Sparrow Press, 1979.

Rich, Adrienne. *Blood, Bread, and Poetry: Selected Prose, 1979–1985.* New York: Norton, 1986.

———. *The Fact of a Doorframe: Poems Selected and New, 1950–1984.* New York: Norton, 1984.

———. *Of Woman Born: Motherhood as Experience and Institution.* Tenth Anniversary Edition. New York: Norton, 1986.

———. *Your Native Land, Your Life.* New York: Norton, 1986.

Riddel, Joseph N. *The Clairvoyant Eye: The Poetry and Poetics of Wallace Stevens.* Baton Rouge: Louisiana State University Press, 1967.

Riding, Laura. *The Poems of Laura Riding.* New York: Persea Books, 1980.

Robinson, Edwin Arlington. *Selected Poems of Edwin Arlington Robinson.* Ed. Morton Dauwen Zabel. New York: Collier, 1965.

Ruggles, Eleanor. *The West-Going Heart: A Life of Vachel Lindsay.* New York: Norton, 1959.

Rukeyser, Muriel. *The Collected Poems of Muriel Rukeyser.* New York: McGraw-Hill, 1978.

Said, Edward. *Orientalism.* New York: Vintage, 1979.

———. *The World, the Text, and the Critic.* Cambridge, MA.: Harvard University Press, 1983.

Sandburg, Carl. *Breathing Tokens.* Ed. Margaret Sandburg. New York: Harcourt Brace Jovanovich, 1978.

———. *The Complete Poems of Carl Sandburg.* New York: Harcourt Brace Jovanovich, 1970.

———. *The Letters of Carl Sandburg.* Ed. Herbert Mitgang. New York: Harcourt, Brace and World, 1968.

Sartre, Jean-Paul. *Critique of Dialectical Reason.* Trans. Alan Sheridan-Smith. Ed. Jonathan Ree. London: Verso Editions, 1982.

Schwerner, Armand. *Seaweed.* Los Angeles: Black Sparrow Press, 1969.

Shapiro, Karl. *Collected Poems, 1940–1978.* New York: Random House, 1978.

———. Preface. *The Harlem Gallery: Book I, The Curator.* By Melvin B. Tolson. New York: Twayne, 1965.

Snowden, Frank M., Jr. *Blacks in Antiquity*. Cambridge, MA.: Harvard University Press, 1971.

Spender, Stephen. *T. S. Eliot*. New York: Viking, 1976.

Stein, Gertrude. *Selected Writings of Gertrude Stein*. Ed. Carl Van Vechten. New York: Vintage, 1972.

Stepto, Robert Burns. *From Behind the Veil: A Study of Afro-American Narrative*. Chicago: University of Illinois Press, 1979.

Stevens, Wallace. *The Collected Poems*. New York: Knopf, 1969.

———. *Letters of Wallace Stevens*. Ed. Holly Stevens. New York: Knopf, 1966.

———. *Opus Posthumous*. Ed. Holly Stevens. New York: Knopf, 1969.

———. *Souvenirs and Prophecies*. Ed. Holly Stevens. New York: Knopf, 1977.

Stock, Noel. *Reading the Cantos*. London: Routledge and Kegan Paul, 1967.

Tarn, Nathaniel. *The Beautiful Contradictions*. New York: Random House, 1970. N. pag.

Tate, Allen. *The Fathers and Other Fiction*. Baton Rouge: Louisiana State University Press, 1977.

———. "The *Partisan Review* Symposium." Giruetz and Ross 91.

———. *Poems*. Chicago: Swallow Press, 1961.

———. *The Poetry Reviews of Allen Tate, 1924–1944*. Ed. Ashley Brown and Frances Neel Cheney. Baton Rouge: Louisiana State University Press, 1983.

———. Preface. *Libretto for the Republic of Liberia*. By Melvin B. Tolson. New York: Collier Books, 1970.

———. "Remarks on the Southern Religion." *I'll Take My Stand* 155–75.

———. *Stonewall Jackson, The Good Soldier: A Narrative*. New York: Minton, Balch, 1928.

Tate, Allen, and Donald Davidson. *The Literary Correspondence of Donald Davidson and Allen Tate*. Ed. John Fain and Thomas Young. Athens: University of Georgia Press, 1974.

Taylor, Henry. *An Afternoon of Pocket Billiards*. Salt Lake City: University of Utah Press, 1975.

Taylor, Mark C. *Erring: A Postmodern A/theology*. Chicago: University of Chicago Press, 1984.

Terrell, Carroll F. *A Companion to the Cantos of Ezra Pound*. 2 vols. Los Angeles: University of California Press, 1985.

Thompson, Lawrance. *Robert Frost: The Early Years 1874–1915*. New York: Holt, Rinehart and Winston, 1974.

———. *Robert Frost: The Years of Triumph, 1915–1938*. New York: Holt, Rinehart and Winston, 1970.

Thompson, Lawrance, and R. H. Winnick. *Robert Frost: The Later Years*. New York: Holt, Rinehart and Winston, 1976.

Todorov, Tzvetan. " 'Race,' Writing, and Culture." *"Race," Writing, and Dif-*

ference. Ed. Henry Louis Gates, Jr. Chicago: University of Chicago Press, 1986. 370–380.

Tolson, Melvin B. *Harlem Gallery: Book I, The Curator*. New York: Twayne, 1965.

Toomer, Jean. *Cane*. New York: Boni and Liveright, 1923.

Unterecker, John. *Voyager: A Life of Hart Crane*. New York: Farrar, Straus and Giroux, 1969.

Van Vechten, Carl. *"Keep A-Inchin' Along": Selected Writings of Carl Van Vechten about Black Art and Letters*. Ed. Bruce Kellner. Westport, CT: Greenwood Press, 1979.

Walker, Alice. *Horses Make a Landscape Look More Beautiful*. New York: Harcourt Brace Jovanovich, 1984.

Wallace, Michelle. Rev. of *Blood, Bread, and Poetry: Selected Prose 1979–1985*, by Adrienne Rich. *New York Times Book Review* 15 March 1987. 18.

Warren, Robert Penn. "The Briar Patch." *I'll Take My Stand* 246–264.

———. *Brother to Dragons*. New York: Random House, 1965.

———. *John Brown: The Making of a Martyr*. New York: Payson and Clarke, 1929. Rpt. St. Clair Shores, MI: Scholarly Press, 1970.

———. *The Legacy of the Civil War*. New York: Random House, 1961.

———. *Segregation: The Inner Conflict in the South*. New York: Random House, 1956.

———. *Selected Poems 1923–1975*. New York: Random House, 1976.

———. *Who Speaks for the Negro?*. New York: Random House, 1965.

Welch, Lew. *Ring of Bone: Collected Poems, 1950–1971*. Ed. Donald Allen. Bolinas, CA: Grey Fox Press, 1979.

Whitman, Walt. *Leaves of Grass*. Ed. Harold W. Blodgett and Sculley Bradley. New York: Norton, 1968.

Wideman, John Edgar. "Charles Chesnutt and the WPA Narratives: The Oral and Literate Roots of Afro-American Literature." *The Slave's Narrative*. Ed. Charles T. Davis and Henry Louis Gates, Jr. New York: Oxford University Press, 1985.

Wieners, John. *Selected Poems*. New York: Grossman, 1972.

Williams, William Carlos. *The Autobiography of William Carlos Williams*. New York: New Directions, 1951.

———. *The Collected Earlier Poems*. New York: New Directions, 1966.

———. *Imaginations*. New York: New Directions, 1970.

———. *In the American Grain*. New York: New Directions, 1956.

———. *Paterson*. New York: New Directions, 1963.

———. *Selected Poems*. New York: New Directions, 1969.

———. *Something to Say: William Carlos Williams on Younger Poets*. Ed. James E. B. Breslin. New York: New Directions, 1985.

———. *Yes, Mrs. Williams*. New York: McDowell Oublensky, 1959.

Williams, William Carlos, Lydia Carlin, and Fred Miller. *Man Orchid. Massachusetts Review* 14 (1973): 77–117.

Worthington-Smith, Hammet. Rev. of *Slavery and Race in American Popular Culture,* by William L. Van Deburg. *Black American Literature Forum* 18 (1985): 181–82.

Wright, James. *To a Blossoming Pear Tree.* New York: Farrar, Straus and Giroux, 1977.

Zukofsky, Louis. *"A."* Berkeley: University of California Press, 1978.

———. *All: The Collected Shorter Poems.* New York: Norton, 1965.

———. *Arise, arise.* New York: Grossman, 1973.

Index